THE BLACK BODY IN ECSTASY

NEXT WAVE: NEW DIRECTIONS IN WOMEN'S STUDIES

A series edited by Inderpal Grewal, Caren Kaplan, and Robyn Wiegman

THE BLACK BODY IN ECSTASY

Reading Race, Reading Pornography | JENNIFER C. NASH

DUKE UNIVERSITY PRESS DURHAM AND LONDON 2014

Designed by Amy Ruth Buchanan
Typeset in Quadraat by Tseng Information Systems, Inc.

Library of Congress Cataloging-in-Publication Data
Nash, Jennifer C., 1980–
The Black body in ecstasy : reading race, reading pornography /
Jennifer C. Nash.
pages cm — (Next wave)
Includes bibliographical references and index.
ISBN 978-0-8223-5605-9 (cloth : alk. paper)
ISBN 978-0-8223-5620-2 (pbk. : alk. paper)
1. Pornography—Social aspects—United States. 2. African
American women in motion pictures. 3. African American
women—Sexual behavior. I. Title. II. Series: Next wave.
PN1995.9.N4N36 2014
791.43′652996073—dc23
2013026381

CONTENTS

ACKNOWLEDGMENTS

This book began as a dissertation directed by a committee of "courage-teachers"—to borrow from Allen Ginsberg—who generously supported the labor of imagination and leaps of faith required to complete this project. Werner Sollors is courage-teacher extraordinaire. He championed this project before it was even a project, offered thoughtful suggestions on numerous drafts, and encouraged me to write fearlessly. I will always be grateful for his support. Evelyn Brooks Higginbotham has been teacher, advisor, and generous mentor; she consistently raised the intellectual bar, pushing me to produce better work. She is my model for scholarly integrity and academic rigor. Kim McClain DaCosta helped me focus on the things that matter, and encouraged me let go of the things that don't. I thank her for insights on how to refine these chapters and—perhaps more important—on how to navigate the academy with sanity and a modicum of grace. This project was also shaped by my undergraduate thesis advisor, Danielle Egan, who seemed to see this moment long before I did. She introduced me to theory, encouraged me to "use my voice," and taught me how to think critically and creatively about pornography. Everything that has happened in my intellectual life since my senior year of college bears her imprint.

While finishing this project, I had two other very important courage-teachers: Sarah Tannenbaum and Darshan Krishna. Sarah's swimming lessons got me out of my head (and into the water) at the time I needed it most. She introduced me to what I now consider one of life's greatest pleasures, never lost her patience when I tried to talk my way out of a Super 500, and encouraged me to be fearless. Darshan-ji's Hindi lessons got me back into my head in an unexpectedly delightful way, and introduced me to the pleasures of chalak bunder stories. Both of them taught me to celebrate playfulness, to embrace new adventures, and to be open to the small mistakes that are part of learning.

This project also owes its existence to the host of institutions that offered me time, space, and resources to research and to write. My first debt is to my fantastic graduate department, African and African American Studies at Harvard University, and to the faculty and graduate students who made it a collegial, vibrant, and fun intellectual community. Thanks also to Women, Gender, and Sexuality Studies at Harvard College; the Graduate School of Arts and Sciences at Harvard University; the W. E. B. Du Bois Institute for African and African American Research; the Woodrow Wilson Women's Studies Fellowship; Columbia University Society of Fellows in the Humanities; and George Washington University's Columbian College. Thanks to my supportive colleagues in the American Studies and Women's Studies departments at George Washington University. I owe special thanks to Tom Guglielmo and Suleiman Osman for friendship and mentorship, and to Libby Anker for her generous and encouraging feedback on many drafts. This project also owes so much to Duke University Press, especially to Ken Wissoker, Leigh Barnwell, Elizabeth Ault, and the two reviewers who posed insightful and challenging questions that pushed me in important ways. Thanks to Robyn Wiegman for encouragement, and Nicole Fleetwood for boundless intellectual generosity.

Many of the ideas that are contained in these pages were first tried out in the classroom. Thank you to my students at Harvard, Columbia, and George Washington. The time that we spend making imaginative leaps and diving into theory reminds me why I do this work. I owe a special thanks to my very first students who taught me how to teach: Shawna Strayhorn, Emily Owens, Tracie Palmer, Sarah Howard, and Vanessa Pratt. I think back on our times together—sipping tea in the Gato and talking feminist theory—with immense fondness.

Amber Musser and Elena Marx helped make this project what it is. They kindly waded through my endless pages of literature review and foot-notes, and helped me locate the story that I wanted to tell. I owe Amber endless thanks for friendship, intellectual companionship, and smart feedback; she is often my first reader, and I am grateful for how she asks hard questions while generously supporting my ideas. I also owe thanks to an amazing group of friends whose kindness sustains me: Peter Geller, Emily Owens, Deb Cohan, Amy Hesse Siniscalchi, Katie Rademacher, Laura Murphy, Brandi Thompson Summers, and Alex and Whitney Van Praagh (and the trio of smaller Van Praaghs).

Thanks to family: Naseem and Ameer Ahmad welcomed this "Ameri-can girl" into their clan with tremendous affection, and introduced me to the pleasures of finger chips, salty lime sodas at the Club, and biscuits from the Petrol Pump Shop. Ken Clinton has always made time to cele-brate life's important events with me, and I am forever grateful. Jonathan Evans has showered me with supportive e-mails over the course of com-pleting this project, and has kindly forgiven me for the many summer afternoons I followed him around insistently asking, "Who's Pete?"

My elders taught me so much about perseverance, courage, and the importance of faith in something beyond the self. Though they aren't here anymore, I carry their stories, their affection, and their wisdom with me as I move through the world. Thanks to my great-grandmother, Mae Thompson; my grandfathers, Maurice Eastmond and Alfred Nash; and my grandmothers, Christine Eastmond and Parthenia Nash. I owe a special thanks to Maurice Eastmond, my Papa, who taught me that a life of ideas was possible. Though our intellectual interests couldn't be more different, the completion of this project is in honor of the dissertation he began at Columbia University in the 1940s.

Finally, thanks to the three who give me the most:

My parents, Carolyn and Douglas Nash, are the most selfless people I know. They have given me the proverbial shirts off their backs more times than I can count. And for as long as I can remember, they have maintained an unshakable faith in me and in my capacity to do good things. They have been there to celebrate every piece of exciting news I've been fortu-nate enough to receive, and they have been there to help me dust myself off after every disappointment. They humble me with their kindness, they sustain me with their love, and I am forever grateful. (Dad, let me publicly say: I promise an extra copy for the 'chives.)

Since Amin Ahmad was there when I wrote the very first words of my dissertation, it seems fitting that the last words I write here are about him. He has held my hand through the many moments of doubt and few moments of revelation that have accompanied this project, read (and edited) countless drafts of this manuscript, supported this project—and me—in every way a person could support another, and always kept me laughing. What I am most thankful for, though, is that a conversation that started ten years ago has become this: a love that deepens and grows. This book is for him because when I see his face every morning, I am reminded that I have a big crush on him.

INTRODUCTION

Reading Race, Reading Pornography

Over the years, a ritual has evolved around my work. Every time I tell curious strangers that I am writing a book about pornographic representations of black women, I am met with great interest. There are often follow-up questions, some titillated and some inspired by a kind of racialized curiosity, a desire to know what is distinctive about racialized pornography, and, at times, a desire to know what is distinctive about black women's bodies and pleasures. The most consistent response, though, is praise for my courage, for my brave willingness to expose pornography's racist exploitation of black women's bodies. My interest in how black women are depicted in pornography is often heard—or *misheard*—as an interest in how black women are violated by pornography. These experiences of being misheard prompted me to wonder if a black feminist project on pornography could articulate a theoretical and political stance that *avoided* a condemnation of the racism imagined to underpin racialized pornography.[1] What would it mean to read racialized pornography not for evidence of the wounds it inflicts on black women's flesh, but for moments of racialized excitement, for instances of surprising pleasures in racialization, and for hyperbolic performances of race that poke fun at the very project of race?[2]

The Black Body in Ecstasy's engagement with these questions requires a critical interrogation of black feminism's approach to representation, which treats visual culture, unless produced by black women, as presumptively problematic. My critique of black feminism's theory of representation is rooted in a particular visual archive that has long troubled black feminists: racialized pornography. In this book, I use the term *racialized pornography* to describe hard-core moving-image pornography featuring black women. It is certainly true, as the film scholar Celine Parreñas Shimizu notes, that "porn shelves are organized by race" and that a host of female bodies—black, Asian, and Latina, to name just a few—generate racial (and sexual) meanings on the pornographic screen, but I am particularly interested in the relationship between black women and pornography's representational economy.[3] Black women's projection on the hard-core pornographic screen has concerned black feminists precisely because it has been imagined to make explicit the exploitation that representation already inflicts on black women. Indeed, if dominant visual culture objectifies black female bodies, racialized pornography is imagined to be particularly demanding in its incessant exposure of black female flesh and its insistence on black female sexual excess and alterity.

In place of reading racialized pornography for evidence of the wound, as is the tradition within black feminist visual culture studies, I develop a new method of analyzing racialized pornography: racial iconography. Racial iconography is a critical hermeneutic, a reading practice that shifts from a preoccupation with the injuries that racialized pornography engenders to an investigation of the ecstasy that racialized pornography can unleash. By reading for ecstasy rather than injury, racial iconography performs what Judith Butler terms an "aggressive counter-reading," one which suspends normative readings of racialized pornography and instead advances readings which emphasize black performances and pleasures represented on the racialized pornographic screen.[4] By *ecstasy*, I refer both to the possibilities of female pleasures within a phallic economy and to the possibilities of black female pleasures within a white-dominated representational economy. I am drawn to the term *ecstasy* in much the same way some feminists have been drawn to the term *jouissance*, to describe pleasures that exceed or transcend the self and to capture a bliss that exceeds language.[5] If jouissance describes an unnamable sexual pleasure, my use of ecstasy aspires to capture forms of racial-sexual pleasure that have heretofore been unnamed (and some that have been too taboo to name), including blissful performances of hyperbolic racialization and uncomfortable

[a method or theory of interpretation]

otherness

enjoyment in embodied racialization. The ecstatic pleasures that this book locates are varied and multiple—pleasures in looking, pleasures in being looked at, pleasures in performing racial fictions, pleasures in upending racial fictions. I am particularly interested in the ecstatic possibilities of racialization, pleasures which are both deeply personal (aesthetic, erotic, sexual) and deeply social, and that form the basis of political communities and identities. To that end, I use ecstasy to consider how race aids pornographic protagonists in staging, enacting, and naming pleasures, even as it always already constrains protagonists' lexicons of desire.

My investment in the term ecstasy also contains a utopian wish for black feminist theory. Drawing on José Muñoz's conception of ecstasy as "an invitation, a call, to a then-and-there, a not-yet-here . . . a collective potentiality," I use ecstasy as a corrective to injury and as a critical response to a black feminist tradition that, as Judith Wilson notes, treats "the Hottentot Venus and Josephine Baker [as] . . . twin poles of visual theory about the black female body."[6] For Muñoz, ecstasy is an "invitation" to "step out of the here and now of straight time" and to embrace the possibility of futurity.[7] For me, ecstasy offers an opportunity to "step out of the here and now" of the logic of injury emphasized by black feminist visual culture studies, and to embrace the potential of *doing* black feminist visual culture studies (and, implicitly, black feminist politics) differently, of organizing around the paradoxes of pleasure rather than woundedness or the elisions of shared injury, around possibilities rather than pain. To be clear, the book does not exculpate racialized pornography or suggest that racialized pornography is the pathway to black women's political freedom. Instead, I use racialized pornography as a tool for shifting the black feminist theoretical archive away from the production and enforcement of a "protectionist" reading of representation, and toward an interpretative framework centered on complex and sometimes unnerving pleasures.[8]

By treating race as both a technology of domination and a technology of pleasure, racial iconography offers a critical departure from scholarly work on race. My conception of race is indebted to the interdisciplinary work of Loïc Wacquant, Michael Omi, Howard Winant, and Edward Telles, which reveals that race is a historically and socially contingent structure of domination, and to the work of Judith Butler, Nicole Fleetwood, Patricia Hill Collins, and Elizabeth Abel, which underscores the centrality of visuality to racial domination.[9] Drawing on their insights, I emphasize two under-theorized aspects of race: pleasure and performance.

When scholars theorize pleasures *in* race, they tend to focus on pleasures in whiteness, as is the case with George Lipsitz's interrogation of white subjects' "possessive investment in whiteness," Cheryl Harris's conception of whiteness as a valuable "property right," or Anthony Paul Farley's description of the "sadistic" pleasures white subjects take in inflicting race on nonwhite bodies.[10] When scholars examine black pleasures, they have focused on black cultural production, envisioning black popular culture as the primary articulation of black pleasure. Moreover, these scholars have imagined cultural appropriations of blackness as particularly pernicious because of the danger that nonblacks will co-opt a significant form of black pleasure. Ishmael Reed's work underscores this approach: "Is there something about black pleasure that attracts members of other races? Do members of other races see something unique about black pleasure, something that can't be found in their own origins? Why is it that 70 percent of the hip-hop market is dominated by white suburban teenagers? Why did whites take such pleasure from minstrel shows, and why did they enjoy getting up in blackface?"[11] Reed's queries suggest that black pleasures and black cultural production are inextricably linked, and that appropriation presents particular challenges for black subjects because it threatens one of the few pleasurable sites that blacks can "own."

Yet black pleasures beyond cultural production remain relatively undertheorized, leading the cultural critic Arthur Jafa to call for an investigation of black pleasure: "What are its parameters, what are its primal sites, how does Black popular culture or Black culture in general address Black pleasure? How does it generate Black pleasure? . . . This whole question of addressing Black pleasure is a critical thing."[12] My work attempts to unsettle the primacy of the appropriation debate to questions of black pleasure. Rather than presuming that black pleasures center on cultural "ownership," I instead ask how black pleasures can include sexual and erotic pleasures in racialization, *even when (and perhaps precisely because)* racialization is painful, and I assert that the racialized pornographic screen is a site that makes particularly visible the complex relationship between race and embodied pleasures. In so doing, I underscore the importance of sexual subjectivity to embodied racialization, and trace the intimate connections between sexual subjectivity and racialized subjectivity.

While pleasure is central to my conception of race, performance is as well. Joining scholars like E. Patrick Johnson, Celine Parreñas Shimizu, Robin Bernstein, and Harvey Young, I am interested in how racial formations are both crafted and disrupted through performance.[13] In particular, my close readings of pornographic films ask how black protagonists' performances of race—some spectacular, some hyperbolic, and some stereotypical—toy with racial fictions, and underscore that race is constituted, at least in part, by a "stylized repetition of acts" that can produce pleasure both for performers and for spectators.[14] These performances demonstrate that race can be entrenched, undone, and rendered hypervisible through repetition, and that racialized performances can be pleasurable for subjects on all sides of the proverbial color line.

While racial iconography foregrounds how pornography renders visible race's pleasurable and performative aspects, it also attends to the historical and technological contingency of how racialized tropes are deployed in pornography. Racial iconography is particularly interested in how pornography engages with black women's bodies, drawing on—and, at times, departing from—prevailing racial-sexual mythologies to generate spectators' viewing pleasures. Racial iconography is also sensitive to the time and place in which pornography is produced and consumed, analyzing how modes of consumption alter both visual pleasures and pornographic viewing experiences. Pornography has proven to be an endlessly malleable genre, routinely taking advantage of new viewing technologies—whether the VCR or the Internet—to reach new consumers, and race has been central to the story of pornography's incessant attempts to reach new consumers, and to generate new (and more substantial) profits.

Because racial iconography is invested in historically and technologically rooted readings of pornography, it implicitly contests a dominant black feminist "overexposure" narrative—an account which asserts that black women have been consistently and violently "exposed" on the pornographic screen.[15] Instead, racial iconography shows that the history of racialized pornography contains moments where black female bodies have been "overexposed," and other moments when black women have been wholly absent from hard-core pornography. In challenging the hegemonic overexposure account, racial iconography asks new and historically specific questions, including how do we interpret black women's absences from the pornographic visual field in particular historical moments? How can we read those absences against pornography's strategic mobilization of black women's bodies in other social, historical, cultural, and technological moments?

While my interest in black women's participation in pornography is, in part, a challenge to ahistorical accounts of racialized pornography, my project is also invested in studying how black women's bodies make race a pornographic subject, placing racial fictions and fantasies on pornography's visual agenda. The films I analyze in *The Black Body in Ecstasy* show black female protagonists rendering explicit racial mythologies, at times toying with them, at times finding pleasure in them, and at times problematizing them. In so doing, they center racial fictions' inextricable connection to sexual fictions, and emphasize that race is necessarily a pornographic fantasy.

Finally, racial iconography advances a theory of representation, one which draws on Shimizu's concept of the "bind of representation." Shimizu's work contests the long-standing presumption that images can be "positive" or "negative," instead considering how minoritarian subjects are both constrained by and potentially liberated through representation.[16] Shimizu uses the term "bind of representation" to argue that Asian-American women (the subjects at the center of her analysis) cannot be "imaged outside of perverse sexuality or non-normative sexuality. . . . Therefore, they must use that sexuality in order to create new morphologies in representation and in history."[17] Like Shimizu, I am interested in how black female pornographic protagonists navigate the "tightrope" of representation, putting to work the sexual stereotypes that often constrain them.[18] Rather than celebrating self-representation, or calling for "positive images in identification and redress in protest," racial iconography asks how black female protagonists negotiate the minefield of representation, and studies how representation can be a site where spectators and protagonists exercise freedom, even within the confines of a visual field structured by race and gender.[19]

If racial iconography is a critical reading practice that troubles black feminism's preoccupation with injury, why use racialized pornography as the visual site for unsettling black feminism's logic of woundedness? Why is racialized pornography a critical site in revealing the limitations of black feminism's engagement with visual culture?

Pornography has implicitly come to structure black feminism's conception of representation. Indeed, black feminism has often read visual culture's treatment of black women even in nonpornographic texts as a kind of pornography; pornography has become both a rhetorical device and an analytical framework, a strategy for describing and critiquing a particular re-presentation of black women's bodies. Alice Walker, for example, notes that "for centuries the black woman has served as the primary pornographic 'outlet' for White men in Europe and America."[20] Here, the "pornographic" comes to signal not the genre conventions of the hard-core, but a mode of sexualizing and objectifying black women. If the "pornographic" describes a way that black women are violated, dominant visual culture is imagined to offer a particularly explicit, uninterrupted gaze at black women's bodies, securing ideas of black women's hyperlibidinousness, ranging from black feminist critiques of blaxploitation to hip-hop feminist critiques of "video hoes" and "video vixens."[21] Engaging with racialized pornography as an actual visual enterprise structured by historical moment and technological shifts rather than as a rhetorical trope is thus necessary for unraveling the assumptions underpinning black feminism's conception of representation.

While pornography has maintained rhetorical and symbolic value for black feminists, some black feminists have been specifically concerned with racialized pornography's pernicious effects. Following Catharine MacKinnon's insight that pleasure can be the "velvet glove on the iron fist of domination," black feminists have often treated racialized pornography as particularly problematic because of its capacity to make racial inequality look sexy.[22] Walker's famous refrain that "where white women are depicted in pornography as 'objects,' black women are depicted as animals. Where white women are depicted at least as human bodies if not beings, black women are depicted as shit" has become emblematic of a prevailing black feminist approach to pornography where critiquing racialized pornography is treated as analogous to critiquing racism.[23] Examining the meaning-making work that black women's bodies have performed in pornography is central for undermining the transhistorical, transtechnological claim that racialized pornography's representational labor is always to represent black women "as shit."

While my work is born from a critique of black feminism's approach to visual culture, it is also indebted to the field and politically committed to crafting space within the black feminist theoretical archive for pleasure. My intellectual coming-of-age was facilitated by an array of black feminists whose work populated my bookshelves. Those scholars—June Jordan, Patricia J. Williams, Audre Lorde, Barbara Smith, Deborah King, and many others—shared a fundamentally important point of departure: "That life is complicated is a fact of great analytic importance."[24] My project is particularly indebted to Mireille Miller-Young's "A Taste for Brown Sugar," a history of black women's participation in pornography, which exposes the "complicated" relationship between black women's bodies and hard-core pornography. Though Miller-Young's work has a different focus than mine—it examines the complex experiences of black women laboring in the sex industry—her archival work laid the foundation for my project. Ultimately, my project does not argue for abandoning black feminism; instead, it is a "loving critique" of the field, one that parts company with many of the questions that have driven black feminist scholarship on representation, and one that hopes to bring renewed theoretical energy to its debates.[25]

Though my work positions itself in conversation with black feminism, it also critically engages other feminist traditions that have taken up, or failed to take up, the significant connections between race and pornography. To underscore the urgency of my intervention—racial iconography— I offer a brief history of feminist theoretical and political engagement with pornography to highlight both the variety of sophisticated analytical tools feminists have used to study pornography and the surprising paucity of analyses of the interplay of race and pornography. While I am critical of the relative inattention to racial meaning-making that permeates the four feminist traditions that I outline—antiporn, pro-porn, sex-radical, and feminist porn studies—this history is not meant to offer a progress narrative, to criticize earlier interventions, or to celebrate newer scholarly innovations. Instead, I endeavor to show that all four traditions have made significant theoretical contributions in tracing pornography's relationship to law, patriarchy, violence, pleasure, and privacy. Moreover, my account is purposefully attentive both to theoretical debates surrounding pornography and to political debates within feminism on how to respond to pornography's ubiquity. In so doing, I underscore that feminist theory and feminist politics are mutually constitutive.

ANTIPORNOGRAPHY FEMINISM

The term "sex wars" has often been used to describe a debate that captivated feminist scholars and activists in the late 1970s and early 1980s, and was at its most visible, and most contentious, at the Barnard College Scholar and Feminist Conference in 1982. The Barnard conference's theme of "pleasure and danger" (from which Carole Vance's now seminal edited collection emerged) attempted to theorize complex experiences of female pleasure under patriarchy, though the effort to capture complexity was threatened by the polarized debates surrounding the conference. Some antipornography feminists, who claimed that they had been excluded from conversations about the conference's planning, protested outside the conference wearing shirts embossed with "For Feminist Sexuality, Against S/M." As a result of the negative publicity, Barnard College halted printing of the conference's publication, *Diary of a Conference*, which contained writing and artwork focused on the politics of sexuality from a number of activist-scholars, including Gayle Rubin, Amber Hollibaugh, and Carole Vance. (Barnard eventually reprinted the volume, but redacted its name from the publication. As Janet Jakobsen notes, "The College effectively paid thousands of dollars to have Barnard's name taken off of the document, thus removing the College's connection to this important body of work.")[26]

While the Barnard conference became the "flash point for a revolution in how feminists could approach questions of sexuality," an antipornography movement (which was part of a larger feminist antiviolence movement) had been gaining momentum for a few years.[27] The legal scholar Catharine MacKinnon and the activist Andrea Dworkin became the centerpieces of a movement that envisioned pornography as a visual celebration of patriarchal power and women's subordination. For antipornography feminists, pornography is not simply an explicit depiction of women's subjugation; it constitutes violence and disguises it as mere representation.

Because pornography functions as an *act* which secures male power, antipornography feminists argue that pornography both mirrors and cements the actual position of women under conditions of patriarchy.[28] MacKinnon asserts, "In pornography, there it is, in one place, all of the abuses that women had to struggle so long even to begin to articulate, all the unspeakable abuse: the rape, the battery, the sexual harassment, the prostitution, and the sexual abuse of children. Only in pornography it is called something else: sex, sex, sex, sex, and sex, respectively."[29] Pornography, then, celebrates male dominance, it eroticizes sexual assault, it glamorizes female subordination, and it "sexualizes women's inequality"—quite simply, it is the linchpin of male control over female bodies.[30]

Antipornography feminists, then, actively rebut the idea that pornography is merely benign fantasy. Dorchen Leidholdt argues, "The environment in which we learn about and experience our bodies and sexuality is a world not of sexual freedom but of sexual force. Is it any surprise that it is often force that we eroticize? Sadistic and masochistic fantasies may be part of our sexuality, but they are no more our freedom than the culture of misogyny and sexual violence that endangered them."[31] Leidholdt shows that the very content of fantasy is shaped by male dominance, suggesting that our affective lives are shaped by "the culture of misogyny." If "sexual force" constitutes the milieu in which our sexual subjectivities develop, antipornography feminists assert, then our sexual practices and pleasures are suffused with the practices of patriarchy.

Nowhere are the dangers of fantasy more apparent than in racialized pornography, a representational site that antipornography feminists have been particularly invested in critiquing. Indeed, antipornography feminists have strategically mobilized claims about race to bolster their arguments about the gendered harms of pornography.[32] These scholars imagine racialized pornography as produced through gendered pornographic representations, asserting that "pornography contains a racial hierarchy in which women are rated as prized objects or despised objects according to their color."[33] For antipornography feminists, pornography oppresses all women, yet it subordinates women differently based on race. Ultimately, this body of scholarship treats race as "an intensifier" which demonstrates the severity of pornography's gender-based injury, and as an analytic tool that helps antipornography feminists secure their claims to pornography's harms.[34]

Despite their interest in using race to bolster claims about pornography's sexism, antipornography feminists have been inattentive to pornography's mobilization of particular racial and ethnic differences. They conflate the variety of racial and ethnic representations within pornography under a theory that the deployment of *any* racial or ethnic trope always renders pornography pernicious sexist representation. MacKinnon's description of racialized pornographic tropes is emblematic of this approach.

> Asian women are bound so they are not recognizably human, so inert they could be dead. Black women play plantation, struggling against their bonds. Jewish women orgasm in reenactments of Auschwitz. . . . Amputees and other disabled or ill women's injuries or wounds or stumps are proffered as sexual fetishes. Retarded girls are gratifyingly compliant. Adult women are infantilized as children, children are adult women, interchangeably fusing vulnerability with sluttish eagerness said to be natural to women of all ages, beginning at age one.[35]

For MacKinnon, there is a basic fungibility to racialized tropes in pornography: all racially or ethnically marked women are exploited "as women" and are the most exploited of women.

Despite the interchangeability of racial and ethnic tropes in antipornography theory, black women have held a special rhetorical and theoretical status for this project. To secure their claims that pornography is a particularly undesirable form of sexist representation, antipornography scholars compare the pornographic treatment of black and white women, advancing the claim that the presence of black women's bodies in pornography makes pornography *more* sexist. Luisah Teish notes, "The pornography industry's exploitation of the Black woman's body is qualitatively different from that of the white woman. While white women are pictured as pillow-soft pussy willows, the stereotype of the Black 'dominatrix' portrays the Black woman as ugly, sadistic, and animalistic, undeserving of human attention."[36] The study of "qualitative differences" in representation has two significant implications. First, antipornography scholars argue that black women are represented "worse" than white women, and that the gendered exploitation of women inherent to pornography is multiplied for black women. This comparison ultimately yields the insights that racialized pornography is doubly dangerous, as it is both racist and sexist, and that black women are exploited more than white women in pornography, entrenching a "black women have it bad" logic with little examination of the historically specific ways that black women are represented.[37] Second, womanhood functions as a unifying common denominator across racial difference. While black women are treated worse than white women, both black and white women are oppressed *as women*. The difference in their treatment is a difference in degree, not in kind.

If antipornography feminism is a robust theory of patriarchal power, it is also a theory of legal action. The movement endorses the abolition of pornography under a theory that pornography has both production and consumption harms: women are injured through their participation in the production of pornography, and all women are injured through the circulation of pornography. The Minneapolis pornography civil rights hearings that took place in 1983—chronicled in MacKinnon's and Dworkin's collection *In Harm's Way*—document the involuntary nature of women's labor in "sex factories," where pornography is produced, and refute the assumption promoted by the pornography industry that women are in pornography because they want to be there.[38] As one woman who testified at the hearing noted, "Every single thing you see in pornography is happening to a real woman right now."[39] Yet antipornography feminists' concerns extend beyond the women victimized by pornography production. MacKinnon writes, "Sex forced on real women so that it can be sold at profit and forced on other real women; women's bodies trussed and maimed and raped and made into things to be hurt and obtained and accessed, and this presented as the nature of women in a way that is acted on and acted out, over and over; the coercion that has become invisible—this and more bothers feminists about pornography."[40] Eliminating pornography entirely, then, is the only way to ensure that women are not subjected to the violent production of pornography—conditions which MacKinnon sees as analogous to prostitution and rape—and that women are not subjected to the continued circulation of images which normalize male violence against women.

These dual concerns animated MacKinnon and Dworkin's attempts to abolish pornography through an ordinance that defined pornography as "the graphic sexually explicit subordination of women, whether in pictures or in words . . . [including representations where] . . . women are presented as sexual objects who enjoy pain or humiliation; or . . . women are presented as sexual objects for domination, conquest, violation, exploitation, possession, or use, or through postures or positions of servility or submission of display."[41] The proposed ordinance, which *American Booksellers v. Hudnut* struck down in 1985 because of its unconstitutional breadth, centered on the elimination of pornography in the service of pro-

tecting all women from pornography's harms, and demo
pornography feminists' commitment to marshal law to pr
bodily integrity and sexual autonomy.[42]

Though their engagement with the state to abolish p
traction after *American Booksellers v. Hudnut,* antipornograpny ......
maintained its cohesiveness as a political moment. Contemporary antipornography feminists extend the work of MacKinnon and Dworkin by
centering the importance of analyses of capitalism on pornography's
omnipresence and by tracing the impact of pornography's omnipresence
on intimate life. Gail Dines, for example, argues that "pornographers are
capitalists and they control much of the speech on sexuality. Anti-porn
feminists are repeatedly censored from mainstream media and silenced by
the capitalist juggernaut that is the porn industry."[43] For Dines, pornography's ubiquity is intimately related to the fact that it is big business; pornographers' tremendous profits afford them to control dominant media
and to effectively silence antipornography critique. Contemporary antipornography feminists also argue that pornography's omnipresence has
come to fundamentally alter the fabric of intimate life. As Dines argues,
"To think that men and women can walk away from the images they consume makes no sense in light of what we know about how images shape
our sense of reality."[44] To that end, the labor of some contemporary antipornography work is to trace how pornography's cultural presence de-
stroys intimacy, commodifies relationships, and glamorizes violence.

While I am deeply critical of antipornography feminism's reliance on
law as an attempt to safeguard women's bodily integrity, its wholesale
neglect of pleasure, and its symbolic use of black women's bodies, my
analysis remains fundamentally interested in two foundational premises
of antipornography thought. First, antipornography feminism convinc-
ingly argues that female subjects' experiences of pleasure are mediated by
patriarchy and its intersection with other structures of domination. This
is not to say that one's experience of pleasure is inauthentic; rather, antipornography feminism uncovers that pleasures are enjoyed against the
backdrop of patriarchy and heteronormativity, and that this context casts
a profound shadow on the pleasures we experience. Second, this scholarly tradition shows that pleasure can mask the pernicious workings of
patriarchy. By critically interrogating pleasure, rather than simply celebrating it as necessarily positive, antipornography feminism shows that

hierarchy often wears the guise of pleasure. Both of these critical interventions underpin my own readings of racialized pornography, spectatorship, and visual pleasures.

PRO-PORNOGRAPHY FEMINISM

Pro-pornography feminism emerged as a response to antipornography's uncritical reliance on the state for redress. Pro-pornography feminists insist that there is a long American tradition of using law to promote sexual puritanism, and argue that state regulation of pornography will hurt sexual minorities and reify sexual hierarchies, continuing the tradition of valuing, indeed sacralizing, some forms of sex and denigrating, even outlawing, others.[45] These feminists point to the "strange bedfellows" pairing of radical feminists and social conservatives in their effort to pass antipornography legislation, exposing the regressive and oppressive underpinnings of the antipornography project.[46]

Moreover, pro-pornography feminists interpret state regulation of pornography as a dangerous form of censorship. In response to MacKinnon's and Dworkin's model antipornography ordinance, a group of feminists formed the Feminist Anti-Censorship Taskforce (FACT), which submitted an amicus brief in anticipation of the Seventh Circuit's decision in *American Booksellers v. Hudnut*. Central to FACT's argument was that the ordinance's breadth allowed the state far too much leeway to define the scope of the pornographic, permitting the suppression of free speech. In the brief, FACT wrote, "Sexually explicit expression, including much that is covered by the ordinance, carries many more messages than simply the misogyny described by Appellants. It may convey the message that sexuality need not be tied to reproduction, men or domesticity. It may contain themes of sex for no reason other than pleasure, sex without commitment, and sexual adventure—all of which are surely ideas."[47] In arguing for pornography's multiple meanings, FACT treated pornography as speech worthy of First Amendment protection (in contrast to antipornography feminists' insistence that pornography is an act and not speech) and characterized antipornography feminists as conservative censors.

In the years following the defeat of antipornography legislation, pro-pornography feminism's political movement began to lose its cohesiveness. Yet in the early 1990s, a cohort of activists and cultural critics, including Camille Paglia, Katie Roiphe, and Naomi Wolf, produced a new brand of pro-pornography feminism that was preoccupied with critiquing so-called victim feminism.[48] These scholars, as Kathryn Abrams notes, "decried the 'victim' status assigned to women by dominance feminism" and "warned—often with marked antipathy toward feminist activists—that depictions of women as sexually subordinated encourage a wounded passivity on the part of women and a repressive regulatory urge on the part of state authorities."[49] More than that, these feminists often celebrated pornography, and women's involvement in it, arguing that participation in pornography constitutes the epitome of female liberation. Paglia exemplifies this position, arguing, "Far from poisoning the mind, pornography shows the deepest truth about sexuality, stripped of romantic veneer. . . . What feminists denounce as woman's humiliating total accessibility in porn is actually her elevation to high priestess of a pagan paradise garden, where the body has become a bountiful fruit tree and where growth and harvest are simultaneous."[50] For Paglia, pornography enables women to cultivate their sexual subjectivities by accessing the "deepest truth about sexuality."[51]

If Paglia, Roiphe, and Wolf constituted a cohort of feminists invested in destabilizing the notion of female victimization, uncoupling feminism from an analysis of women's subordination, and celebrating female liberation through commodified sex, contemporary pro-pornography feminisms have built on this tradition. With the advent of third-wave feminism and its embrace of sex-positive feminism, an iteration of feminist praxis that celebrates sexual freedom has allowed a new era of pro-pornography feminism to emerge.[52] This new epoch, with its fetishization of choice, views the consumption and production of pornography as potentially liberatory and celebrates subjects' "choice" to consume or produce whatever they enjoy.

Surprisingly absent from pro-pornography feminism is an engagement with how race (and other structures of domination) fundamentally alter and constrain women's access to sexual pleasure and agency. Fortunately, a new and more complex form of sex-positivity has begun to take hold within the parameters of black feminism, with work by scholars like LaMonda Stallings, Siobhan Brooks, and Shayne Lee asking how "a pro-sex vision can supplement the feminist quest for social and sexual equality by delving into popular culture to see the production of proactive scripts for female sexuality and erotic agency."[53] The development of sex-positivity within black feminism has productively bracketed older black feminist conversations about respectability and sexual conservatism, instead attempting to place black female sexual agency at the heart of black feminist conversations.

While my work challenges pro-pornography feminism's tendency to neglect the context in which the decision to participate, or not participate, in sex work occurs and its unproblematized celebration of the language of choice, I share with this tradition a great suspicion of state regulation of pornography and the injuries it can inflict on sexual minorities. In fact, my work is underpinned by the idea that law is an imperfect device, a blunt instrument, which often forecloses the rights of far too many in an attempt to safeguard the liberties of some. Moreover, my work builds on (and aspires to contribute to) the chorus of scholars working within black feminism who draw upon sex-positive theory to advocate for a black feminist politics of pleasure.

THE SEX-RADICAL REJOINDER

Sex-radicalism disrupted the contentious anti-pornography/pro-pornography debate that marked the early 1980s. Emerging from two canonical volumes—*Pleasure and Danger: Exploring Female Sexuality* (1984) and Ann Snitow's *Powers of Desire: The Politics of Sexuality* (1983)—sex-radicalism destabilized the tendency to view pornography as exclusively a site of women's subordination or a locus of women's agency. Instead, sex-radicals studied how arousal, pleasure, subordination, and dominance are co-constitutive, and emphasized the contingent and complex meanings inherent to each pornographic text.

This attention to pornography's multiple meanings allowed sex-radicals—including performer Annie Sprinkle, filmmaker Candida Royalle, and scholar-activists Jill Nagle, Wendy Chapkis, and Vicky Funari—to investigate how feminists could challenge the dominant pornographic aesthetic from inside the parameters of the genre, producing a plethora of feminist pornographies that drew on the aesthetic conventions of the hard-core, but imbue them with feminist sensibilities. Sex-radicals prioritized feminist work that claimed the female subject's affirmative rights to sexual autonomy, sexual pleasure, and sexual subjectivity, rather than staking out her negative rights to be free from sexual violence. Unlike pro-sex feminists, though, sex-radicals emphasized sexuality as a fraught site for female subjects (rather than simply a site of agency), a space where pleasure and danger bleed into each other in messy ways, particularly for multiply marginalized subjects.

Because sex-radicals were particularly interested in creating cultural space for women's pleasures, they were committed to dismantling sexual hierarchies and promoting sexual diversity.[54] As a result, this project actively contested the installation of certain sexual practices as "feminist." Indeed, sex-radicals refused to interpret either viewing pornography or opposing pornography as necessarily feminist, and instead argued that feminism's purview did not include moral judgments. Amber Hollibaugh asserts, "Feminism cannot be the new voice of morality and virtue, leaving behind everyone whose class, race, and desires never fit comfortably into a straight, white, male (or female) world. . . . Instead of pushing our movement further to the right, we should be attempting to create a viable sexual future and a movement powerful enough to defend us simultaneously against sexual abuse."[55] Rather than condemning particular sexual practices, sex-radicals challenged feminism to develop a politics that opens up sexual possibility.

Sex-radicals often crafted creative political strategies to protect women's bodily autonomy while simultaneously helping women unleash their sexual subjectivities. The legal scholar Drucilla Cornell, for example, advocates zoning pornographic displays to prevent unwanted viewing of pornography. Zoning, she argues, "keep[s] pornography safely resting in its jackets, out of the view of those who seek to inhabit or construct an imaginary domain independent of the one it offers," and yet ensures that it is accessible for those women who long to see it, who find hard-core pornography important to the development of their "imaginary domains."[56] Cornell's strategy is underpinned by the idea that pornography might constitute freedom for some subjects and oppression for others; the labor of law is thus to ensure access for those who desire it and freedom from viewing for those whose bodily autonomy and sexual integrity require it.

Sex-radical feminists were also staunchly committed to including sex workers' experiences in feminist conversations about pornography's meanings. In fact, sex-radicals refused to treat "sex worker" and "feminist" as oppositional identities, instead asking how sex workers infuse their daily labor with feminist ideologies (this is most visible in Jill Nagle's provocatively titled anthology *Whores and Other Feminists*). In viewing sex workers as agents and sex work as a form of labor, these scholars consider the multiplicity of ways that sex workers exploit sex work's interstices, staging resistance from within paid erotic labor.[57]

My work embraces sex-radicalism's interest in complexity and its fundamental commitment to treating both pornography and sexuality as contingent and fraught terrain. Though I find that sex-radicalism lacks a robust method for decoding pornography's multiple meanings, my own analyses are fundamentally connected to sex radicalism's insistence that pornographic texts have multiple—rather than singular—meanings. Moreover, I am inspired by sex radicalism's fundamental investment in treating sex work as labor and in treating sex workers as feminists without either romanticizing or condemning the practice of sex work or the labor of sex workers.

FEMINIST PORN STUDIES

Born with the release of Linda Williams's *Hard Core: Power, Pleasure and the "Frenzy of the Visible"* in 1989, feminist porn studies takes as its point of departure the fact that pornography is "on/scene," that "culture brings on to the public scene the very organs, acts, 'bodies and pleasures' that have heretofore been designated obscene, that is, as needing to be kept out of view."[58] Feminist porn studies treats pornography not as an aberration, but as a ubiquitous part of public life that insistently makes visible that which is supposed to be "out of view." In so doing, feminist porn studies scholars have ushered in an era of theorizing pornographies, with an attention to pornography's historical and technological context, pornographic genre conventions, and pornography's multiple meanings.[59]

Feminist porn studies' theoretical approach to grappling with pornography's meanings has been staunchly Foucauldian. Pornography is imagined as a phallocentric discursive project, a kind of *scientia sexualis*, which seeks to elicit the "truth" of pleasure, particularly female pleasure, by asking female bodies to make their pleasures knowable.[60] Williams captures this, noting that "the history of hard-core film could thus be summarized in part as the history of various strategies devised to overcome this problem of invisibility within a regime that is . . . an 'erotic organization of visibility.'"[61] Ultimately, the pornographic aesthetic is a frustrated one because it cannot capture quantifiable, legible proof of female pleasure—the female orgasm—in the way that it so easily captures visual evidence of male pleasure through the money shot, a close-up of the ejaculating penis.[62] Though the male spectator seeks the "truth" of women's pleasures, he sees only a reflection of his own pleasure, witnessing the male protagonist's sexual climax. It is the will-to-know the "truth" of the female body, and the incessant frustration of that will, that most clearly displays the pornographic repetition compulsion.

Unlike the other feminist theoretical traditions, feminist-porn-studies scholars including Williams, Constance Penley, and Nguyen Tan Hoang have been particularly interested in studying how race produces meanings and engenders pleasures on the pornographic screen. Feminist-porn-studies scholarship draws on the same Foucauldian framework when it turns its attention to racialized pornography, arguing that the presence of the black body (or any racially marked body) on the pornographic screen performs a confessional role, promising to display the "truth" of its ostensibly different pleasures and practices to the spectator. Williams's work epitomizes this deployment of a Foucauldian theoretical framework to understand racialized pornography: "If pornography is a genre that seeks to confess the discursive truths of sex, then what happens when racialized bodies are asked to reveal their particular 'truths'? And what does it mean when the taboos enforcing the racial border are systematically violated and 'black cock' penetrates 'white pussy'?"[63] For Williams, racialized pornography can best be understood as a racialized *scientia sexualis*, an attempt to make both racial and sexual difference knowable to its spectator.

While my project—like nearly every academic project on pornography written in the last twenty years—is indebted to Williams's groundbreaking analyses of pornography, I part company with feminist porn studies in important ways. I aspire to problematize the reliance on a Foucauldian paradigm which presumes that difference—both gender and racial—structures the relationship between spectator and protagonist, with the spectator seeking the "truths" of something unknown. This effectively erases black pornographic spectatorship (male or female) and implicitly presumes that pleasure-in-looking hinges on difference, rather than analyzing how spectators might take pleasure in sameness, in seeing themselves—their bodies, their pleasures, their longings—projected onscreen. More than that, this insistence that the pornographic scene is fundamentally structured by difference elides all of the ways that the pornographic promise of difference gets interrupted, ruptured, and troubled, sometimes by the very protagonists whose bodies are rhetorically and visually evoked as sites of difference.

The problem with feminist porn studies' emphasis on difference is particularly apparent in Williams's conception of the interracial scene as one that features "black cock" penetrating "white pussy." Here, Williams suggests that the pleasure that the interracial scene generates is one of visually and materially "violating" a racial border. But this articulation of racialized pornography's pleasures effectively erases black women from the analytic and visual frame. By treating "interracial" as synonymous with a black male–white female configurations of bodies, Williams ignores the plethora of pornographies that feature black women, and the erotic, aesthetic, and political charges that different gendered arrangements of interracial sex produce. I respond to black women's erasure from feminist-porn-studies scholarship by centering the meaning-making work that black female protagonists perform on the pornographic screen.

Moreover, while feminist-porn-studies scholarship has provided important insights into the historical and technological specificity of pornography imagery, and identified the panoply of meaning-making work that bodies perform on the pornographic screen, when this body of work turns to racialized pornography, it tends to foreground the racism ostensibly inherent to racialized pornography. For example, Williams's analysis of the Kinsey Institute's collection of stag films endeavors to stake out a "historically nuanced way of reading female agency in stag films, something that can be located *between* white slavery and the ethnography of sex workers."[64] Yet when Williams turns to considering a racialized stag film, questions of agency are wholly bracketed, and her analysis instead centers on the racism inherent in one of stag's most terrifying films. Williams offers a close reading of KKK *Night Riders* (ca. 1930s), a film which represents a Klansman (who remains hooded for the duration of the film) breaking into a black woman's house and raping her. The sex, which initially appears forced, is quickly transformed into something pleasurable for both the black female protagonist and, of course, for the hooded Klansman.[65] For Williams, the film is significant because it makes clear the shortcomings of feminist engagements with agency in the context of the stag film, a term which she argues "says too little about the historically determined, coercive context of black female and white male sexual interactions depicted here under the very sign of a white supremacy designed to reassert the race- and gender-based prerogatives of white men."[66] While KKK Night Riders deserves critical attention to its terrifying representation of racial-sexual violence, my interest is in how Williams's insistence on "historically nuanced" readings of agency gets bracketed in a conversation about race. Clearly, KKK Night Riders is a film where (black) female agency is absent and a film that brutally eroticizes racial violence. Though I suspect Williams's deployment of the film is to demonstrate the importance of race in conversations about agency on the pornographic screen, I am interested in how black female protagonists are analytically used as the outer limits of conversations about agency. The presence of black women on the pornographic screen (in the context of a stag film that sexualizes the most terrifying forms of racial violence) means agency is absent. My impulse, of course, is not to critique Williams for documenting (and criticizing) pleasurable viewings of deeply painful scenes or for underscoring the presence of racial violence in stag films. Instead, my interest is in how black women appear in Williams's account as evidence of agency's absence, and how their presence in other pornographic contexts is elided.

While my work is committed to many of feminist porn studies' foundational tenets, particularly its commitment to studying pornographies, my project pushes against the Foucauldian hegemony that has marked feminist-porn-studies scholarship. By interrogating the notion that black bodies appear in pornography exclusively to confess difference or to bare their bodies' imagined truths, my project unravels a host of assumptions about spectatorship, visual pleasure, and race that have been smuggled into feminist-porn-studies scholarship.

Notes on Method

Unlike earlier scholarly traditions which either wholly bracket an analysis of pornography's varied use of racialized images or presume that race is a kind of "intensifier," treating racialized pornography as particularly pernicious form of pornography, I approach racialized pornography as a visual form that tells us something about "who we are as a culture," as a rich repository of information about collective fantasies and racial fictions.[67] If, as Laura Kipnis argues, "pornography is the royal road to the cultural psyche," the contemporary equivalent of Clifford Geertz's Balinese cock-fight, then racialized pornography contains at least some of the stories we tell—or *like* to tell—ourselves about our bodies and pleasures, and about "other" people's bodies and pleasures.[68] Ultimately, I use racialized pornography as a window through which I can ask new questions about the complex relationship among race, gender, and pleasure.

My method for analyzing racialized pornographic texts is close reading. Because I am invested in closely reading texts, I have largely bracketed engagement with the biographies of pornographic filmmakers or pornographic actors, and instead focused on the racialized meaning-making performed by various pornographic texts. I am also cognizant of the important critiques of close readings of film generally, and of pornographic texts more specifically, including critiques that close reading neglects pornography's complex social functions. John Champagne's work on queer pornographies persuasively argues that close reading "obscure[s] some of the social functions of gay pornography in particular," eliding consideration of the ways that pornography "makes possible a social space in which dominant forms of (sexual) subjectivity might be (re)produced, challenged, countered, and violated."[69] By ignoring the conditions under which pornography is screened and the variety of guises—or disguises— its public display takes, textual analyses often neglect the social context of its production and consumption.[70] While Champagne's work focuses on the queer (counter) public viewing cultures that pornography produced, his intervention informs my commitment to grapple with interpretation, reception, and production, alongside close readings of scenes. My analyses move back and forth between text and context, between representation and the multitude of possible spectator responses.

My interest in the variety of spectatorial responses is particularly significant, as pornographic spectators are generally presumed to screen pornography with their penises in their hands. Indeed, as MacKinnon notes, pornography is generally imagined to be simply "masturbation material."[71] This analytical assumption ignores the host of nonmasturbatory pleasures pornography engenders and the complexity of consumption, particularly the psychic and intellectual "labor" of interpretation.[72] Jennifer Wicke describes this as "the shuffling and collating and transcription of images or words so that they have effectivity within one's own fantasy universe—an act of accommodation, as it were. This will often entail wholesale elimination of elements of the representation, or changing salient features within it; the representation needs to blur into or become charged with historical and/or private fantasy meanings."[73] The dominant perception that pornography is used exclusively to produce (male) arousal and to aid in (male) masturbation ignores the variety of social and cultural uses to which pornography might be put, and the interpretative labor that the consumer engages in to transform the on-screen narrative into something that can produce a coherent, engaging, and exciting fantasy. In my close readings I attempt to decenter the prevailing assumption that pornography is exclusively "masturbation material," instead asking about the hosts of pleasures—visual, comical, aesthetic, racial, political—pornography can engender.[74] In so doing, I heed Kipnis's warning: "Pornography isn't viewed as having complexity, because its *audience* isn't viewed as having complexity, and this propensity for oversimplification gets reproduced in every discussion about pornography."[75] Taking Kipnis's insight as a point of departure, my close readings are infused by an attention to the personhood, the messy subjectivity, of *all* pornographic spectators, even as they are limited by the paucity of scholarly information available about actual spectatorship.

As I am interested in pornography's "social functions," its spectators' complexity, and the spaces in which it is consumed and enjoyed, I am also interested in the relationship among history, technology, and representation. My close readings of Golden Age (1970s) and Silver Age (1980s) films are committed to tracing how viewing technologies shaped representational practices and viewing pleasures in both epochs. For example, the Golden Age fundamentally transformed pornographic viewing experiences. In the wake of *Miller v. California* (1973), which defined the obscene as materials that cultivate "prurient interest" and lack "redeeming" scientific, artistic, or cultural importance, pornographers labored to produce films filled with "redeeming" narratives. These new films, which resembled feature-length Hollywood films, were screened publicly (and legally) in urban theaters that attracted mixed-sex and mixed-race audiences.[76] My analysis of Golden Age films—*Lialeh* and *Sexworld*—is explicitly invested in the pleasures that collective public viewing engendered, in the similarities between the films and mainstream feature-length Hollywood films, and in pornographers' narrative attempts to capitalize on a new and more diverse audience. In my attention to historical moment I aspire to heed Elizabeth Freeman's insight that "close reading is a way into history, not a way out of it, and [is] itself a form of historiography and historical analysis."[77]

If my close readings are invested in pornography's social functions and historical context, they are decidedly a departure from earlier feminist close-reading practices, which were invested in the male gaze. The lengthy history of male-gaze scholarship, beginning with Laura Mulvey's seminal "Visual Pleasure and Narrative Cinema," draws on "psychoanalytic theory . . . [as] a political weapon, demonstrating the way the unconscious of patriarchal society has structured film form."[78] Even as feminist work on film has shifted from the psychoanalytic model of Mulvey's work to a media-studies model, the "male gaze" continues to inform much of the work on pornography. However, the male gaze has become so predominant—particularly in analyses of pornography—that there is little engagement with why the gaze is the primary unit of analysis for analyzing the relationship between the on-screen object and the spectator. In particular, the male-gaze framework's simplistic mapping of gender onto looking positions, its inattention to the possibilities of cross-sex identification, and its implicit normative judgment—the "male gaze" is, as Edward Snow notes, "a fixed and almost entirely negative term"—suggests the importance of rethinking the very premises underpinning this scholarship.[79] My close readings tug at the seams of conventional feminist film scholarship, critiquing the hegemony of particular analytical frameworks, while remaining attentive to the messy relationship between looking and power.

Throughout the book, my close readings are supplemented with images from the films, a decision I made after considering the extensive debate among feminist-porn-studies scholars as to the role of images in scholarly writing about pornography.[80] Williams's first edition of Hard Core explicitly avoided the inclusion of pornographic images because "there is no getting around the ability of such images, especially if quoted out of context, to leap off the page to more viewers and thus to prove too facilely whatever 'truths' of sex seem most immediately apparent."[81] In "forgo[ing] the luxury of illustration," Williams gestured both to the marginal and often-times stigmatized place of feminist porn studies in the academy and to the argumentative force (and shock value) of pornographic images.[82] Writing twenty-five years after Williams's work has legitimized, if not institutionalized, the academic study of pornography, I need not "forgo the luxury of illustration." While I recognize the power of images to "leap off the page" and the danger that the images included here might trouble or unsettle some readers, my hope is that viewing images alongside my interpretative work will invite readers to engage in close readings *with* me and will allow readers to hold me accountable for providing rigorous proof to support my interpretations. More than that, though, I hope the images—and their power to unsettle and excite, offend and titillate, humor and disgust—will make grounded my insistence that pornography generates a multiplicity of complex (and sometimes contradictory) reactions.

If close reading is my method for engaging with pornographic films, it is also my method for analyzing the black feminist theoretical archive, a collection of texts and images which, I argue, actively produces and enforces the idea of wounded black female flesh. My understanding of the importance of close reading the black feminist theoretical archive is informed by Clare Hemmings's work.[83] Hemmings's *Why Stories Matter* offers a compelling account of why feminists must attend to the "political grammar of our storytelling" and recognize the "amenability of our own stories, narrative constructs, and grammatical forms to discursive uses of gender and feminism we might otherwise wish to disentangle ourselves from if history is not simply to repeat itself."[84] While our scholarly preoccupations are different, I heed Hemmings's caution to closely analyze black feminist "storytelling," paying careful attention to the "political grammar" of black feminist theory, to the ways that certain analytical frameworks—injury and recovery—have *become* predominant. Following Hemmings's lead, I resist reducing the black feminist theoretical archive to a singular perspective or agenda; instead, I argue that a vibrant and varied archive that contains different theories of representation still manages to collectively perform the black female body as an injured site, producing an archive that is structured by a "grammar" of woundedness. Ultimately, as my commitment to close reading *both* pornographic texts *and* the black feminist theoretical archive shows, this volume is underpinned by an investment in close reading as a practice that can unsettle ossified narratives and expose analytical frameworks that are so entrenched as to seem naturalized.

I begin with a close reading of the black feminist theoretical archive's engagement with representation, arguing that it has become oriented toward twin logics of injury and recovery which make theorizing black female pleasures from within the parameters of the archive a kind of impossibility. In the remainder of this volume I turn the practice of close reading toward hard-core pornography with an interest in staging black feminist readings of racialized pornography *outside of dominant black feminist interpretative paradigms.* In chapters 2 and 3 I examine two Golden Age pornographic films—*Lialeh* and *Sexworld*—with an interest in the kinds of pleasures those films engender for black pornographic spectators and for black pornographic protagonists. In chapter 4 and 5 I examine two Silver Age films—*Black Taboo* and *Black Throat*—analyzing how race becomes the subject of pornographic humor in both films, and arguing that black female pornographic protagonists are the subjects who comically, hyperbolically, and productively poke fun at the very project of race. My hope is that these close readings both disrupt the prevailing logic of the black feminist theoretical archive and create space for crafting a black feminist theoretical archive oriented toward ecstasy.

important

1 | ARCHIVES OF PAIN

Reading the Black Feminist Theoretical Archive

In Renee Cox's self-portrait *Hot-En-Tot*, Cox re-enacts the nineteenth-century public display of the so-called Hottentot Venus, Saartjie Baartman (figure 1.1).[1] At the dawning of the nineteenth century, European audiences were fascinated by Baartman, a Khoikhoi woman who was an object of caged display at exhibitions in London and Paris.[2] In an era where locating the other's imagined racial, sexual, physiological, and moral differences justified colonialism and slavery, Baartman's body functioned as a "master text" that allowed audiences to access and assess the "primitive" other.[3] Of particular interest were her breasts, her buttocks (her imagined steatopygia), and her labia (her imagined "Hottentot apron"), all of which were thought to indicate an abundant sexual appetite.[4]

In *Hot-En-Tot*, Cox wears an "armature" of buttocks and breasts to call attention to the most mythologized portions of Baartman's body and to underscore what Baartman's viewers (and perhaps contemporary viewers of Cox's portrait) *thought they would see*: black female sexual excess.[5] The strings that attach the exaggerated breasts and buttocks to Cox's body call attention to the artifice of racial mythologies—which are always, it seems, spectacular and larger than life—while also reflecting how these mythologies are worn and even imposed on black female bodies. If black female

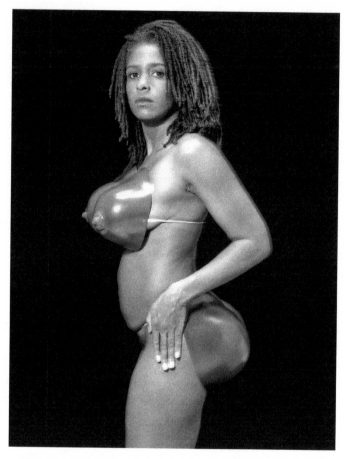

1.1 Renee Cox, *Hot-En-Tot*, 1994. Courtesy of the artist.

flesh has acted as the canvas onto which ideas of difference have been projected, Cox's self-portrait pokes fun at the search for the "truth" of racial difference that animated nineteenth-century racial pseudoscience, and underscores the violence this search has repeatedly inflicted on black women. In so doing, she reveals that the logics underpinning Baartman's display also undergird contemporary racialized representation, which continues the search for the "truth" of black female difference. Cox's embodiment of Baartman's exhibition acts as a vehicle for a larger critique of visual culture; it demonstrates both that representation is a practice which consistently makes demands on black women to expose their imagined differences and that representation is a racialized practice because visual technologies—most notably the photograph—emerged, at least in part, to make imagined racial and sexual difference visible.[6] The Hottentot Venus story becomes Hot-En-Tot's "touchstone" for a robust theory of sexuality, race, history, and representation.[7]

Of course, Cox is not simply reenacting the objectifying conditions that marked Baartman's brutal display; instead, she emphatically and defiantly matches the spectator's difference-seeking gaze, undermining a visual tradition of black female accessibility.[8] Describing her artistic process, Cox notes, "I was able to return the gaze to the Hottentot Venus. I felt that was the triumphant moment. . . ."[9] In "returning the gaze," Cox's portrait allows the Hottentot Venus to boldly look back at those who relentlessly observed her, and reveals the genre conventions of a black feminist counter-aesthetic which uses the visual field as the site for contesting black women's hypervisibility. By striking what Janell Hobson calls a "Venus pose," Cox uses the body—the site of Baartman's degradation— as a way of recovering Baartman's history and as a strategy for connecting Baartman's history to contemporary black women's embodied experiences.[10] As Hobson notes, Cox's portrait "suggest[s] ways in which historical imagery of the body lingers in the present and in which an alternative aesthetic might disrupt such imagery."[11]

I treat Cox's Hot-En-Tot as my point of departure because it epitomizes one interpretative strategy black feminists deploy to theorize visual culture: they use the Hottentot Venus story as a method both for making visible the connection between the past and an unfolding present, and for staging a larger critique of dominant visual culture that emphasizes representation as a practice that references and reenacts historical traumas. Black feminist retellings of the Hottentot Venus story, like Cox's portrait, treat Baartman as the paradigmatic case of racialized sexuality and as a "crucial element in black female contestations of the common perceptions and misconceptions of black female sexuality."[12] While Cox's portrait epitomizes one black feminist mode of interpretation, it mobilizes other dominant black feminist interpretative practices as well, including the presumption that black female flesh can be recovered through the visual field and the assumption that representation degrades black women by treating part of their bodies—here, the mythologized breasts and buttocks—as evidence of black women's deviance generally, and by treating one black woman—here, Baartman—as representative of all black women's alterity.

This chapter uses close readings of seminal black feminist texts as a strategy for uncovering the dominant interpretative modes that black feminist theory has deployed to critically examine the politics and pitfalls of representation. While various black feminist texts read visual culture differently, and maintain distinctive political commitments, the black feminist theoretical archive—a collection of scholarly texts and visual images created by cultural producers invested in recovering black female bodies—collectively presumes the meaning of the black female body in the visual field and assumes that representation injures black women. Of course, black feminist scholars grapple with the nature and origin of dominant representation's violence differently, crafting distinctive approaches to visual culture's harm; yet, what these texts share is the fundamental belief that representation inflicts violence on black female bodies.

This archive also dedicates itself to what might be understood as the flip side of a preoccupation with injury: a practice of visual defense and recovery. Indeed, the architecture of the black feminist theoretical archive is undergirded by twin logics of injury and "protectionism," marked by what Carol Henderson calls "signs of wounding and signs of healing."[13] These "signs of healing" presume that the labor of black feminism is to adopt recovery strategies which shield black women from further visual exploitation. Black female cultural producers like Cox use the imagined terrain of violent objectification—visual culture—as the space of recovery, so that their own self-representation is imagined to resolve (or, at the very least, expose and circumvent) the trouble of representation. Black feminist cul-

tural producers' belief that the visual field is both a problem
remedy constitutes its own theory of representation.

The black feminist theoretical archive is not simply a r
theoretical innovation; it also enacts and enforces a view o
ture that makes it impossible to theorize black female ple
within the confines of the archive. My understanding of impossibility is
informed by Gayatri Gopinath's work which uses the term to describe the
"unthinkability of a queer female subject position within various map-
pings of nation and diaspora" and "scrutinize[s] the deep investment of
dominant diasporic and nationalist ideologies in producing the particular
subject position as impossible and unimaginable."[14] Gopinath uncovers
how "dominant" discursive projects render particular subjects not simply
invisible but also "unthinkable." The dominant black feminist theoretical
project similarly renders ecstasy—the messy and sometimes uncomfortable nexus of racial and sexual pleasures—"unthinkable," and the black
feminist theoretical archive's "deep investment" in foregrounding the
black female body's woundedness comes at the expense of capturing the
possibilities of black women's pleasure.

My conception of the black feminist theoretical archive is decidedly
broad. I draw on scholarly work that falls within conventional understandings of theory—including work by Patricia Hill Collins, Hortense Spillers,
Nicole Fleetwood, and Janell Hobson—and a set of work by artists including Cox, Lyle Ashton Harris, and Carla Williams, all of whom use cultural
production as a site for grappling with the problem of representation. My
investment in an expansive conception of the black feminist theoretical
archive is informed by black feminism's long-standing critique of conventional and narrow conceptions of theory.[15] Barbara Christian's work epitomizes this scholarly tradition, asserting that the intellectual privileging of
particular forms of theory has overlooked the ways that "people of color
have always theorized—but in forms quite different from the Western
form of abstract logic." She continues, "And I am inclined to say that our
theorizing (and I intentionally use the verb rather than the noun) is often
in narrative forms, in the stories we create, in riddles and proverbs, in the
play with language, since dynamic rather than fixed ideas seemed more to
our liking."[16] Christian interrogates which knowledge gets to lay a claim
to theory, exposing that claims to theory are always claims to power. As
a way of disrupting this logic, Christian embraces an expansive concep-

tion of theory, one which treats a variety of kinds of intellectual and creative labor—the "riddle and proverb," the "narrative form"—as theoretical innovations. My capacious conception of theory, which analyzes black feminist cultural production as a kind of theory-making, shares Christian's investment in destabilizing an imagined "Western form of abstract logic" and in championing forms of intellectual production that are regularly deemed untheoretical—like images—but that actively shape black feminist epistemology.

This chapter traces four interpretative strands that permeate the black feminist archive's conception of visual culture: representation as pedagogy, as a temporal practice, as a metonymy, and as a site of recovery. Though I trace these interpretative strands separately, they intersect in significant ways and bolster each other, collectively crafting a black feminist theoretical archive organized around the violence of representation. My investment in untangling these strands is part of a commitment to closely examining the contours of the black feminist theoretical archive and to showing how each strand places emphasis on distinct problems of representation. By reading this archive as one preoccupied by logics of injury and recovery, I hope to create analytical breathing room for scholarship that moves beyond either exposing the wound or recovering from the wound. Indeed, my profound faith in the promise and possibility of black feminist theory leads me to advocate not an abandonment of it, but instead a concerted effort to craft an alternative black feminist theoretical archive, one that can imagine black female ecstasy in all of its complexity, paradoxes, and—at least at times—uncomfortable contradictions.

Representation as Pedagogy: Reading Patricia Hill Collins

Patricia Hill Collins's *Black Feminist Thought: Knowledge, Consciousness, and the Politics of Empowerment* (1990) is a field-defining book, one which established black feminism as a theoretical perspective that emerges from black women's distinctive standpoint, from "the knowledge gained at intersecting oppressions of race, class and gender," and as a recovery project that recognizes the importance of "discovering, reinterpreting, and analyzing the ideas of subgroups within the larger collectivity of U.S. Black women who have been silenced."[17] Collins's work amplified a set of "core themes" that have come to constitute the foundation of contemporary black feminist thought, including the idea that representation is one of the preeminent sites in the production of racial and sexual inequality.[18] In the years following the publication of *Black Feminist Thought*, the notion that representation is central to black women's subordination has become so prevalent as to be unremarkable, despite the fact that earlier black feminist texts invested in analyzing black women's particular experiences of subordination (or what Deborah King termed "multiple jeopardy") had relatively little interest in representation.[19] Instead, they located myriad other sites—capitalism (Frances Beale), sexual violence (Darlene Clark Hine), sexual hierarchy (Audre Lorde), simultaneous oppressions (Combahee River Collective, Deborah King, Barbara Smith), and law's inattention to black women's experiences of discrimination (Kimberlé Crenshaw), to name a few—as the loci of black women's marginalization. When Collins emphasized representation, then, she ushered in a new moment in black feminist thought, one which treated visual culture as a particularly pernicious technology where black female bodies are "viewed as object[s] to be manipulated and controlled."[20] This conception of representation's singularity—its unrelenting and single-minded pursuit of objectification—allows Collins to treat visual culture as an instructive site, one which both creates patterns of wounding and teaches viewers how to repeatedly injure black female flesh.

Collins develops the term "controlling images" to describe an ideologically consistent set of visual practices which insist on black women's sexual deviance and train viewers to interpret black women's alterity. For Collins, images of deviant black maternity (the mammy, the matriarch, the welfare queen) and of an excessive black female libido (the jezebel, the hoochie, the video ho) present black female sexuality as uncontrollable, even as they point to different sites of sexual excess. For example, if the mammy is masculine, effectively feminizing (and possibly queering) her male children, the jezebel is excessively desirous and hyper-reproductive. Even though these images are, in some ways, at odds, the underlying ideological consistency is that both contain an excessive performance of gender and sexuality, which endangers the viability of the state, the heteronormative family, and conventional gender roles. In their uniformity, these images render "racism, sexism, poverty, and other forms of social injustice . . . natural, normal, and inevitable."[21] Collins imagines that consistency underpins all "controlling" images, a belief that assumes both that images work on all viewers in similar ways and that ostensibly heterogeneous dominant representations are all embedded with a singular meaning. Controlling images are thus pedagogical insofar as they work to make "natural, normal, and inevitable" a dominant racial order, offering instruction on the hierarchy that marks daily life and providing viewers an analytic framework for interpreting black female flesh.

If dominant images injure black female subjects, then black women have developed a set of strategies to resist being wounded. While white women are often seduced into complicity by representation, black women, Collins argues, have never been offered opportunity to find pleasure in their oppression. Indeed, the very idea that black women might locate pleasure of any sort—aesthetic, sexual, political, or racial—in controlling images is an impossibility for Collins, showing her investment in the idea that black subjects never take pleasure in what confers pain or perpetuates subordination (and her investment in the idea that pleasure and injury are mutually exclusive). Like bell hooks's now canonical work on the "oppositional gaze," which asserts that black female spectators actively reinterpret dominant cinema, Collins underscores that black women are critical readers who "construct social realities" that counter "controlling images."[22]

When Collins analyzes black women's resistance to controlling images, she moves from the visual register toward literature, insisting that literary texts authored by black women offer "one comprehensive view of Black women's struggles to form positive self-definitions in the face of derogated images of Black womanhood."[23] It is only *outside* of the visual register that black women find cultural space to craft and circulate "positive self-definitions" of black womanhood. Indeed, Collins concludes her analysis of visual culture by arguing that "one way of surviving the everyday disrespect and outright assaults that accompany controlling images is to 'turn it out.' This is the moment when silence becomes speech, when stillness becomes action. As Karla Holloway says, 'no one wins in that situation, but usually we feel better.'"[24] Collins advocates an abandonment of visual culture, and her celebration of "turn[ing] it out," reveals precisely how powerfully and dangerously determining she imagines controlling images to be: black women's resistance to visual culture has to be staged outside of the visual field.

What is most significant about Collins's reading of representation is

that at a critical moment in the history of black feminism's i
alization, her text installed a conception of dominant repres
a singular instrument of violence that produces and reprodu
of black female sexual alterity. By creating a set of framewor
which viewers can interpret black female flesh, controlling images instruct viewers on how to injure black female flesh and naturalize notions
of black female sexual alterity. However, Collins's seamless ideological
universe exposes that virtually all images are "controlling" unless they are
produced by black women and outside the trappings of a regime invested
in rendering black female bodies spectacular. In so doing, Collins demonstrates that the word controlling which modifies images is a redundancy
since the labor of dominant representation is to control, to objectify, and
to injure black female flesh.

Representation as Epistemology: Reading Patricia Hill Collins II

If the labor of images is to instruct viewers on how to repetitively inflict the wound of racial and sexual alterity on black women's bodies, the
paradigmatic case of visual culture's violent insistence on black women's
deviance is the nineteenth-century display of Saartjie Baartman, the so-
called Hottentot Venus. Collins's retelling of Baartman's story connects
the Hottentot Venus exhibition to what many scholars interpret as the
most pernicious of controlling images: racialized pornography. Even before Collins wrote "Pornography and Black Women's Bodies," a portion of
Black Feminist Thought devoted to the relationship between Baartman and
pornographic representation, the Hottentot Venus had emerged as one
of the most significant figures in contemporary black feminist scholarship.[25] The recent explosion of interest in Baartman can be traced, at least
in part, to Sander Gilman's seminal article "Black Bodies, White Bodies:
Toward an Iconography of Female Sexuality in Late Nineteenth-Century
Art, Medicine, and Literature," which documents the nineteenth-century
European fascination with Baartman's body.[26]

Gilman details the myriad ways that Baartman's body—particularly her
buttocks—was proffered as a site of racial-sexual difference, preoccupy-
ing and pleasuring European audiences. Baartman's exhibitors required
her to wear costumes that emphasized her buttocks "in order to render
her strange and sexual," and advertisements promoting her display regu-

larly called attention to her mythologized rear.[27] In what is perhaps the most famous image in the Baartman archive, a French comic from 1814 entitled *Les Curieux en extase ou les cordons de souliers* (The Curious in Ecstasy or Shoelaces) depicts Baartman standing on a small pedestal while two British soldiers and a young woman curiously gaze at both her genitalia and her buttocks. The soldier studying her buttocks proclaims, "What roast beef!"[28] T. Denean Sharpley-Whiting notes that in the comic, Baartman "becomes, all at once, roast beef, a strange beauty, [and] an amusing freak of nature."[29] The oft-reprinted comic is regularly interpreted as providing evidence of a European "fascination with the buttocks" in an era where, according to Gilman, the buttocks were "a displacement for the genitalia. . . . When the Victorians saw the female black, they saw her in terms of her buttocks and saw represented by the buttocks all the anomalies of her genitalia."[30]

Baartman's imagined steatopygia also attracted scientific attention, as scientists sought to trace connections between Baartman's body, the Hottentot physiology generally, and animals.[31] In 1815 she was observed by professors from the Muséum national d'Histoire naturelle who endeavored to document her body's imagined peculiarities for their "scientific" textbooks, and ultimately placed her image alongside pictures of monkeys in their treatises.[32] As Anne Fausto-Sterling notes, "Bartmann's buttocks, [Georges] Cuvier believed, bore a striking resemblance to the genital swellings of female mandrills and baboons which grow to 'monstrous proportions' at certain times in their lives."[33] Scientific interest in similarities between Baartman's "deviant" buttocks and genitalia and animals' genitals continued even after her death, in 1815, when Georges Cuvier and Étienne Geoffroy Saint-Hilarie petitioned to "retain [her] corpse on the grounds that it was a singular specimen of humanity and therefore of special scientific interest."[34] When the request was approved, Cuvier conducted an autopsy, produced a plaster mold of Baartman's body, and dissected her genitalia. Sharpley-Whiting notes that as Cuvier explored Baartman's body, "the mystery of the dark continent" was also "unfold[ing]," as his violent exploration of her body was an attempt to explore (and even conquer) Africa.[35] Her preserved genitalia (along with her brain and her skeleton) were displayed in Paris at the Musée de l'Homme until 1974, when mounting criticism forced the museum to place her skeleton and body cast into storage.[36] Ultimately, Gilman's canonical work offers the important insight that Baartman's body became the quintessential Hottentot body, and the Hottentot body became the quintessential African body, such that "in the course of the nineteenth century, the female Hottentot comes to represent the black female *in nuce*."[37] In other words, Baartman became a symbol of a symbol, the primary metaphor for imagined racial and sexual difference.

Curiously, Baartman's body has also become a symbol for black feminists, including Collins, who use Baartman's story as the quintessential example of the violence of the visual field.[38] Collins reads Baartman's exhibition as a kind of racialized pornography, one where Baartman's flesh was "reduced to . . . sexual parts."[39] She treats Baartman's history as a critical data point in crafting a theory of pornography, taking as a point of departure the idea that racism, rather than sexism, organizes the pornographic visual field, and uncovering that black women's bodies are "key pillar[s] on which contemporary pornography itself rests."[40] She writes,

> The pornographic treatment of Black women's bodies challenges prevailing assumptions that since images of White women prevail in pornography, racism has been grafted onto pornography. African-American women's experiences suggest that Black women were not added into a preexisting pornography, but rather that pornography itself must be reconceptualized as a shift from the objectification of Black women's bodies in order to dominate and exploit them, to one of media representations of all women that perform the same purpose.[41]

Collins's intervention contests the notion that black women's bodies were "added into a preexisting pornography," and instead suggests that black women were the very foundation of pornography, so that the contemporary objectification of *all* women in pornography took as its training ground the violent objectification of black women.

If black women's bodies are essential to pornographic meaning-making, Baartman's exhibition created a kind of representational template for how to exploit black female flesh. Her caged display is mirrored in contemporary pornography, where, as Alice Walker notes (and Collins cites), "white women are depicted . . . as 'objects,' black women are depicted as animals."[42] Similarly, Collins argues that black women are regularly represented in pornography in ways that reference and sexualize racial traumas. She writes, "African-American women are usually depicted in a situation of bondage and slavery, typically in a submissive posture, and often with two White men. . . . White women and women of color have different pornographic images applied to them."[43] Collins's contention emphasizes that the violent racial traumas of the past—slavery and Baartman's display, for example—are made into technologies of fantasy in contemporary sexualized representation.

Collins's first radical contention is to argue that Baartman's display was the genesis of contemporary pornographic tropes; her second is to argue that racialized pornography is more than a set of representational strategies that reinforce historical violence and reduce black women to objects, to animals, and to excessive desires. Pornography is also a racialized episteme or "way of thinking" and a mode of "treatment."[44] What makes this conceptualization of pornography so radical is that Collins treats pornography as far more than a set of images projected on-screen. Instead, pornography is a "site of intersecting oppression" that produces knowledge by relating "portrayed individuals" and "the general qualities ascribed to that class of individuals."[45] Pornography is thus a quintessential "controlling image," a way of thinking that exceeds a representational practice; it is a mode of seeing black female bodies and a mode of knowing, or rendering knowable, black female flesh.[46]

If pornography is an episteme for Collins, it is also a set of actions inflicted on black female bodies.[47] Collins's brief selection on pornography routinely refers to pornography as a "treatment," not simply a set of visual practices.[48] That is, pornography is both a way that black female protagonists are treated on-screen (by pornographers, and by male pornographic protagonists) and a way that black female protagonists are treated by desirous (ostensibly white) spectators who are encouraged to interpret black female flesh as animalistic. In Collins's hands, pornography becomes a shorthand for a practice of racialized degradation that is violently inscribed on black female flesh. In imagining pornography as a set of debasing actions that are inflicted upon black women, rather than as simply a set of representational practices that constitute a genre, Collins's account resonates with antipornography work, particularly MacKinnon's attempts to undermine the synonymous-ness of pornography and speech. Like MacKinnon's claim that pornography is a doing akin to hate speech, rather than "only words" worthy of First Amendment protection, Collins's insistence that pornography is a racist practice shows that it is the infliction of a kind of wound on black female flesh, not simply a representation of the wound.[49]

Collins's reading of pornography as a visual practice that emerged from black women's experiences of subordination, and as a "habit of thinking" and "treatment" that entrenches black women's subordination, reveals an expansive conception of the "controlling images" that permeate dominant representation. The harms of controlling images are not simply that they instruct viewers in how to wound and rewound black female flesh with the injury of alterity; controlling images are also structures of knowledge which shape how black female bodies are known and knowable both on-screen and, perhaps most problematically, off-screen. Ultimately, Collins demonstrates that controlling images are not symptoms of a broader injury—the images *are* the injury, and constitute the brutal act of violence, the wounding itself.

Representation and Temporality: Reading Hortense Spillers

For Hortense Spillers, representation is always an encounter with history. Representation is not only crafted in time and space; it also acts as the connective tissue between the past and the unfolding present through its insistent wounding of black female flesh. Indeed, what distinguishes Spillers's interpretative work is precisely its preoccupation with the repeated wound of representation, a wound that she traces carefully, with her emphasis on the relationship between history and black female fleshiness.

Spillers's two canonical pieces—"Mama's Baby, Papa's Maybe: An American Grammar Book" and "Interstices: A Small Drama of Words"— were each written in distinctive moments and for particular audiences. "Mama's Baby, Papa's Maybe" appeared in the literary criticism journal *Diacritics* in 1987, and as Spillers later noted, the piece was an attempt "to generate a discourse, or a vocabulary that would not just make it desirable, but would necessitate that black women be in the conversation. And that is a theoretical conversation about any number of things but one of the things is certainly the feminist project."[50] "Interstices" was written five years earlier, for the contentious Barnard Scholar and Feminist conference that took place in 1982.[51] Spillers notes that "Interstices" was born of a certain recognition: "I didn't see a vocabulary that would make it possible to entertain the sexuality of black women in any way that was other than traumatic. Before you could have a conversation about sexuality of black women you had to clear the static, clear the field of static."[52] What both pieces share is an interest in "clear[ing] the static" and in creating new vocabularies for black women's experiences to be named and amplified. Together, they perform a theory of representation which draws out the intimate relationship between the racial traumas of the past and the present, a conception which emphasizes what Christina Sharpe calls the "long psychic and material reach" of slavery.[53]

If Collins located Baartman's display as the origin for contemporary representation, Spillers traces contemporary representational practices to the Atlantic, the site where the logics underpinning racialized and gendered representational tropes were produced. The violence of the Atlantic, Spillers argues, effectively degendered black bodies so that "the female body and the male body become a territory of cultural and political maneuver, not at all gender-related, gender-specific."[54] Even as the Atlantic unraveled gender, it sexualized black bodies, converting black bodies into black flesh. For Spillers, the transformation of body into flesh is relegation to a marketplace; it is the process of being made into a commodity, into something that can be "seared [and] divided" and left in state of "ripped-apartness,"[55] and an exercise in boundary-making, effectively distinguishing the captor from the captive, the white subject from the black object. Most important, as a technology of distinction fleshiness operated—and continues to operate—in gendered ways.

> Slavery did not transform the black female into an embodiment of carnality at all, as the myth of the black woman would tend to convince us, nor, alone, the primary receptacle of a highly-rewarding generative act. She became instead the principal point of passage between the human and the non-human world. Her issue became the focus of a cunning difference—visually, psychologically, ontologically—as the route by which the dominant male decided the distinction between humanity and "other."[56]

When Spillers uncovers the gendered aspects of fleshiness, she reveals that it is a sexual state as well. Fleshiness is a state of sexual availability and use; it is having one's body located as the preeminent site of racial-sexual difference.

For Spillers, this transformation of body into flesh is termed "pornotroping," and it is through this concept that she advances a theory that connects representation, gender, histories of racial violence, and the pornographic. She describes this process.

(1) The captive body [becomes] the source of an irresistible, destructive sensuality; (2) at the same time—in stunning contradiction—it is reduced to a thing, to *being* for the captor; (3) in this distance *from* a subject position, the captured sexualities provide a physical and biological expression of "otherness"; (4) as a category of "otherness," the captive body translates into a potential for pornotroping and embodies sheer physical powerlessness that slides into a more general "powerlessness," resonating through various centers of human and social meaning.[57]

Pornotroping is, of course, a process of objectification (or being "reduced to a thing"), but it is also a process of being reduced to "sensuality." Pornotroping hinges on the ability of the captor to presume the "destructive" sexuality of black female flesh and on the fundamental availability of black female sexuality—to meaning-making, to cooptation, to violence. Here, Spillers underscores that the creation of sexual alterity is fundamental to the creation of racial difference; indeed, the production of racial otherness is a pornographic process—a process of visuality—that requires seeing black female bodies, reducing and categorizing them, and making them into "sensual" flesh. If pornotroping shows the sexual labor that undergirds the production of racial difference, it also demonstrates the pornographic pleasure that is taken in producing race. In Spillers's hands, race is constituted by a repeated sadistic white pleasure in black female suffering.[58] Moreover, as the pornographic is a mode of knowing bodies that is intimately connected to the visual, Spillers asserts that the pleasurable production of racial difference for white subjects, and the infliction of racial brutality on black female flesh, is a quintessentially visual practice.

Though Spillers locates the transformation of black female bodies into black female flesh in a particular site—the Atlantic slave trade—she demonstrates that this process is replayed in our present moment because this initial "act of commodification [was] so thoroughgoing that the daughters labor even now under the outcome."[59] In so doing, Spillers shows that the strategies of race-making perfected in the Atlantic continue to be reproduced and practiced. This conception of temporality and history imagines critical connections between the racial and visual practices of the unfolding present and those forged in the past; the historical moment in which captors were trained in how to see black female flesh continues to shape current practices of viewing and practices of representing. Pornotroping, then, is a modality of using the visual field to incessantly delineate what Michael A. Chaney calls "culture and cultural exclusion," to mark black women's bodies as sites of sexual difference.[60]

If pornotroping is a historically rooted erotic practice of race-making that wounds black female flesh and insists on black female sexual alterity, black women's freedom, Spillers advocates, comes through subverting the visual register entirely. Like Collins, Spillers indicates that visual culture can never function as the locus of black women's liberation. Instead, a "truer sexual self-image," one that captures "the poetry of black female sexual experience," can only be located in "the domain of music and America's black female vocalists, who suggest a composite figure of ironical grace."[61] Spillers also concludes that the singer serves a pedagogical purpose: "Black women have learned as much (probably more) that is positive about their sexuality through the *practicing* singer as they have from the polemicist."[62] For Spillers, the visual field is saturated with the injuries of the past and their extension into the unfolding present; freedom requires an embrace of an alternative site that amplifies black female subjectivity.

Spillers's work offers a theory of representation that situates contemporary representation's racial-sexual wounding in its point of origin: the violent traumas of the past. If Collins emphasizes the unfolding present and the proliferation of controlling images that wound, Spillers underscores the past—the slave trade and its transformation of black female bodies into flesh—as the basis of black women's experiences of multiple marginalization. "Clearing the static," to borrow from Spillers, requires an engagement with the violence of the Atlantic and its fundamental reorientation of gender and sexuality. The continued transformation of black women's bodies into consumable, objectified, degraded flesh shows that the past lives on and rewounds black women; the only escape is to surrender the terrain of visuality altogether. She epitomizes a black feminist interpretative tradition which insists on the long shadow of history, a shadow which renders all dominant representation fundamentally structured by racial logics of the past.

Representation as Metonymy: Reading Janell Hobson and Nicole Fleetwood

If black feminists have been interested in the epistemological and historical problems of visual culture, others have been invested in analyzing the *representational* problems of dominant imagery, critically interrogating how particular icons come to stand in for black women. From this perspective, the violence of representation lies in the fact that it is a reductive practice that renders black female bodies synonymous with certain images, oftentimes images of the spectacular, the exaggerated, the hyperbolic, and the grotesque. Two black feminist scholars who have engaged with the metonymic problem of representation—Janell Hobson and Nicole Fleetwood—offer very different views of representation and diverge in their political concerns, yet, taken together, they reveal a third black feminist interpretative tradition: a preoccupation with how singular black female bodies are asked to speak *for* all black female bodies in the visual field, and how particular icons come to stand for black women generally.

For Hobson, the Hottentot Venus has become the paradigmatic representation of black women's bodies. Indeed, Baartman's display, Hobson argues, continues to form the contours of the unfolding present—here, her work resonates with Spillers's investment in treating representation as a temporal project—fundamentally "shap[ing] representations of blackness and beauty" and exiling black women from conventional conceptions of beauty.[63] Part of the violence of Baartman's display, as well as the violence of its continued effect, is the way that her "presumed ugliness and heightened sexuality" came to stand for the "presumed ugliness and heightened sexuality of the African race during her era."[64] According to Hobson, if Baartman was called on to stand for "the African race," her body—particularly its imagined steatopygia—has come to stand in for black women, forever suturing the image of the black female body to the image of corporeal excess. Hobson asks,

> Who else but Baartman would be forced to represent all of humanity in a voluminous scientific study of mammals, as in Frederic Cuvier and Geoffrey St. Hilair's 1824–27 *Historie naturelle des mammiferes?* Who

else but Baartman served as the quintessential black woman—cutting across continents and cultures—subjugated under slavery and colonialism? Finally, who else but Baartman could inspire a wholesale stereotype in which black women, en masse, are "known" to have big behinds.[65]

What Hobson traces is a kind of triple (and triply violent) metonymy: Baartman's buttocks stand for Baartman; Baartman's body stands for all black female bodies; the buttocks come to stand for black female difference. The profound reductiveness of this exercise constitutes the violence of the visual field.

The metonymic problems of representation show a profound connection between the past and the unfolding present. Here, Hobson's intellectual commitments resonate with the temporal concerns of Collins and Spillers: for Hobson, Baartman's brutal display creates the template for black women's continued "overexposure" and establishes the conditions that permitted black women's continued "exile" from ideas of beauty.[66] As Hobson notes, "The presentation of the unfeminine black female body as grotesque links back to the spectacle of the Hottentot Venus, whose body is presented . . . in terms of hypersexuality, or excessive femininity through the emphasis on her supposedly prominent buttocks."[67] If Baartman's display is the origin—or at least one point of origin—of black women's degradation, black women continue to be subjected to a set of images developed in and through Baartman's exhibition which "distort the ways black women see themselves and each other."[68]

Nicole Fleetwood's work also grapples with the problem of the metonym, which she conceptualizes as the problem of the icon, though she traces representation's violence quite differently than Hobson. For Fleetwood, the visual field has long been understood as "a punitive field—the scene of punishment—in which the subjugation of blacks continues through the reproduction of denigrating racial stereotypes that allow whites to define themselves through the process of 'negative differentiation.'"[69] If the visual field is the site where controlling images are violently deployed to regulate black bodies, it is also a space that is imagined to resolve the "problem" of race. The black body captured in the visual field is always called on to "do something," to produce a set of affective, cultural, and political "results." This call to "do something" constitutes "the weight placed on black cultural production to produce results, to do something to alter a history and system of racial inequality that is in part constituted through visual discourse."[70] Nowhere is this weight more visible than in the iconic labor black bodies are compelled to perform; for Fleetwood, the icon is a prevailing visual practice through which "singular images or signs come to represent a whole host of historical occurrences and processes."[71] Exceptional images of singular black bodies become the vehicles through which black bodies in general are known, and what is often made knowable through those bodies is a narrative of racial progress. What distinguishes Fleetwood's work from Hobson's (and even from Collins on "controlling images") is that, from her perspective, iconic images do not serve exclusively to shore up black alterity; instead, she argues, exceptional black bodies are regularly captured and decontextualized in the visual field to offer an account of the waning power of racism and to visually manage a history of racial violence. Icons are reductive, to be sure, but their meanings are multiple and complex for Fleetwood.

Nowhere is the violence of the icon more visible than in the case of black female bodies, which, Fleetwood argues, are regularly called on as images of excess. Like Hobson, Fleetwood connects contemporary displays of imagined black female excess, at least in part, to Baartman's display, noting that "the specter of the 'Hottentot venus'—Saartje Baartman, the much-written-about Khoisan (South African) woman exhibited as a spectacle in nineteenth-century Europe—casts a broad shadow over both cultural production and scholarship on the black female body: representation as excessive and degenerate, as well as the body's commercialization."[72] Black women's representation, then, is staged in the "broad shadow" of Baartman's history, which has engendered a visual field that presumes black women's bodies as "excessive and degenerate." Indeed, the "broad shadow" cast is so visible that Fleetwood can draw an iconographical lineage—"from the Hottentot Venus to Josephine Baker to Millie Jackson, Pam Grier, and Serena Williams in her cat suit"—of black women whose bodies have come to "register as excessive in public culture" and who are often reduced to a singular image, that of the buttocks, as in the case of Baartman, Baker, and Williams.[73] For Fleetwood, as for Hobson, the violence of the visual field is its reductive work, its insistence that black women can be rendered synonymous with "excess," and that this "excess" is located in the buttocks.

However, unlike Hobson, Fleetwood shows that the visual field can be a site where black women recover their bodies from the violence of representation; in so doing, her work bridges a black feminist investment in woundedness and a black feminist commitment to recovery.[74] She argues that some black female cultural producers—including Cox, Lil' Kim, and Ayanah Moor—actively engage with the prevailing fantasy of their own excess, effectively using spectacular performances to disrupt conceptions of black female deviance. These cultural producers expose the "very problem[s] that their bodies pose as visible and corporeal bodies."[75] While Fleetwood cautions that "excess flesh" performances are not "necessarily . . . liberatory enactment[s]," she celebrates these performances because they "acknowledge black women's resistance of the persistence of visibility."[76] The very site of injury—the visual field—becomes a space that black female artists can use to "reflect" on their injuries, to account for the history of displaying black female flesh, and to recover black female subjectivity.

Both Hobson and Fleetwood highlight and critique the violent reductiveness of representation, even as they analyze that problem, its origins, and its manifestations differently. For Hobson, representation presumes that one body can speak for all black female bodies and that one imagined part of the black female body—the buttocks—can speak of black women's corporeal deviance more generally. Hobson's work thus connects a black feminist tradition invested in the connections between the past and contemporary representation with one committed to exposing the problem of metonymy. Fleetwood, like Hobson, establishes that black female bodies are reduced in the visual field, but uses the concept of the icon to show that black bodies represent both racial problems and, at times, imagined racial progress. The icon, then, is a flattening of complexity, an insistence on violently reducing black bodies to the simplistic and, often, the stereotypical. Yet Fleetwood embraces the possibility that the spectacular can be staged in transgressive ways that undermine the metonymic problem of dominant representation. What both scholars share, though, is a vision of visual culture's capacity to violently reduce black women to singular signifiers, images, or icons.

If the black feminist theoretical archive has been preoccupied with tracing how representation produces injury, it has also celebrated the flip side of woundedness: recovery work. By *recovery work*, I refer to black feminist representation that attempts to salvage the black female body from the violence of the visual field. At times, the visual "unmirroring" strategies deployed by black feminist artists "hold up a mirror that reveals a different image divorced from this iconographic history in dominant culture," and at times, they "chronicle the 'spectacle of blackness'" and engage in "tactics of counter-appropriation."[77] As Michael Bennett and Vanessa Dickerson argue, this body of work "explores the ways in which black women have confronted this assault by reclaiming and representing their own bodies" and "focuses . . . on the ways in which the black female body has been covered, uncovered, discovered, and recovered."[78] Unlike Collins and Spillers, both of whom insist that black women's wholeness will only come through abandoning the visual, this countergenre is deeply invested in drawing upon visual conventions, particularly the use of self-portraiture, referencing and sometimes embodying historical trauma, and performing blackness in ways that expose the constructedness of race and evidence a belief that the visual can be the register for redressing and healing representation's fleshy wounds. Most important, this genre is marked by a significant paradox which its cultural producers are always navigating: while the visual field may be the terrain of objectification, it is also imagined as the site for countering that objectification. How cultural producers navigate this "tightrope" can be traced in two pairs of images — one pair by Cox and one pair by Carla Williams. In each set, one image satisfies the demands of the black feminist recovery genre and one does not, acting instead as an indictment of the violence of controlling images.

Cox's self-portrait *Hot-En-Tot* is emblematic of the black feminist recovery work I trace: It locates the visual field both as a site where racial-sexual traumas are inflicted, and as a space where those traumas can be exposed and even undone. Indeed, the image contains a rich repository of information about how "black female cultural producers [engage] with the imago of black female excessiveness," offering their own "critique[s]" of the racializing and gendering apparatuses of the visual field."[79] It is notable that Cox's self-portrait has been canonized in the black feminist theoretical archive and celebrated for its successful recovery of Baartman's body, as well as for its profound critique of the relationship among history, embodiment, and visuality. However, a similar portrait of Cox, produced collaboratively by Cox and Lyle Ashton Harris, is instead treated as an indictment of the visual field: a critique, but not necessarily a recovery.

Cox's use of Baartman's story as a way of framing Cox's self-representation suggests that the conditions of Baartman's exhibition continue to frame how black female bodies are imagined. The title of the portrait, Hot-En-Tot, is indicative of the variety of claims the portrait makes about the relationship between Baartman's display and the representational practices of the present. First, it explicitly ties Cox's "tits-and-ass armature" to the nineteenth-century fantasies of Baartman's imagined "Hottentot apron" and steatopygia, demonstrating that contemporary racial fictions have historical underpinnings. Cox shows that the same collectively held fantasies that allowed Cuvier and Saint-Hilarie to search Baartman's body for definitive proof of her sexual differences animate an ongoing cultural fascination with black women's imagined differences.

Second, with its deconstruction of the label "Hottentot," the image's title places analytic pressure on the very idea of Baartman *as* Hottentot, exposing the artifice of the invented name and our continued lack of knowledge about Baartman's origins, and calling into question a preoccupation with racial classification more generally.[80] As Zine Magubane argues, racial categories were the subject of intense debate in the era of Baartman's display. Though contemporary scholars presume that Baartman's body was interpreted as black, for a nineteenth-century audience she was a Khoikhoi, a group that was considered "not Black or brown but yellow or tawny and thus different in important respects from Africans living further North, as well as those on the West Coast."[81] In fact, Magubane shows that nineteenth-century travelers even drew classifications among Khoikhois "based on their color, culture, geographic location, and appearance," with some arguing that the Khoikhois could be divided into a number of races.[82] The debates surrounding racial classifications of Khoikhois problematizes the prevailing notion that Baartman's body came to stand *for* blackness, exposing that "Blackness is less a stable, observable, empirical fact than an ideology that is historically determined and, thus, variable."[83] Like Magubane, Cox's title poses larger questions about the taxonomies of race, about how we come to know some bodies as black (or not black), and about the centrality of visuality to racial "knowledge."

While Cox pays homage to Baartman's display and the visual tradition it established—one where representations of black female bodies were thought to provide visual access to black women's imagined difference—she also inserts her body into a lengthy tradition of black-and-white ethnopornographic images which sought to capture black bodies' imagined differences.[84] As Debra S. Singer notes, Cox "recalls both 'scientific' illustrations of Baartman—including the oft-reprinted comic—and later anthropological black-and-white photographs depicting non-Western individuals from front, side, and rear views."[85] Cox shows that viewing the black body is often a process of insisting that it confess its differences, and that visuality's incessant demands emerge from racial pseudoscience.

But in "recalling" those illustrations and making the comically absurd "truths" that ethnopornographic images sought to capture larger than life, Cox pokes fun at the "scientific" discourse which presumed black women's steatopygia and excessive sex. Indeed, the highly visible white strings that attach the breasts (made even more visible since the image is in black and white) render hypervisible the artifice of racial fiction, and coupled with Cox's defiant and direct stare at the viewer, fundamentally problematize the very fantasies of race. Cox both exposes the violence of the visual field which reduces black women to buttocks and breasts, and dismantles the very project of visuality: its unrelenting search for difference. The visual becomes both the terrain of violence and the site of redressing that violence, a space of exploitation and a locus of redemption.

Cox's self-portrait has been championed by black feminist scholars who interpret the image as both a searing critique of racialized representation and as an effective recovery of the black female body, particularly because of Cox's insistence that her body is not simply an object to be looked at. Hershini Young celebrates the self-portrait, noting that it "reclaims the black woman's (sexual) subjectivity from the scientific gaze that dissected and reduced it to beast of burden and mechanism of labor."[86] Similarly, Singer notes, "While drawing on various strains of documentary photographic practices, Cox's image complicates these references to past traditions: as she looks straight out and meets the viewer's gaze, the image resists assumptions about the structure of 'the gaze' as an active male scopic drive onto a passive female object."[87] Their collective admiration of Cox's self-portrait—their treatment of the image as successful recovery work—centers on Cox's insistence that her body is not simply to-be-looked-at; instead, both note that Cox defiantly matches the spectator's gaze, rupturing the long tradition of black female accessibility.

This same praise, however, is not extended to a very similar image, Cox's collaboration with Lyle Ashton Harris (figure 1.2).[88] In order to reveal the generic underpinnings of black feminist recovery work, it is necessary to underscore this disjuncture and interrogate why Harris's image is not as readily interpreted as black feminist recovery work.

Like Cox, Harris is invested in retelling Baartman's story; the title of Harris's image, *Hottentot Venus 2000*, demonstrates a commitment to showing the legacy of Baartman's display, and to capturing how historically rooted racial traumas are reenacted in the present. Yet *Hottentot Venus 2000* has a very different visual style than Cox's self-portrait. The Harris-Cox collaboration is shot in color, with Cox's strap-on breasts and buttocks in a shimmery bronze. Cox again returns the viewer's gaze, but this time the viewer is acutely aware of Cox's made-up face—her pink-glossed lips and makeup-smudged eyes—and the row of bracelets which adorn her wrist. In this image, her fingers cup her hips rather than pointing straight down as in an ethnographic mug shot. If the black-and-white image serves to desexualize the fantasy of black women's hypersexuality, the color image showcases black female sexuality. In Cox's and Harris's hands, Cox's body becomes the object of desire, not a critique of the object of desire.

The Harris-Cox collaboration fails to perform the labor of black feminist recovery work, operating instead as an indictment, a searing commentary on black women's continued sexualization, and a profound revelation of the host of ways in which the visual field continues to objectify and degrade. Indeed, the image's sexualization of Cox's body—particularly the fact that Cox sexualizes herself, a fact made more acute by the image's title, which gestures to how black female bodies are Hottentotted in a visual economy fueled by a longing to see them—operates not to insist on black women's wholeness in a visual field that insistently breaks black bodies down into their constitutive pieces. Instead, the image reflects how black women are enlisted in their own sexualization, invited to Hottentot themselves. Moreover, the image suggests that the invitation to self-sexualize comes from a particular moment—the one where Baartman was an object of caged display. The image thus showcases the particular

1.2 Lyle Ashton Harris and Renee Cox, *Hottentot Venus 2000*,
1994. Courtesy of the artist and CRG Gallery.

and limited scope of black feminist recovery work: its task is to visually locate black female bodies outside of a sexual economy, to insist on black women's sexual and corporeal wholeness, not to further sexualize black women's bodies or to assert black women's embodied fleshy pleasures.

Like Cox and Harris, the artist Carla Williams is invested in using the legacy of the Hottentot Venus story as a medium for theorizing the racial and gendered politics of representation. In *Venus*, Williams sits sideways, her head thrown back in quiet pleasure (figure 1.3). The black-and-white portrait emphasizes the sensual curves of Williams's body: her breasts, the roundness of her hips and stomach, and the bend of her knee. The image's attention to the smooth fleshiness of Williams's arms, the thickness of her hair, and the gentle curves of the fabric only enhance the portrait's investment in capturing Williams's quiet pleasure. What is significant about the image's depiction of pleasure, though, is that Williams's ecstasy is contained, inward, not at all performed for the spectator. Unlike in Cox's self-portrait, Williams's head is pointed away from the viewer and her eyes are closed. Indeed, the logic of the image makes viewers feel as though they are peering in on a private moment, on an encounter between Williams and her body.

If Williams's image showcases her body-in-pleasure, it also stakes a claim to black women's beauty, a political strategy that places it squarely in the black feminist recovery genre. The image's title locates Williams's body in a tradition of Western art which simultaneously celebrates (and objectifies) the white female nude and ignores the black female body as an object of desirability. The art historian Lisa Collins argues that the history of the nude image—the "central subject in Western art since it was constructed as a subject in ancient Greece"—is marked by an overwhelming absence of black flesh.[89] When black bodies appear, they are often simply "erotica and exotica" or "allegories for freedom and its necessary inverse, enslavement," but rarely representations of classical beauty.[90] By inserting her body into a tradition from which black women have been nearly absent, Williams stakes a claim to beauty for black women, even as she paradoxically suggests that black women's claims to beauty come from locating themselves in a tradition that hinges on women's availability, accessibility, and objectification. If the title *Venus* insists on black women's desirability, it also references Baartman's exhibition, a display of black female flesh that equated black women with corporeal grotesqueness. In

1.3 Carla Williams, *Venus*, 1994. Courtesy of the artist.

so doing, she shows that black women's assertions of desirability require an engagement with a tradition that not only excluded them, but insisted on their ugliness.

Williams's self-portrait also makes a claim about pleasure and its relationship to the black feminist recovery genre. The image emphasizes the sensual, but unlike Cox's collaboration with Harris, it is a quiet, private eroticism, one that hinges on Williams's enjoyment of *herself* (rather than on another's enjoyment of Williams). This conception of pleasure resonates with Audre Lorde's work on the erotic, which carves out a space for female pleasure (and even self-pleasure) that is explicitly outside of the phallic economy of pornography. Lorde writes, "The erotic is a measure between the beginnings of our sense of self and the chaos of our strongest feelings. It is an internal sense of satisfaction to which, once we have experienced it, we know we can aspire."[91] The erotic is a practice of self, a way of feeling in one's body, a kind of self-actualization that recognizes the "lifeforce of women," and a practice that is articulated in a host of sites, in "our language, our history, our dancing, our work, our lives."[92] Williams's quiet pleasure, with its emphasis on self (rather than other), and with its inward focus, shows that though the black feminist recovery genre problematizes black women's sexualization, it has space for black women's pleasures in their own corporeality.

If *Venus* performs the labor of the black feminist recovery genre, insisting on black women's wholeness, gesturing toward the violent racial injuries of the past, and celebrating black women's eroticism, Williams's untitled self-portrait from the *How to Read Character* series (a title that she took from a phrenological handbook by Lorenzo Niles Fowler) functions as an indictment of the visual field. The image, with its textured, collage aesthetic, shows only the oft-fetishized black buttocks displayed "in a gilt frame, juxtaposing photography's honorific function in portraiture with its surveillant and objectifying function in science" (figure 1.4).[93] Williams's image visually performs the critique of metonymy that scholars like Hobson and Fleetwood theorize. The collage aesthetic, with its "visible seams" and slashes, enacts the cutting away of the black female body that the image represents.[94] The black female body is sliced again and again, each time reduced more profoundly so that the fetishized buttocks come to stand for black female corporeality.

Like Cox's *Hot-en-tot*, Williams's *How to Read Character* self-portrait un-

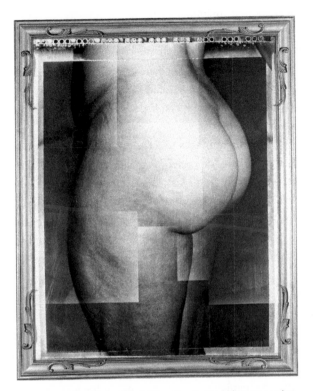

1.4 Carla Williams, Untitled from *How to Read Character* series, 1990–91. Courtesy of the artist.

covers the saturation of the visual field with "racial science" and exposes the myriad ways that black women's bodies are objectified and subjected to scrutiny, underscoring that the buttocks are always already racially coded. The self-portrait's provocative title, *How to Read Character*, shows the host of ways that imagined racial sexual alterity has been taken up as a sign of character, and of moral fitness. Williams often displays the image next to drawings of Baartman which purport to be scientific but instead call attention to her so-called steatopygia; Williams uncovers photography's complicity in racial pseudoscience and interrogates the role of photography in producing racial knowledge (about libido, about longings, and about character).

By reading these two images together, it is possible to trace the labor of the recovery genre: if *Venus* celebrates black women's wholeness, *How to Read Character* showcases how black female bodies are taken apart and violently reduced. It is a visual enactment of metonymy and a performance of how images of black female alterity are celebrated and glorified (seen in Williams's use of an ornate frame, which one would expect to see reserved for the most honorific of portraits). Reading the two images against each other shows that the black feminist recovery genre's work is to insist on black women's autonomous wholeness, their bodily integrity, over and against a history of images like *How to Read Character* which detail the violence of the visual field. It also shows the limited place of sexuality in the black feminist recovery genre; though a certain kind of quiet sensuality and self-contained eroticism (as in Williams's *Venus*) maintains black female wholeness, explicit articulations of longing and desire (as in Cox's and Harris's *Hottentot Venus 2000*) do not.

Black feminist celebrations of recovery work offer a fourth interpretative framework that is the flip side of the logic of injury, an insistence that wounds can be remedied through a sustained counteraesthetic. Recovery work shows that the visual field can be both the locus of injury and the site for salvaging black female flesh, both the space of objectification and the locus of remedying objectification. Recovery work maintains an unshakeable political faith in *self*-representation, which is imagined to undo the violence of dominant representation. Allowing black women to represent themselves — despite the fact that self-representation is shaped by prevailing logics of race, gender, and sexuality, which might even provide lexicons for black women to represent themselves — is thought to counter the violence of dominant representation, to expose and to redress the wound. As Carla Williams notes,

> Given the legacy of images created of Black women, it is an especially complex task for contemporary Black women to define their own image, one that necessarily both incorporates and subverts the stereotypes, myths, facts, and fantasies that have preceded them. . . . It is to all of the aforementioned artists and writers that the task falls to incorporate visual legacies with contemporary realities in order to present images of black women who are no longer acted up but who possess, in one body, both active voice and visual self-presentation.[95]

Williams's investment in "active . . . self-presentation" and self-authorship shows that recovery work imagines itself as outside of a dominant representational economy because black women craft it, and it assumes that black women must be outside of this dominant economy because they are often injured by it. It is in this outsider space—this self-authored space—that black women can heal the wound.

Theorizing Black Feminist Theory: Beyond Impossibility

By a close reading of a set of black feminist theoretical texts, I have carefully traced four interpretative strands which, I argue, constitute the theory of representation that subtends the black feminist theoretical archive. My close readings are attentive to the heterogeneity of texts and debates that pervade the black feminist theoretical archive, yet expose that this varied set of texts produce a singular idea about representation—that it wounds black female flesh—even as they differently trace the nature of that violence (and the possibility of remedying that violence). These texts engender and enforce a black feminist theoretical archive that presumes that dominant representation injures black female flesh and that black women's pleasure in representation comes through self-representation focused on restoring black women's wholeness, or through an active resistance of dominant representation's violence. Even the conditions of effective self-representation are narrowly defined by the black feminist theoretical archive, which celebrates work that traces connections between the violence of the past and the unfolding present, and which condemns images that further sexualize black female bodies. In its preoccupation with injury and recovery, the black feminist theoretical archive is, I argue, an archive of pain, one which traces a set of harms and injuries, exposes a set of violences, and champions strategies of redress.

If this chapter excavates a long tradition of black feminism's engagement with injury and recovery, the remainder of my project shifts the archive away from pain by performing a set of close readings of pornographic texts, the very texts that the black feminist theoretical archive approaches with tremendous scrutiny. My close readings are invested in using the paradigmatic imagined site of injury, racialized pornography, as a platform for imagining black women's sexual ecstasy. My interest is not in imagining pleasure as a site outside of pain or injury, nor do I deny that pleasure is fraught terrain; instead, I consider the complex, sometimes uncomfortable, racial and sexual ecstasies that pornography can produce for black female spectators and for black female pornographic protagonists. Because my political and theoretical investments are always oriented toward black feminism, a project that I consider imaginative, restorative, world-making, generative, and politically necessary, my aim is to remake the black feminist theoretical archive so that we no longer need to leave it to take pleasure seriously. Surely it is possible to transform this archive into a home not just for locating and healing wounds, but for naming and claiming desires, for speaking about the complex ways that pleasure—both racial and sexual—moves under our skin.

2 | SPEAKING SEX / SPEAKING RACE

Lialeh and the Blax-porn-tation Aesthetic

Nineteen seventy-three was a landmark year for hard-core pornography, featuring the release of the genre's first all-black film, *Lialeh* (dir. Barron Bercovichy).[1] Two years earlier, the commercial success of the mainstream blaxploitation hit *Shaft* (dir. Gordon Parks) revealed the economic viability of films marketed to black audiences. *Lialeh* borrowed *Shaft*'s soul-music soundtrack and cool black protagonists, and merged them with the genre conventions of the hard-core pornographic, producing a story that "speaks race" as much as it "speaks sex."[2]

Lialeh begins with its black female protagonist, Lialeh, auditioning for a role in an all-black sexual revue. She tentatively steps onto a dimly lit stage and begins to sing for Arlo, the revue's creative director. Her thin crackly voice disappoints Arlo, and he interrupts her audition by vigorously shaking his head and exclaiming "No, no, no! If you sing like that, ain't nobody gonna use you! Sing from that black throat of yours." Arlo instructs her to "open up wide like this," and as he pushes her lips apart with his fingers, he slides his tongue into her mouth. Then he quickly says, "Now that's how wide you gotta open up. Do it right this time." When Lialeh begins to sings again, her voice is huskier, and richer. She dances in front of Arlo, flirtatiously singing, "Touch me again where it feels good." She leans in to him as her voice rises, and places his hands on her breasts and then her buttocks. Lialeh then kneels in front of Arlo, unzips his pants, and begins to perform fellatio on him. The opening scene shows that Lialeh's "black throat" has a double-meaning: it is the locus of Lialeh's "authentic" soulful voice and a sexual site that can confer pleasure on black men. The film's treatment of Lialeh's black throat as a space of both racial authenticity and sexual pleasure encapsulates how *Lialeh* draws on the genre conventions of both hard-core pornography and blaxploitation to "speak sex" to black spectators.

While much has been written about the particularities of the Golden Age and its aesthetic and economic investment in narrative-driven pornography, little has been written about its relationship with its "mainstream" cinematic contemporaries.[3] I argue that the Golden Age borrowed from other genres—particularly blaxploitation—to craft a distinctive pornographic vernacular intended to pleasure black spectators (and, of course, to profit from pleasuring them).[4] By uncovering Golden Age pornography's investment in speaking sex to black spectators, I intervene in a black feminist conversation which presumes both that black bodies populate the pornographic screen exclusively to pleasure white male spectators, and that black spectatorial pleasures are limited to pleasures in critically interrogating the on-screen world. While spectatorship was once a primary analytic framework for feminist film scholarship, it has waned in popularity as the field has moved from a psychoanalytically rooted feminist film theory approach toward a media-studies approach interested in the transnational circulation of images, and in what Linda Williams terms "the 'massness' of cinema, the importance of film as a sensory as well as a meaning-producing medium, its existence as an alternative public sphere."[5]

Yet spectatorship has retained its analytical purchase within black feminist visual culture studies. In particular, black feminist approaches to pornography tend to presume—and to condemn—white male spectatorship, and thus to implicitly foreclose the possibility of black *pleasurable* spectatorship generally, and black pleasurable pornographic spectatorship specifically. When the black feminist theoretical archive has turned its attention to black spectatorship, it has been preoccupied with the strategies that black viewers, particularly black female viewers, deploy to engage a cinematic world that has been constructed around their objectification.[6] bell hooks's now canonical work on the "oppositional gaze" epitomizes this tradition; she presumes that black female spectators critically look back at dominant cinema because the world unfolding on-screen is not designed for their enjoyment. If white spectators enjoy a "dominant gaze," a pleasure in identification (or perhaps a pleasure in racial fetishism, which hooks terms "eating the other"), black female viewing pleasures stem from an oppositional "interrogation."[7] This critical encounter with representation constitutes both a productive reading practice and a survival strategy adopted because, as hooks notes, cinema "constructs [black women's] presence as absence."[8] Similarly, Patricia Hill Collins argues that black women actively "resist . . . ideological justifications for [their] oppression" and craft strategies for rereading or wholly circumventing dominant visual culture.[9] The black feminist theoretical archive's consistent celebration of black women's "oppositional" reading strategies is underpinned by two problematic and under-interrogated assumptions: the on-screen world is not designed to please black spectators (indeed, it is created for white male spectators), and black viewing pleasures are extraordinarily limited, emerging only from actively re-interpreting dominant texts.

While black feminists have imagined critical black female spectators who actively reread dominant cinema, they have also envisioned black female viewers who craft "empowering" interpretations of seemingly problematic representations.[10] Jacqueline Bobo's reading of Steven Spielberg's The Color Purple (1985) asserts that the film adaptation distorted Alice Walker's novel, eliminating "the empowering aspects of the strong Black women."[11] Black women viewers thus had to "'read through the text' to reconstruct satisfactory meanings from a mainstream cultural product created by a White male filmmaker."[12] The practice of "reading through the text" is a learned strategy developed by black women because "society . . . places little value on their situation."[13] This training renders black women cultural decoders who can "extract images of power and relate them to their lives."[14] The "reconstructive" interpretative work that Bobo highlights is the flip side of the oppositional spectatorship hooks traces; black female spectators are imagined both to critically interrogate what is on-screen and to remake on-screen narratives into something palatable.

Lialeh marked a critical moment in hard-core pornography's history, one that fused the genre conventions of pornography and blaxploitation to allow black spectators to find themselves, and their pleasures, represented on the pornographic screen. I use the film and its interest in speaking race and speaking sex simultaneously to challenge the prevailing black feminist reading practice, which effectively limits black viewing pleasures to oppositional ones. Of course, the mere presence of black bodies on-screen will not necessarily please all, or even most, black viewers; instead, I trace how the very particular fusion of the pornographic and blaxploitation demonstrates *Lialeh*'s anticipation of pleasurable black spectatorship, an investment in black pleasures enjoyed not through "oppositionality" or critical rereadings of the film.

While I argue that the generic merger between pornography and blaxploitation serves as evidence of *Lialeh*'s investment in capturing and pleasuring black audiences, I also analyze how the incomplete and imperfect fusion of the genres—what I call generic failure—open up spaces for multiple and complex black viewing pleasures. Indeed, the film's black female protagonist, Lialeh, explicitly contests the generic intersections of the pornographic and the blaxploitation, troubling and, at times, wholly undermining blax-porn-tation's celebration of the black male phallus. These failures create spaces for distinctive black female pornographic viewing pleasures outside of identification with the black male pornographic protagonist, Arlo, and far removed from oppositional and dis-identificatory readings of the film. Ultimately, this chapter's close readings unsettle the black feminist logic of oppositionality by examining how *Lialeh* can excite and titillate the black viewer when read both "against the grain" and "with the grain," and can open up possibilities for myriad pleasurable black viewing experiences.

Crafting Blax-porn-tation

During the Golden Age, a period spanning the 1970s, pornography was transformed from an underground genre consisting of illegal, short stag films to a mainstream genre consisting of feature-length, narrative-driven films, most notably *Deep Throat* (1972), *Behind the Green Door* (1972), *Debbie Does Dallas* (1978), and *The Devil in Miss Jones* (1972).[15] This significant shift was enabled, at least in part, by changing legal conceptions of obscenity.[16] The Supreme Court's decision in *Miller v. California* (1973) defined the obscene as materials that cultivate "prurient interest" and lack "redeeming" scientific, artistic, or cultural importance. In response, pornographers constructed films with sophisticated storylines that insisted on social and aesthetic value beyond the "prurient." This new style of pornography refused to simply "splice together a series of 'beaver shots,'" and instead, as Mireille Miller-Young notes, "engaged the narrative style of feature films—and the paying theatrical audience they garnered—as a focus for hardcore media."[17] Pornography thus began to resemble mainstream Hollywood films in style and form.

Golden Age films shared two other qualities with Hollywood films: they were screened publicly (and legally) in urban theaters, and they attracted mixed-sex, mixed-race audiences.[18] As Linda Williams notes, before the Golden Age, the American public had "very little experience of watching graphic sex in a mixed-gender public theater."[19] During the Golden Age, films like *Deep Throat* and *Behind the Green Door* provided a kind of public "education of desire" cloaked, at least in the case of *Deep Throat*, in comic absurdity.[20] Pornography's sudden public-ness coupled with its resemblance to mainstream films shattered the taboo of viewing pornography, such that "the screening of graphic sex [seemed] almost necessary to sexual citizenship in the early 1970s."[21] Thus, Golden Age pornographers ushered in an epoch of "porno chic," which made consumption of the era's most popular films "fashionably chic."[22]

In the years during which Golden Age films received mainstream attention, the success of blaxploitation films like Gordon Parks's *Shaft* led to Hollywood's "discovery" of black audiences. *Shaft* is the quintessential blaxploitation narrative: it tells the story of the black hero, John Shaft, "a slick, pretty, sexy dude," whose skillful navigation of multiple worlds— the black world of Harlem, the underground world of the mafia—allows him to rescue a black gangster's kidnapped daughter.[23] Along with *Shaft*, Melvin Van Peebles's *Sweet Sweetback's Baadasssss Song* (1971) and Gordon Parks Jr.'s *Super Fly* (1972) crystallized the "blaxploitation formula": gritty urban settings, distinctive soul soundtracks, black popular fashion, and cool black heroes who triumphed over white villains.[24] These motifs would be replicated in nearly sixty blaxploitation films released between 1969 and 1974, and in *Lialeh*, hard-core pornography's first blax-porn-tation film.[25]

Lialeh's effective merger of the conventions of the pornographic and the blaxploitation was not without aesthetic precedent. Blaxploitation was itself a kind of pornographic genre, just skirting the conventions of the hard-core. Van Peebles filmed *Sweetback* in less than three weeks for merely $500,000 by pretending it was a pornographic film, which allowed him to lower his production costs by using non-union staff. While calling his film pornography allowed him to film quickly and cheaply, it also added to the film's sexual and racial charge. Though Van Peebles did not officially submit his film to the Motion Picture Association of America (MPAA) in 1971, he marketed *Sweetback* with the slogan "Rated X by an All White Jury" (a slogan that stuck until he formally submitted the film to the MPAA, in 1974, and the film received an R rating). The slogan suggested that a racist film industry relegated his racy film to the adult market, and proposed that black consumption of the film was a radical act of racial solidarity.[26]

If the conditions surrounding *Sweetback*'s production flirted with the pornographic, the content of the film did as well. The film's opening scene, which features a barely adolescent Sweetback, the film's male protagonist, having sex with a prostitute, continues to prompt scholarly debate about the film, including scholarship which analogizes the film to pornography. Mikel Koven, for example, writes,

> It also occurs to me that, despite Van Peebles' claim that the film was rated X due to the film's unrelenting realism, that his "all-white jury" wanted to suppress the ideas of the film, the truth is more banal — the film is more pornography than Blaxploitation. Conventional wisdom on the film (i.e., Film and Media Studies folk) likes to note that the film's box-office success indicates that it spoke to a contemporary black audience. It strikes me that the $1.5 million it made domestically was due more to curiosity about the sex in the film, than an engagement with the socio-politics of it.[27]

Activists' critiques of *Sweetback* focused not just on the film's explicit sexual imagery; the formation of the Coalition against Blaxploitation (CAB) in 1972 drew attention to "the transformation from the stereotyped Stepin' Fetchit to Super Nigger on the screen," calling the film "another form of cultural genocide."[28] Blaxploitation was imagined to traffic in the very stereotypical images of black bodies — black men as drug dealers and pimps, black women as hypersexual prostitutes — that it purported to disrupt.

If blaxploitation had a prolonged flirtation with the pornographic, *Lialeh* pushed it one step further, creating a distinctive blax-porn-tation aes-

2.1 John Shaft in Times Square

thetic aimed at pleasuring a black pornographic viewing audience. As a film straddling two genres, *Lialeh* uses its opening moments to authenticate itself by gesturing to the genre conventions of both the blaxploitation and the pornographic. *Lialeh* secures its position as a blaxploitation film by explicitly referencing Parks's *Shaft*, which begins with Isaac Hayes's now famous lengthy soundtrack introducing the viewer to its protagonist, John Shaft (figure 2.1). As Shaft emerges from the subway, skillfully navigating his way through Times Square's crowds with his brown leather trench coat unbuttoned and flapping behind him, Hayes's deep voice sings, "Who's the black private dick that's a sex machine to all the chicks? Shaft! Who is the man that would risk his neck for his brother man? Shaft!" Hayes's cool track coupled with Shaft's cool strut secures the notion of Shaft as the quintessentially nonchalant, tough blaxploitation protagonist. *Lialeh* begins in much the same way: with a long musical interlude performed by Bernard Lee "Pretty" Purdie. As Purdie's band plays, the viewer sees the film's male protagonist, Arlo, traversing Times Square (figure 2.2).[29] Like Shaft, Arlo is dressed in the cool fashion of the day—a striped zebra blazer and a large red hat. In the midst of the lights and chaos of Times Square, Arlo is self-assured and poised. *Lialeh*'s opening sequence establishes Arlo as the blax-porn-tation equivalent of the blaxploitation hero Shaft.

Lialeh also authenticates itself by drawing on one of blaxploitation's fundamental principles: an unrelenting celebration of black male phallic power. The day after her audition, Lialeh telephones Arlo and playfully confesses, "I'd love to see your cock again. You know it's the most beauti-

2.2 Arlo in Times Square

ful cock in the world. I'd like to have it right here, right now. Just riding it."
Lialeh says, "Talk to me," then masturbates while listening to his voice.
While Arlo is fully clothed in the scene, not titillated by his conversation
with Lialeh, she is clearly overcome by sexual excitement. The juxtaposition of Lialeh's naked body and Arlo's clothed body, Lialeh's breathy voice
and Arlo's calm voice, only entrenches ideas of the black male phallus's
power: it can arouse even when it is not aroused.

What makes the scene particularly emblematic of the blaxploitation
tradition is that it shows the power of the black male phallus to enable
socially prohibited desires, particularly interracial desires. As Arlo "talks"
to Lialeh, the scene cuts to a white female phone operator who eaves-
drops on their conversation. She urges her colleague to listen in with her,
exclaiming that there is "some guy who is turning his chick on!" As the
two operators listen, they, too, are overwhelmed by sexual excitement.
The film then juxtaposes images of Lialeh masturbating with images of
the two white operators undressing each other and performing mutual
cunnilingus (figures 2.3 and 2.4).

The black male phallus, then, is so powerful—and so desirable—that
it need not even be present to arouse either Lialeh or the two operators;
instead, with merely his voice, Arlo can pleasure multiple women simultaneously. Finally, and most important, the scene implies that white
women's contact with the black male phallus can release their repressed

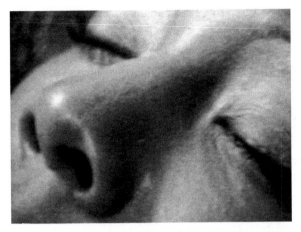

2.3 Lialeh in pleasure
2.4 Phone operators in pleasure

desires, including same-sex attractions and interracial longings. The notion that Arlo's seductive voice could encourage the operators to pleasure each other (and themselves) suggests that black male sexuality is so alluring, so exciting, that it encourages white women to transgress entrenched racial and sexual boundaries.

While *Lialeh* explicitly references earlier blaxploitation films like *Shaft*, and celebrates the black male phallus in the tradition of blaxploitation, it simultaneously establishes itself as a quintessentially pornographic film. In the film's opening scene, Lialeh arrives for her audition and catches a quick glimpse of the act auditioning before her: a piano is playing, and a black heterosexual couple contorts their bodies into various positions while having sex. As Arlo shouts out various positions—"rocking chair, helicopter, thinking man"—the couple alters their physical arrangement, moving their bodies in tempo with the pianist's music. It is this endless variation of sexual positions—and the film's commitment to showing the panoply of ways that bodies experience pleasure—that quickly establishes *Lialeh* as a hard-core film committed to what Williams terms the "maximum visibility principle."[30]

What distinguishes *Lialeh* from other blaxploitation films, and from other Golden Age pornographic films, is how it fuses the conventions of both genres, yielding a distinctive blax-porn-tation aesthetic. As the auditioning couple continues to arrange their bodies in tempo with the music, Arlo talks to his pianist about the challenges of running a black revue.

> I don't give a shit what happens to the white folks. I'm just interested in making that goddamn dollar work for us. That brother there [looking at the man performing on stage], I want to put him in his own Playboy jet. And that sister out there [looking at Lialeh sitting in the audience], I want to make her the first lady in the White House. Are you into that? I want to take big black tits, cunts, dicks, pricks, and make them into a good-time money-making show.

Arlo's monologue connects blaxploitation's political project and pornography's aesthetic commitments by its suggestion that transforming "big black tits, cunts, dicks, pricks . . . into a good-time money-making show" is a racially progressive project which challenges white dominance. By placing the economic challenges of running an autonomous sexual black production—"making that goddamn dollar work for us"—at the center of

2.5 Johnnie Keyes in *Behind the Green Door*

the pornographic narrative, *Lialeh* provides a nationalist justification for the visual display of black bodies, particularly black female bodies.

The success of the film's blax-porn-tation aesthetic, its fusion of the hard-core and the blaxploitation, is most evident in the scene's climax, where *Lialeh* references the Golden Age hit *Behind the Green Door* and adds a distinctly blaxploitation twist.[31] *Behind the Green Door* begins when Gloria Saunders, a young white woman, is blindfolded and abducted. When her captors remove her blindfold, she finds herself in an unnamed place surrounded by unknown people. A woman quietly tells her to prepare for "the most exquisite moment of [her] life." Saunders is then ushered onto a stage, through the proverbial green door, and her body is sexually consumed by men and women, who penetrate her, kiss her, suck on her nipples; all the while, an audience masturbates while watching the scene. One of the unimaginable pleasures that Gloria experiences is sex with an unnamed black man who enters the stage wearing a bone necklace, complete with "African" face paint, and a skin-tight white leotard with a hole through which his already erect penis is visible.[32] Performing the role of the hypersexual, animalistic "African," this unnamed black man shows that the promise of life behind the "green door" is one of sexual liberation, of unbounded ecstasy, of forbidden interracial sex (figure 2.5).[33]

While *Behind the Green Door* gestures to the stage as a site of sexual liberation, *Lialeh* demonstrates that the stage can act as a site of sexual *and*

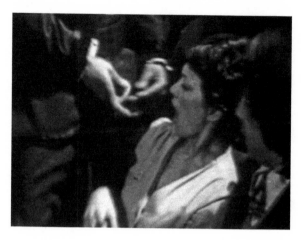

2.6 Audience member in shock

racial liberation. As *Lialeh* concludes, Lialeh performs her signature song on a stage in front of an excited audience. When she finishes her song, she enters the audience to perform a strip tease, dancing suggestively in front of a black male audience member who slides money into her underwear. She continues her provocative dance in front of a white male audience member who also adds money to her G-string. Yet she reprimands the white man, exclaiming, "That's a fiver, not a c-note." Lialeh's unwillingness to accept money from a white man signals the race loyalty narrative that underpins the blaxploitation: she is willing to sacrifice financial gain to maintain her sexual allegiance to black men. Moments later, *Lialeh* tethers this insistence on black economic solidarity to sex by uncovering the sexual power that black subjects, particularly black men, hold over white subjects. As Lialeh and the other dancers perform, Arlo walks through the audience, collecting tickets from audience members. He quickly zeroes in on a white couple pointing to the woman and exclaiming, "My, my, my, this lady here is a winner! Don't you want to know what you win, sweetheart?" Without waiting for a reply, Arlo removes his penis from his pants and thrusts it toward the woman (figure 2.6).

The insistent visual presence of Arlo's penis is contrasted with the white man's inability to protect his partner from Arlo and from the threat of sexual violence. When the couple, visibly threatened by Arlo's violent gesture, tries to leave the revue, they are physically barred from exiting.

2.7 Audience member onstage

Arlo then rips off the woman's shirt and carries her onstage, ignoring her audible, frightened protests. After he pins her down, kissing her and fondling her, her fear yields to pleasure, and her screams are replaced by the moans and whimpers of longing. Arlo declares, "She's all yours," and three black male dancers appear. As in *Behind the Green Door*, the black male dancers wear face paint, presumably to call attention to an imagined primitive black sexuality. The men encircle her, continue to strip her, and then have sex with her. Much as Gloria's resistance is transformed in *Behind the Green Door*, in *Lialeh* the white female audience member's initial terror quickly yields to desire, with the stage becoming the site of her sexual and racial liberation (figure 2.7). *Lialeh* shows that black men's sexual appeal overpowers both white men's ability to protect white women from black men and white women's culturally prescribed resistance to black men. As in the earlier scene with the telephone operators, this scene demonstrates the power of the black male phallus to unleash white women's "real" desires for black men. More than that, the authenticity and virility of the black phallus neuters white men, exposing their weakness, their inability to protect white women from the power—and pleasures—of the black male phallus.

Both scenes—of Lialeh's sexual dancing and of the unnamed white woman who is transported onstage—show that the pornographic and the blaxploitation easily coincide to buttress a narrative of black male phallic power. Blaxploitation lends the pornographic its unrelenting celebration of the black phallus, while the pornographic lends the blaxploitation a commitment to "maximum visibility," to making bodies and their pleasures hypervisible.[34] The easy union of blaxploitation and the pornographic is particularly significant in its unrelenting anticipation of a black spectator. By speaking sex *and* speaking race, and in showing how speaking sex is *always* speaking race, the film anticipates and even engenders ecstatic black spectatorship. Indeed, the pleasures of black spectatorship (as, for example, in watching Arlo's revue succeed) only bolster the pleasures of pornographic spectatorship (as, for example, in watching bodies expose and pleasure each other), so that speaking sex and speaking race enhance each other for the imagined black spectator.

Many scholars have argued that blaxploitation's and pornography's easy merger produces a particularly patriarchal visual project, as both genres circulate narratives of phallic power and patriarchal authority at the expense of a meaningful development of female protagonists. These scholars presume that blax-porn-tation is constructed around a black male sexual imaginary, foreclosing the possibility of black female viewing pleasures and neglecting black female protagonists' sexual pleasures. Donald Bogle, for example, asserts, "Like most pornographic films, *Lialeh* obviously exploits its female characters."[35] Similarly, Mireille Miller-Young concedes that "the film [*Lialeh*] ends without fully exploring the intriguing and sexy secrets of the main female character, sacrificing her development to the conquests and desires of the black male characters."[36] Yet it is precisely *Lialeh's* incomplete intersection of the pornographic and the blaxploitation, its imperfect convergence, that provides spaces for the black female protagonist's "intriguing and sexy" pleasures, a set of pleasures which, at times, trouble the promises of both the blaxploitation and the pornographic.

The complex and incomplete generic intersections that mark *Lialeh* raise a number of questions: in what ways do the genre conventions of the blaxploitation and the pornographic collide both to produce narratives about black phallic power and to trouble black phallic power? How do these collisions and collusions both anticipate and disrupt black male spectatorship? How might these fusions and failures anticipate pleasurable black female spectatorship? And in what ways do black women's bodies exploit the interstices of this generic marriage, troubling the black phallic reign that blax-porn-tation purports to solidify?

Things Left Unseen

While Lialeh shows the blaxploitation and the pornographic collabora-tively producing a narrative that celebrates the sexual underpinnings of black male power and offering a nationalist rationale for the display of female bodies, the film also depicts moments where the respective genre conventions fail to coincide in ways that produce fissures in their respec-tive fundamental promises: pornography's commitment to make bodies and their workings visible, and blaxploitation's commitment to affirming black male power. These moments of discontinuity, like when blaxploi-tation's race loyalty narrative—which, at least in the context of Lialeh, re-quires black men to withhold sex from white women—collides with por-nography's "maximum visibility" premise, produce spaces for multiple black viewing pleasures. To be clear, as Williams notes, blaxploitation heroes have long "[made] a point of having sex with both the sisters of the black community and appreciative white women" even as "the female heroes are never portrayed having interracial sex except under duress."[37] That is, black male–white female interracial sex has never been taboo on the blaxploitation screen; yet in the context of Lialeh, a film which hinges on Arlo's political insistence on displaying "big black tits, cunts, dicks, and pricks," Arlo's sexual loyalty to black women signals his racial poli-tics, even as it undermines pornography's incessant display of bodies.

In an early scene, Arlo travels to visit Rogers, the club owner, to discuss Rogers's incessant attempts to shut down the all-black revue. Rogers's white female secretary brusquely tells Arlo that he is not in the office, and when Arlo tries to sidestep her desk, she jumps up from her chair, per-forming a swift martial arts move and declaring, "I'm warning you I have a brown belt! Local ordinance requires me to tell you that my hand is a deadly weapon!" Arlo responds, "I bet you got deadly thighs too, but I'm warning you, I'm a black belt" (figure 2.8). The two engage in highly styl-ized comical martial-arts fighting, which concludes when Arlo throws her to the floor and begins to kiss her.

When Arlo pushes away from her, she asks, "Wait a minute, you mean

2.8 Arlo and the secretary fighting

you're not going to rape me?" The secretary then transforms the fiction of
the black male rapist into a site of her own sexual excitement, telling Arlo,
"Now come here before I put a karate chop on your cock." Arlo refuses her
sexual invitation, clearly insulted by her invocation of the racial stereotype, and decides to teach her a lesson. As Arlo fondles her, she closes
her eyes in excitement, and he penetrates her with the remainder of her
lunch, a hot dog. Mistaking the hot dog for Arlo's penis, she continues to
moan with pleasure, until Arlo jumps up and says, "So long bitch, enjoy
your lunch!"

This scene shows how profoundly the respective goals of the pornographic and the blaxploitation can collide. While the scene celebrates
racial loyalty through Arlo's refusal of interracial sex and investment in
upending the "myth of the black male rapist," it frustrates pornography's
promise to make bodies visible.[38] The viewer is denied visual access to
the secretary's body, and thus left without the (potentially transgressive)
thrills of watching interracial sex. In its place, the trick that Arlo plays
on the secretary, penetrating her with a simulacrum of his black penis,
is also a trick on the viewer, who is left with the image of the hot dog instead of the image of the black penis. While the secretary's body is partially displayed, Arlo's body remains entirely covered, and the viewer is left
to speculate as to whether the secretary aroused him, and left to imagine
what their bodies in pleasure would resemble.

Similarly, *Lialeh*'s final scene is marked by aesthetic failures that frustrate the merger of the pornographic and the blaxploitation. On the morning of the revue, Rogers comes to collect his money from Arlo, shouting, "No bucks, no fucks." Arlo attempts to stall Rogers by offering sexual access to one of the women in his cabaret. When Rogers refuses, Arlo sighs, "Mr. Rogers, you're so uptight, I'm sure we can work something out," and Rogers replies, "I'm no faggot, man! No offense if you are!" When Arlo implies that Rogers's "uptightness" might be a sign of an inauthentic, or even queer, masculinity, Rogers quickly insists on the authenticity of his masculinity. Yet Rogers's "real" masculinity is called into question moments later. When Rogers warns Arlo that unless he receives his payment, he will let the police know about the revue, the scene quickly turns violent: Rogers calls Arlo a "dirty black motherfucker," and Arlo retaliates by punching him in the face. Rogers seems stunned, resting his hands on his cheeks and crying out, "Oh my face, not my face. Here! [pointing to his buttocks] I like it here," gesturing that Arlo should slap Rogers's buttocks. Much like other scenes in the film, this initial moment of violence is transformed into something pleasurable. When Arlo strikes Rogers's buttocks, Rogers's moans—whether of pain, sexual pleasure, or both— fill the aural space of the scene.

While this scene celebrates black male triumph over white male dominance, it also troubles mainstream hard-core pornography's fundamental promise that male bodies never seek pleasure from each other.[39] The very presence of Rogers's queer desires secures the blaxploitation mythology of inauthentic white masculinity, yet it upsets the homophobic pornographic promise that male-male desire will never be represented on-screen. Moreover, while Arlo's participation in the scene can be read as one where a black man exposes white men's effeminacy, it can also be interpreted as gesturing to Arlo's own queer desires. Unlike the scene where Arlo refuses to participate in sex with the white secretary, here Arlo willingly disciplines Rogers and seems to locate his own pleasures—certainly political, and perhaps even sexual—in the encounter. By placing Arlo's pleasures in Rogers's queer desires at the center of the scene, *Lialeh* suggests that insistently heterosexual black male pleasures might also be queer pleasures, a fundamental disruption of the insistent heterosexist logic that underpins the blaxploitation.

It is not that blaxploitation simply transfers its homophobia onto pornography (or vice versa). In fact, both mainstream hard-core pornography and blaxploitation are often read as homophobic genres, though in distinctive ways; hard-core pornography has long been marked by an insistence on avoiding representations of male-male desires and pleasures, and blaxploitation has long celebrated excessive heteronormative masculinity and denigrated effeminacy. My own reading of blax-porntation—informed by Joe Wlodarz's work—is invested in how the imperfect intersections of pornography and blaxploitation produce space for "diverse versions of black masculinity that confound the presumed cultural 'authenticity' of the black macho of the early 1970s."[40] The incomplete merger of these two genres upends the promises of both genres, creating space for multiple and heterogeneous black spectatorial pleasures, including black queer viewing pleasures.

Lialeh's moments of generic failure also feature its female lead. In the scene immediately following the fight between Arlo and Rogers, Lialeh sits in the dressing room, preparing for her performance. The revue's pianist enters and asks, "Would you like to put your hands in my pants?" When Lialeh shows her lack of interest, saying that she has to "save herself for the show," the pianist says,

> You don't understand my problem. I had a girl once. She was fine, oh my God! She had large boobs and well, anyway, I would see her every night and we'd sit on the couch and just make out, boy, and she could grind and it just made me, oh my goodness! Well, this went on for a couple of weeks and I tried to get up enough courage to try and fuck her. So I kissed her and put my hand under her skirt and she looked up at me with a smile and I just knew I could get it. I just took my dick out and I just whipped it around and got hard, got big, that I stuck my other hand up her crotch and she had a dick and balls and everything!

As the pianist begs Lialeh to touch him, she pushes him away from her. He then continues his confession, sharing his anxieties about the size of his penis.

> *Pianist:* Do you think my dick is small?
> *Lialeh:* No, it's normal.
> *Pianist:* Honest to God?
> *Lialeh:* It's big, it's really something.

Pianist: Yeah, I guess it is something.

Lialeh: It's beautiful.

Pianist: That's not an ordinary site you're looking at. This is pure love
   muscle!

Lialeh: I know.

Pianist: I never thought you'd like me, that's why.

Lialeh: I like you.

The camera then cuts away to the revue, which has already begun with
Bernard Purdie singing "sweet sexy Lialeh." When the viewer returns to
Lialeh and the pianist, they are already in the midst of a silent, clumsy sex
act that concludes not with a view of the pianist's ejaculating penis, but
with a close-up of Lialeh's silver stilettos, which she wears for the duration of the sexual encounter. While the demands of the pornographic require that the spectator see visual proof of sexual pleasure, generally in
the form of the money shot, this scene curiously fails to provide a close-up
of either the ejaculating penis or of bodies in pleasure. In fact, though the
sex act is fully on-screen, it is effectively hidden, with both Lialeh's and the
pianist's sex organs off-screen, rendering impossible the pornographic
climax. And so the money shot is replaced with the pianist's quick breathy
utterance, "Oh my God, oh my God. Deeper, more." Most surprisingly, the
spectator is denied evidence of the pianist's penis size; instead, the viewer
is told only that the pianist has a "pure love muscle," a descriptor which
takes the place of a display of the penis. The pianist's absent penis coupled
with the pleasure he took in his "fine" girlfriend who turned out to be
a hermaphrodite shroud his masculinity (much like Rogers's and Arlo's
masculinities in the preceding scene) in questions about its authenticity.

   In failing to meet the genre conventions of the pornographic, this
scene also fails the genre conventions of blaxploitation. The pianist's
"love muscle" concerns demonstrate that the black male phallus can indeed be inadequate, undersized, and even anxiety ridden. More than that,
the scene exposes that the black male phallus—so often represented as
self-assured and confident—can require reassurance from black women.
Lialeh's essential role in assuaging the pianist's anxieties shows the very
dependence of black hetero-masculinity on black women, indicating that
the black male confidence projected throughout the film actually relies on
black women's approval and support. Lialeh, then, becomes instrumental

to rescuing the black male phallus in a moment of crisis, even if it is never visually vindicated on screen.

Ultimately, while *Lialeh* clearly marshals a blaxploitation aesthetic to speak sex to a black spectator, the speaking sex is, at least at times, troubled by the imperfect union of the blaxploitation and the pornographic. Blaxploitation's race loyalty narrative and pornography's maximum visibility imperative seem to only partially overlap, creating a messy and imperfect vernacular for speaking sex to black spectators. *Lialeh* not only anticipates pleasurable black spectatorship, but its moments of imperfection engender heterogeneous forms of black spectatorship. Indeed, it is these moments of failure—moments where the merger of genres renders it impossible to fulfill their respective demands—that produce the possibility both of multiple, incomplete forms of identification and, as I discuss in the chapter's final section, of pleasurable black female spectatorship. This failure, which is particularly evident in scenes featuring Lialeh, opens up pleasurable spaces for black female spectatorship.

"Beware, Beware of Lialeh"

The film's soundtrack warns its listeners to "beware of Lialeh, sweet, sweet sexy Lialeh," and it is Lialeh's capacity to seek pleasure outside of the blaxploitation and pornographic representational economies that might be the most transgressive aspect of the film. While it is true that Lialeh's body becomes a site that destabilizes the pornographic and the blaxploitation, there is nothing inherently transgressive about the idea that black women and their sexuality can produce the downfall of men. In fact, this trope pervades dominant cinema, entrenching the conception that female sexuality is duplicitous and dangerous.[41] Where the figure of Lialeh is transgressive, though, is in her capacity to trouble the generic union that the film attempts to present, providing the black spectator opportunities for viewing pleasures outside of simple identification with the film's black male protagonist, engendering, and perhaps even anticipating, pleasurable black female viewing.[42]

In the scene preceding the film's climactic revue, Lialeh sings "Give Me That Old Time Religion" with her church's choir. When the rehearsal ends, Lialeh approaches the reverend and whispers something in his ear. The reverend encourages her to have confidence in her ability to sing, leaving

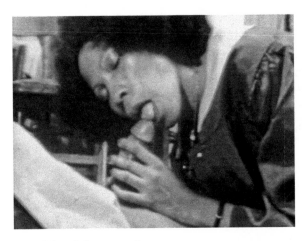

2.9 Lialeh and the reverend

the spectator to deduce that Lialeh has just confessed anxiety about her
upcoming performance. After offering Lialeh this advice, the reverend ex-
cuses himself to use the bathroom. Lialeh talks to two friends, and they
ask if they can perform in the show with her, exclaiming that they can be
"three sisters, just like we sing in church." Just as Lialeh begins to explain
that the show involves more than mere singing, the reverend runs into the
room screaming. He asks the women to call a doctor and quietly confesses
that his penis has become stuck in his zipper. Although he begs them not
to touch it, Lialeh and her friends immediately disobey, insistently working to dislodge his jammed penis. At first, their efforts seem thoughtful and concerned, focused on the reverend's comfort. Yet within a few
moments the mood changes, and Lialeh and the other choirgirls use the
reverend's mishap as an opportunity for enjoying their own sexual pleasures. While Lialeh provides the reverend with a blowjob, one of the other
choirgirls clutches his head to her now bare chest (figure 2.9). Lialeh then
mounts the reverend and has sex with him.

This scene is particularly revealing of the "trouble" Lialeh can produce
for the generic marriage of the blaxploitation and the pornographic. As in
the scene with Lialeh and the pianist, the black male phallus is again under
siege—this time the film shows the black phallus can be undermined in
the most absurd of ways, by a faulty zipper—and seems to require black
female intervention to save it. Here, while the viewer sees evidence of the

reverend's phallic power—his prominently displayed erection—it is Lia-leh who takes advantage of the black phallus's troubles to satiate her own longings. The trouble Lialeh brings to the scene is even more significant in light of the reverend's position as a social, religious, and cultural authority figure. In this case, Lialeh and her choral friends literally expose the reverend, willfully ignoring his request to leave his injured penis undisturbed. While the reverend eventually takes pleasure from the rescue of his penis, it is also clear that Lialeh and her female friends initiate the act to fulfill their own longings. The women's strategic unwillingness to yield to black authority shows black masculinity's vulnerability and disrupts the imagined patriarchal order at the heart of the black Church. As Miller-Young argues in her analysis of the film, this scene acts as a "subversion of the sexual conservatism within the black Church."[43] More important, the scene is also a "subversion" of the blaxploitation foundational myth of black phallic power.[44] In representing the vulnerability of the black male phallus, this scene (like that in which the pianist confesses his penile anxieties) reveals that the hypermasculine blaxploitation aesthetic is undergirded by a surprising insecurity about black masculinity. Finally, the scene concludes without a resurrection of black male phallic power, instead focusing on Lialeh's longings and pleasures. While aural clues imply a sexual climax, the scene concludes without a money shot and without evidence that the fallen black phallus has been restored to a position of supremacy.

This lack of visual proof of phallic triumph permeates *Lialeh*, showing that the film creates space to capture female pleasures, often at the expense of celebrating black male pleasures. For example, while the "lesbian" telephone operator scene is arguably a pornographic genre convention—ostensibly heterosexual women performing "lesbianism" for an imagined male pornographic spectator—it showcases women pleasing each other without the intervention of a penis. Though Arlo's voice is the catalyst for the same-sex encounter, he is wholly absent from the scene as the women engage in cunnilingus and bring each other to orgasm. Similarly, Lialeh's masturbation scene is initiated by the sounds of Arlo's voice, yet as the camera pans her extended body, showing her penetrating herself with her recorder (ostensibly designed to visually resonate with an image of the black penis), it is revealed that Lialeh has put the phone down, no longer using—or needing—Arlo's voice to pleasure herself.[45]

When the "lesbian" scene is read alongside Lialeh's masturbation scene, it becomes clear that the film represents the possibility of female pleasure both alongside and outside of the black male phallus.

Both the blaxploitation and the pornographic represent male phallic power that is achieved through interactions with female protagonists. One could easily assume that the merger of the two would produce a doubly patriarchal logic, a hyper-phallic aesthetic that champions male pleasure at the expense of black women. Yet, it is in Lialeh's generic failures—in the moments when the collision of the blaxploitation and the pornographic yields a hybrid form that fails to satisfy the demands of either—that the film engenders space for heterogeneous black spectatorial pleasures. While the film's deliberate deployment of the genre conventions of the blaxploitation clearly illustrates a commitment to pleasuring black spectators, the film's failures open up space for a variety of black spectators and their heterogeneous and varied longings.

Rethinking Black Spectatorship, Rethinking Black Pleasures

My reading of Lialeh has emphasized the black viewing pleasures that the union of the pornographic and the blaxploitation produces. Indeed, in the very moment in which pornography sought to become a mainstream genre, Hollywood "discovered" black audiences. My analysis of Lialeh investigates how Golden Age pornographers borrowed visual and narrative conventions from blaxploitation filmmakers, producing a distinctive pornographic vernacular designed to "speak sex" to black viewers. Though the blaxploitation and the pornographic easily buttress each other, producing a film that celebrates phallic power, they also have an imperfect union, one that often upsets the promise of both genres. Indeed, the film's theme song, reminding the viewer to "beware" of Lialeh, signals the dangerous possibility that black women can find spaces for pleasure outside of a phallic economy and, perhaps more troubling, can locate spaces for pleasure within a phallic economy by troubling the supremacy of the black male phallus. In the many moments where blaxploitation's and pornography's respective projects collide, black women's bodies play a central role in exposing the instability of this generic union, troubling pornography's insistent will-to-know-bodies and blaxploitation's insistent celebration of the black phallus. In so doing, they insist on space for the black female protagonist's pleasure and anticipate space for a kind of spectatorship wholly ignored by black feminist scholarship: nonoppositional, nonresistant, pleasurable black viewing. The black spectator need not peer in on a world that was not created for her; instead, there is space for black pleasures—pleasures in watching Arlo, pleasures in watching Rogers, pleasures in watching the actors contort their bodies, and pleasures in watching Lialeh achieve her own pleasure—within the parameters of the film. In underscoring these multiple possible pleasures, I do not presume (and, in fact, reject) that black spectators can locate pleasure only by watching black pornographic protagonists; instead, I register the variety of pleasures depicted on the blax-porn-tation screen, and the multiple identifications that *Lialeh* both anticipates and engenders for its black viewers, particularly its black female viewers.

Ultimately, my reading of the film places analytic pressure on the narrow viewing pleasures that the black feminist theoretical archive has carved out for black spectators. Rather than presuming that black spectators always labor to re-interpret films and to read texts "against the grain," I ask how black viewers might locate pleasures reading pornographic texts "with the grain." In so doing, I reject the idea that critical reinterpretation and disidentification are the hallmarks of black spectatorship; instead, I endeavor to shift black feminist conversations toward an examination of the multiple ways that the pornographic screen can pleasure black spectators.

3 | RACE-PLEASURES

Sexworld and the Ecstatic Black Female Body

If vacation is a space where people reimagine and reinvent themselves, then Anthony Spinelli's *Sexworld* (1978) documents the quintessential vacation.[1] In the film, guests board a bus that transports them from the routines of their ordinary lives to a remote sex mansion, Sexworld. When the guests arrive, the resort's manager announces Sexworld's philosophy: "If you can imagine it, we can arrange it. Don't be inhibited or embarrassed, we're not doctors or therapists to judge you. We're here to pamper you."

Released six years after the Golden Age hit *Behind the Green Door* (dir. Mitchell Brothers, 1972), *Sexworld* contains many of the same elements as its predecessor.[2] Like *Behind the Green Door*, *Sexworld* is a feature-length, narrative-driven film that documents the unspeakable pleasures made possible by leaving the constraints of daily life, including the pleasures of traversing racial boundaries.[3] *Behind the Green Door* features the taboo coupling of its white female protagonist, played by the former "Ivory Soap girl" Marilyn Chambers, and an unnamed black male protagonist, played by the Golden Age star Johnnie Keyes. *Sexworld* reverses the conventional gender roles of Golden Age interracial pornography, featuring a white male protagonist, Roger, who locates unspeakable pleasure in a sexual encounter with the film's black female protagonist, Jill.[4]

As proof of Sexworld's promise to "arrange" anything, the film's narrative centers on Roger, whom the Sexworld experts quickly identify as a "special case," a man whose desires are hard to discern. When a Sexworld technician suggests that he might enjoy "aggression in a woman," Roger bemoans the technician's lack of creativity, noting that he has already "hooked up with a dame like that." Finally, the Sexworld staff concludes that he needs to be challenged, and that he should be matched with "someone he hates." They remember an uncomfortable encounter on the Sexworld bus: when Jill noticed Roger staring at her, she playfully puckered her lips and blew him a kiss (figure 3.1). In return, he looked visibly uncomfortable and quickly turned away (figure 3.2). Based on this information, the Sexworld staff orchestrates a sexual encounter between Roger and Jill, an encounter which ultimately transforms Roger.

By representing its white male protagonist finding transformative pleasure in a sexual encounter with a black woman, Sexworld can easily be read (and even dismissed) as following a pornographic tradition where white male subjects inflict the violent injury of racialization on black female bodies and take pleasure in that objectifying difference-making exercise. Yet even as Sexworld depicts Roger locating pleasure in incessantly naming and then consuming Jill's imagined difference, it also shows Jill's pleasure in eroticizing her imagined difference. In its representation of Jill's hyperbolic performance of blackness as a source of her own excitement, Sexworld serves as a point of departure for considering how the pornographic screen depicts the relationship among blackness, embodiment, and pleasure, and as a platform from which the black feminist theoretical archive can imagine blackness beyond an embodied wound.

To describe Jill's pleasure, I borrow the legal scholar Anthony Paul Farley's term "race-pleasure," but I inflect it very differently. For Farley, race-pleasure refers both to embodied pleasures in whiteness that white subjects garner from inflicting the wound of race on black bodies—a pleasure that is only heightened by denying the incessant practice of injuring black bodies—and to a pathological black "pleasure in humiliation."[5] Much like antipornography critiques of women's illusory pleasures under conditions of patriarchy, Farley presumes that false consciousness is the only explanation for black subjects who garner pleasure from race; locating pleasure in blackness is relishing the "velvet glove" which cloaks the "iron fist of domination."[6] Instead of pathologizing black pleasures,

3.1 Jill blowing Roger a kiss

3.2 Jill and Roger on the Sexworld bus

I analyze how blackness becomes a vehicle for black pornographic protagonists to name pleasures, to speak desires, and to amplify longings. In short, I trace how blackness can function as a lexicon of desire and a locus of eroticism for black pornographic protagonists.

My understanding of race-pleasure is informed by queer-of-color studies scholarship which underscores the possibilities of pleasures in blackness. Kathryn Bond Stockton, for example, draws on the queer theorists Leo Bersani and Eve Sedgwick to study the relationship among blackness, abjection, shame, and pleasure.[7] She writes, "I . . . ask of my texts what they imagine debasement produces, at certain moments, for those people who actually undergo it, who, in a manner of speaking, practice it. How does debasement foster attractions? How is it used for aesthetic delight? What does it offer for projects of sorrow and ways of creative historical knowing?"[8] Indeed, Stockton's very project is to analyze "why certain forms of shame are embraced by blacks and queers, and also black queers, in forceful ways."[9] Similarly, Darieck Scott locates blackness's abjection as a site of intense pleasure for black (male) subjects, arguing, "Though sexuality is used against us, and sexual(ized) domination is in part what makes us black, though sexuality is a mode of conquest and often cannot avoid being deployed in the field of representation without functioning as an introjection of historical defeat, it is in and through that very domination and defeat also a mapping of political potential, an access to freedom."[10] For Stockton and Scott, pleasures in blackness are pleasures in abjection, where the wound of blackness is taken up as a site of ecstasy.

Other scholars interested in questions of pleasures in blackness, like the anthropologist Margot Weiss, have examined racialized performances as loci of eroticism. Weiss studies how some BDSM practitioners perform sexual scenes that garner their erotic charge from enacting racial injuries, including, most controversially, practitioners who stage the slave auction block. Though Weiss reflexively documents her ambivalence about these scenes, she concludes that these profoundly complex racialized performances show that

> it requires a certain spectacular dramatization to unsettle whiteness as the universal basis of community belonging, of normalness. And so, for me, focusing on the social, economic, and political investments

in maintaining the invisibility of whiteness . . . finally dislodged my concern for the black slave and my discomfort with her white master's commanding grasp on her hair, and instead prompted a closer look at my simultaneous attraction to and revulsion from such loaded scenes.[11]

Weiss's rich ethnography attempts to circumvent (and trouble) the binary between fantasy and reality, between sexual race play and "real life," by insisting that sexual play is always already race play.

While I draw on Stockton's and Scott's respective commitments to thinking about the pleasures race confers on black subjects, and on Weiss's investment in studying the kinds of racial play that lie at the heart of sexuality, my point of departure is far from debasement and abjection. Rather than considering how "dirty details" are transformed into pleasure, I theorize the relationship between race and sexuality differently. Like other scholars, I view race as a "pre-eminently socio-historical concept" where "racial categories and the meaning of race are given concrete expression by the specific social relations and historical context in which they are embedded,"[12] and I understand race as a technology of violent hierarchy which wields the language (and fantasy) of difference to sustain itself. Where I part company with other scholars is in my interest in the potentially *productive* nature of racialization for all subjects. Here, my work is informed by the performative turn in feminist theory, which has been marked by a commitment to viewing gender as a performance which engenders "anxiety and pleasure."[13] Far more than simply a locus of violent domination, gender is a space that confers a set of aesthetic, corporeal, and even erotic pleasures on its performer. Similarly, I treat blackness as a fraught, complex, and potentially exciting performance for black subjects, as a *doing* which can thrill, excite, and arouse, even as it wounds and terrorizes.

In uncovering black female pornographic protagonists' embodied race-pleasures, I am purposefully engaged in what Judith Butler terms an "aggressive counterreading," an intentional attempt to read strongly "against the grain"—against prevailing conceptions of racialization—in an attempt to engender theoretical and political space to imagine black subjects' erotic attachments to blackness.[14] With so few cultural avenues open for black subjects generally, and black women particularly, to speak sex, my reading of *Sexworld* concludes that speaking race can become an essential, albeit limited, way of speaking sex, a strategy for naming one's pleasures, longings, and desires.[15]

"Between My Thighs Is Where My Rhythm Lies"

When the Sexworld guests arrive at the remote mansion, it becomes clear that Roger's suite is designed to provoke him. The room is shrouded in dim light, and decorated in a jungle motif, and the bed is circled by fake palm trees and covered in a zebra-print spread. Roger sits on the edge of the bed, wrapped in a white bathrobe, and calls the Sexworld technicians to complain about the suite's décor: "This room with these stripes all over the place, the plants, the spears. What, are you going to have some Zulu raisinettes come out and dance with me?" As Roger lodges his complaint, Jill quietly enters his room, leaning against the doorframe with a hand resting on her hip (figure 3.3). When Roger turns around and sees her, he brusquely asks, "What do you want? Are you here to clean up the room? Well, if you're gonna clean up, clean up!" She replies, "Clean your wet cock when *we's* done, sir." Roger quickly realizes that Jill is not the maid and that the Sexworld technicians have arranged precisely what he wishes to avoid: a sexual encounter with a black woman.

A conversation ensues between Roger and Jill.

> Roger: Oh no, you can't be my trick!
> Jill: Surprise, honey!
> Roger: There goes the fucking neighborhood. [She moves closer to him.] Now look fat lips, you got the wrong room, the wrong boy.
> Jill: No, they told me to go find that honky boy. Ain't that you?
> Roger: Ain't that me?
> Jill: Ain't that *you*?
> Roger: No, but I tell you a secret. At Thanksgiving, I wait for the white meat. I say give me the breast, period.
> Jill: . . . What's the matter, you ain't never had no *black* pussy before?
> Roger: Not yet. Not now. Not ever. [Runs to the other side of the room.]

The scene's beginning is marked by Roger's evident racial panic: he has come to Sexworld to have his fantasies unleashed, not to confront what he detests. When he realizes that Jill is his "trick," he clumsily utters, "I wait for the white meat" to mark his preference for intraracial sex. And

3.3 Jill entering Roger's suite

in refusing the title of "that honky boy," he paradoxically (and comically) makes visible his disgust for interracial sex (and his commitment to white superiority) yet disavows Jill's charge of racism.

While these first moments are marked by Roger's obvious discomfort, the visual framing of the scene hints that Roger's beliefs will be undermined in the moments that follow. Both Roger and Jill wear identical white ropes, their respective (and differently raced) bodies cloaked in matching outfits. This symmetry serves as an emphatic reminder of their shared place at the Sexworld resort. While the sexual encounter seems designed to pleasure only Roger—he refers to Jill as "my trick"—the fact that both Jill and Roger are guests at a resort that promises to fulfill their every desire suggests that the encounter should be designed to please them both.

The scene takes a quick and notable turn when Jill persists in engaging with Roger despite his obvious repulsion. Significantly, Jill adopts a vocabulary familiar to Roger (and, possibly, to the viewer) to counter his aversion: she makes use of the racialized fictions that have shaped Roger's sexual imagination, and perhaps her own, insisting on the racial and sexual distinctiveness of her black body.

> Jill: You don't know what you've been missing. Haven't you ever heard, the darker the meat, the sweeter the juice?
> Roger: I never heard that.
> Jill: Don't you want to see where I keep my juices at, honey?

3.4 Roger's excitement

> Roger: I don't want to see nothing from you.
>
> Jill: Oh you just think like that. [Loosens robe.] This ain't too shabby, is it?
>
> Roger: [His mouth falls open with surprise and excitement; see figure 3.4. Jill is wearing a white bustier and garter belt, her genitals exposed.] Oh my god. [He runs to other side of bedroom.] Black and white went out with Wallace Beery, it's all big widescreen color for this kid!
>
> Jill: Well, if I ain't got me a first-class honky bigot here, whoowee!
>
> Roger: Now wait a minute, you can't call me—I am not prejudiced. I just don't happen to like you people.
>
> Jill: Take a chance white boy. [She puts her knee on the bed.] I'll prove your spigot ain't no bigot. [Takes off her robe.] Let's get your faucet out and see if we can get it flowing.

Jill resorts to racial folklore—"the darker the meat, the sweeter the juice"—as a strategy to convince Roger of the merits of her "dark meat." The racial fictions she draws upon, promises of "sweet juice" and of the particularity of her racialized body, are precisely the mythologies that have shaped Roger's repulsion. Yet Jill senses the fictions that produce disgust might also produce longing, and she capitalizes on the conflict between Roger's desire, visually marked by his mouth hanging open in pleasurable surprise, and his revulsion at the idea of sexually traversing the racial border. Jill attempts to mediate this conflict by hinting that Roger's masculinity hinges on his ability to "prove [his] spigot ain't no bigot." Jill transforms the threat of interracial sex into an act that can affirm the power (and normativity) of Roger's "spigot."

Their conversation continues.

Roger: Well, you are built kinda nice, I'll say that.

Jill: You're fucking A I am, Cecil. These jugs are filled with honey, and down here is my honey pot just for you. This is home grown.

Roger: Alright, I'll give you the benefit of the doubt. What are you supposed to do for me?

Jill: [Raising one eyebrow as camera zooms in on her face.] Me, I *provides* entertainment, sir.

Roger: Alright, entertain me! You're supposed to have such rhythm, do a little dance!

Jill: The rhythm I got ain't in my feet, it's about three or four feet high, between my thighs is where my rhythm lies, fine as wine, so divine.

At various moments in Roger's and Jill's encounter, Jill resorts to stereotyped and hyperbolic racialized performances—a term I use to highlight the deliberateness of Jill's performance of racial stereotype—as a tool to transform Roger's aversion into desire. Jill reminds Roger that "the darker the meat, the sweeter the juice" and then encourages him "to see where I keep my juices," drawing on Roger's preexisting racial "knowledge" and using it as an invitation to discover the particular and distinctive pleasures that black women can provide. Similarly, when Jill responds to Roger's question by telling him, "Me, I *provides* entertainment, sir," she purposefully retreats into black vernacular as a way of fulfilling his expectations that black women exist to subserviently provide "entertainment," while willing him away from his racial bigotry and urging him to partake in the sexual pleasures black women can provide. More than that, her exaggerated emphasis on *provides*, coupled with the eyebrow she cocks as she delivers the statement, underscores that Jill is a knowing, willing participant in the exaggerated performance.

Once Jill has lured Roger in, she then relies on her vernacular performance to further her seduction. When Roger asks her to "entertain" him because blacks are "supposed to have such rhythm," Jill responds in rhyme, and later encourages him to "dip into the valley, dally into the valley for a while." Jill thus packages her attempts to "convert" Roger from bigotry to interracial intimacy in a language that is familiar to him, in the linguistic, aesthetic, and sexual terms he expects from a black woman. In so doing, Jill masks the transgressive component of her labor—moving Roger from his insistence on "white meat" to an enjoyment of black female bodies.

Dominant black feminist readings of the interracial scene in *Sexworld* would analyze Jill's willing submission to racial abuse as emblematic of a pornographic fantasy where women generally, and black women particularly, willingly comply with their degradation. More than that, the notion of a black woman performing hyperbolic racial stereotype for a white male protagonist's enjoyment resonates with a black feminist critique of the very notion of representation—that it is a regime which naturalizes and eroticizes racial and sexual violence at black women's expense. Feminist porn studies scholar Mireille Miller-Young gives specific attention to *Sexworld*, and argues that Jill enacts the role of the hyperlibidinous black woman for the pleasurable consumption of both the white male protagonist and the ostensibly white male spectator. She argues that the Roger/ Jill scene "is significant for being exceedingly illustrative of the ways in which black sexuality was fetishistically represented as openly repulsive but secretly desired, an ambivalence shaping the politics of interracial sex during the period."[16] While Miller-Young interprets the scene as crafted by a "white pornographic imagination of black women's sexuality" she also argues that Sexworld exists *exclusively* for white subjects, whose desires are fulfilled at the expense or sublimation of black subjects' sexual longings.[17] This interpretation of *Sexworld* aligns with a black feminist interpretative convention which presumes that the on-screen pornographic world is designed to pleasure white (male) spectators by objectifying black female flesh, and that assumes that black women are represented through "trope[s] of black female sexual domination and licentiousness."[18] According to this tradition, Jill's hyperbolic performance of blackness resonates with prevailing views of black female sexuality as excessive, and Jill's willingness to continue to engage with Roger despite his obvious and repulsive racism shows the logic that underpins the hard-core: that black women find pleasure in injury, that no matter what is inflicted on their bodies by men, they will find a way to moan, whimper, and groan in pleasure.

Certainly Jill does enact a particularly exaggerated racialized performance for Roger's pleasure, embodying the very stereotypes in which he is so deeply invested. Yet Jill's hyperbolic racialized performance confers a set of pleasures on her as well, even as the film represents her pleasures differently from Roger's. How do we understand the fact that Jill describes her own embodied pleasures in highly racialized and highly stereotypical ways (the "rhythm" between her thighs, her delectable "honey pot")? How do we analyze the ways that Jill's use of racial rhetoric seems to excite her, to provide a way for her to locate pleasure in the encounter? How do we interpret the fact that Jill takes pleasure in representing her body as a black female body and in being seen as a black female body? And what might Jill's investment in racial fictions reveal about the relationship between race and pleasure for black subjects more generally?

Central to understanding Jill's race-pleasure is the moment in which she tells Roger that her task is to "*provide* entertainment." As Jill promises Roger that she will enact the role of black female subservience, she cocks her eyebrow and stares directly into the camera. The raised eyebrow places Jill and the spectator in conversation—it is the moment when she makes visible to the spectator that her deployment of the trope of the subservient black woman is deliberate. In fact, in willingly performing the role for Roger, Jill inhabits it for herself; the cocked eyebrow shows that her engagement with racialized stereotypes is a conscious performance. Jill's knowing glance into the camera suggests that the Roger and Jill scene can be reread as a staged racialized performance, one where Jill's stereotypical enactment of blackness becomes a vehicle for her own pleasure as much as it serves as a vehicle for Roger's pleasure.

As the scene begins and Jill advocates for her body's virtues, alerting Roger to precisely what makes her body distinctive, she also rehearses her body's virtues for herself. While she describes her dark meat, her "jugs filled with honey," and the rhythm between her thighs, she stretches herself across Roger's bed, closing her eyes in excitement. It is as if the racialized rhetoric she uses to ensnare Roger also arouses her, becoming essential to the sexual pleasure she takes from the encounter. Similarly, as she offers Roger her "home grown honey pot," she runs her fingers down her torso, shutting her eyes and moaning, demonstrating that racial fictions have shaped not just Roger's imagination, but her own as well, that they act, at least at times, as a powerful imaginative strategy for her. *Sexworld* thus illustrates that the racialized labor of converting Roger also serves as a tool for Jill's own arousal, with the trappings of hypersexual and hyperbolic blackness working as a vocabulary with which Jill can voice her own longings and pleasures.[19] Speaking race, then, becomes a strategy for Jill to name a set of longings and to describe a set of cravings and desires that she might not otherwise be able to voice.

It is not only her embodied blackness, but the insistent rhetorical gesturing toward blackness that is central to Jill's race-pleasure. In fact, her enjoyment of the encounter with Roger hinges both on having him read her body as black and on her insistence that he do so. Roger refuses to read Jill as anything but "you people," a member of a group he initially detests; rather than resisting the label "you people," Jill demands her inclusion in that group. So she tantalizes Roger with the promise of "*black pussy*" and "*dark meat*," insisting that Roger *see* her as a black woman, and as a very particular kind of black woman—one who performs and embodies hyperbolic stereotypes of black femininity. Jill demands legibility from the scene, requiring Roger to name her as black, to recognize her place in the category he disavows, and she finds pleasure in being named, in being seen as black.

The scene concludes with evidence of Roger's conversion, and his initial disgust is transformed into longing.

Roger: You sure have some long legs.

Jill: Just ready to wrap around your head. Just think you'll get one thigh against each ear, ooh.

Roger: Well, let me take a look at you. Turn over or something.

Jill: Now that's the way. Now ain't these about the finest biggest tits you've ever seen? [Holds her breast.] And these thighs, don't these thighs make your peter rise? And this ass, ain't this a class ass, best ass you've ever had stuck in your face, ain't this a class ass?

Roger: You people do have nice asses.

Jill: Go ahead put your hand on it, feel it, bet you never felt one, come on, feel it, there you go, you got nice hands too, there you go, dip into the valley, dally into the valley for a while.

Roger: [He smells his hand.] Hmm, you don't smell funny. I thought you people smelled funny.

Jill: Not this ass, it just smells like ass. Go on, smell it, go on, stick your nose down there.

Roger: I'll touch it, but I don't want to smell it.

Jill: Don't be mad, just be glad, come on, I saw you sneaking a peek at these titties a long time ago. They're yours, ain't nobody gonna know, it's just for you.

As Jill encourages Roger to enjoy her body—her "class ass," her "finest biggest tits"—she continually reminds him that the encounter is private, that it is "just for him." Indeed, it is Sexworld's distance from the trappings and taboos of ordinary life that make the sexual scene, and ostensibly the pleasure both take in it, possible.

The Roger and Jill scene ends abruptly, with Jill offering Roger "a peek at [her] titties," but the film returns to them four more times, providing concrete evidence of the resort's capacity to unleash its guests' sexual imaginations. In the first return, Jill sits on top of Roger, placing her crotch over his mouth as he says, "I didn't say I wanted to." She replies, "You didn't say you wanted to do what, white boy? Come on, suck that stuff!" The camera then cuts to another Sexworld liaison. In the second return, Roger and Jill are in the midst of vaginal intercourse, with Roger remarking, "What's a nice black girl like you doing in a place like this?" In both returns, a kind of racialized play is central to the pleasure they both take in the encounter. In the first return, Jill locates pleasure in ordering Roger to do what disgusts him; in the second return, Roger locates a kind of pleasure in imagining Jill as a "nice black girl," a description clearly at odds with their sudden and ostensibly dirty sexual encounter. For both Roger and Jill, reading the other as merely a "white boy" or a "nice black girl"—and performing that role for themselves and each other—becomes central to the pleasure they take in the encounter. The categories that constrain—"black girl" and "white boy"—become devices that animate the erotic encounter. In the penultimate return to Roger and Jill, they are having "doggie-style" sex, and Roger proclaims, "I didn't think you had this much class!" Despite Roger's invocation of class, Roger and Jill seem to locate pleasure precisely in the classlessness of their quick, anonymous sexual encounter (which is rendered only more ironic by the fact that Sexworld prides itself on its classiness and on the expense that guests have paid to enjoy the sex resort).

The final return to Jill and Roger features the climactic money shot: documentary evidence of Roger's transformation. The money shot is

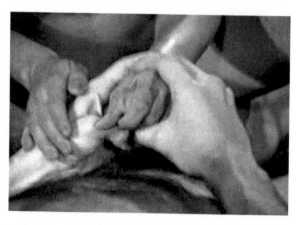

3.5 Roger's money shot, with Jill's hands

hypervisible to satisfy the ethnographic impulses of the genre, and, as is often the case in interracial pornography, the scene's lighting emphasizes the color contrast between Roger's and Jill's bodies. In the tradition of the hard-core, Roger removes his penis from Jill's vagina before ejaculating, and they both rub Roger's penis, facilitating the viewer's proof of his satisfaction. As the four hands—two white and two black—hold Roger's white penis, the viewer has incontrovertible evidence of Roger's pleasure and of Roger's "conversion" from a position of interracial disgust to interracial longing (figure 3.5). As is the pornographic tradition, evidence of Roger's pleasure stands in for Jill's pleasure, with the ejaculating penis signifying both parties' sexual satisfaction. Yet here the ejaculating penis held by black and white hands also comes to signify the transgression of a racial boundary and the transformative element of the sexual encounter. The four hands cupping Roger's ejaculating penis stand as a kind of metaphor for what the Roger and Jill scene has accomplished: the coming together of differently racially marked bodies in a shared pleasure, a pleasure that is fundamentally linked to Jill's performances of hyperbolic blackness.

While the money shot provides visual evidence of Roger's sexual pleasure, *Sexworld*'s closing moments foreground Jill's pleasure in the sexual encounter. The film ends with Sexworld guests again boarding a bus, this time to return to their ordinary lives. Unlike the movie's opening shot, however, the Sexworld guests seem profoundly relaxed now, as though

3.6 Roger begging for a second chance

their time of mediated sexual seclusion has left them content and re-freshed. As Roger walks toward the bus, he approaches the bus driver and offers him money in exchange for one last visit to Sexworld and, osten-sibly, one last chance to have sex with Jill (figure 3.6). Unbeknownst to Roger, Jill watches the scene with a knowing smile, seemingly amused by the lasting impression their sexual encounter left on him. As Roger runs toward the house again—to find Jill, perhaps, or to petition for another sexual encounter—Jill stops and smiles again, this time staring into the camera (figure 3.7). This final moment underscores the fact that Roger and Jill both took pleasure in the encounter, even though their respective pleasures were different. While Roger's money shot and his pleas for an-other evening at the resort become emblematic of his pleasures, Jill's sug-gestive smile reveals her own pleasures—which include exposing Roger to the imagined distinctiveness of the black female body and perform-ing black female hyperlibidinousness for her own pleasure. Indeed, her knowing glance at the camera (much like her cocked eyebrow during their sexual encounter) indicates Jill's active and pleasurable participation in the racialized sexual scene.

Sexworld concludes with a smiling Jill boarding the departing Sexworld bus, a moment that serves as an emphatic reminder of Jill's status as a guest at the exclusive resort. Jill's place as a guest, rather than an em-ployee, means that while Roger's most secret longing might have been interracial sex, her desires were also satisfied by their encounter. After all,

3.7 Jill boarding the bus

visitors travel to the resort to experience their most secret desires, because "if you can imagine it, [Sexworld] can arrange it." Jill's presence boarding the bus underscores the fact that "converting" Roger *and* performing blackness for her own excitement were precisely the kind of pleasures she was seeking. The film illustrates that as much as blackness could titillate and arouse Roger, it could also titillate and arouse Jill, generating distinctive sexual pleasures for them both. It also shows that racial stereotype, as violent and reductive as it is, could be a vehicle for pleasure for both Roger and Jill, even as their pleasures are differently represented in the film. Racial fiction, then, becomes the grammar that allows both characters to locate and name their desires, even as they both deploy racial fictions differently.

Reading across the Screen

Jill's race-pleasure—her embodied sexual pleasure in hyperbolic blackness—is particularly evident when contrasted to the film's representation of its other black character, a black male Sexworld employee. While the Roger and Jill scenes act as the film's narrative spine, *Sexworld* features another interracial scene: the coupling of an unnamed black employee (the actor Johnnie Keyes) with a white woman guest, Lisa, in a scene which constitutes the film's climactic sexual number.[20] A comparison of the film's treatment of its two black protagonists demonstrates

3.8 Johnnie Keyes in *Behind the Green Door*

the variety of ways that the black body can be positioned vis-à-vis pleasure on the pornographic screen, and shows the centrality of embodied race-pleasure to Jill's performance. Though both Jill and Keyes perform stereotyped blackness, Jill performs it for both herself and Roger, while Keyes's performance is staged simply for the pleasure of a white female Sexworld guest.

The film's second interracial scene commences when Lisa confesses her sexual secret to the Sexworld technicians: she regularly attends pornographic movies and has a particular predilection for interracial films. She tells the technician, "Well, there's this film, *Behind the Green Door*, and there's a black man in it all dressed in white except for down there. The crotch is cut out, cut away, his, his—." Lisa's confession refers to Keyes's *Behind the Green Door* costume: skin-tight white leggings which act as a kind of racial condom, cloaking his legs in whiteness and displaying his always erect penis (the costume has a cut out for his penis so that his erection is always visible) (figure 3.8). This hole serves an important visual purpose: his dark penis contrasts with the stark whiteness of his pants, underscoring the visual emphasis the film places on his always erect, always visible black penis.

In a testament to Sexworld's power to arrange for the fulfillment of any sexual fantasy, Sexworld technicians coordinate Lisa's sexual liaison with Keyes. Keyes silently enters Lisa's room wearing his famous costume, his

3.9 Johnnie Keyes in *Sexworld*

face painted with "tribal" makeup (figure 3.9). He quickly embraces Lisa, initiating a sexual encounter that reenacts Lisa's *Behind the Green Door* fantasy. Keyes's immediate purpose on-screen is clear: he inhabits the screen for Lisa's pleasure. Keyes's role as a facilitator for Lisa's pleasure is made representationally evident by the film's subversion of the primary principle of hard-core representation: the "maximum visibility" rule. According to this rule, evidence of male pleasure (through the close-up of the money shot) comes to stand in for female pleasure, which "refuses" to provide quantifiable, visual evidence of pleasure. Instead, female pleasure is represented aurally, through moans and whimpers, such that the hardcore's soundtrack acts as evidence of female pleasure. In lieu of visual proof of phallic pleasure, the scene provides extensive evidence of Lisa's pleasure, featuring close shots of her face, her mouth opening in the surprise of enjoyment as Keyes performs cunnilingus on her, and her teeth grinding into his shoulder in ecstasy (figure 3.10).

Surprisingly, evidence of his pleasure is wholly absent from the scene; in fact, the viewer rarely sees him, except for his fingers reaching toward Lisa's nipples or his tongue penetrating her vagina. As in the Roger and Jill scene, the lighting seems designed to emphasize (and eroticize) the color differences between Lisa's and Keyes's bodies, so that his dark hand reaching for her pink nipple or his dark penis against her white face becomes a visual symbol of a transgressive interracial encounter.

The only moment when Keyes's body is emphatically present is in the

3.10 Lisa in pleasure

scene's climactic money shot. Even this generic convention, normally read as documentary evidence of the male protagonist's pleasure, centers on Lisa. Because her fantasy is to reenact *Behind the Green Door*, a film which famously ended with an erect penis streaming ejaculate into the white female protagonist's mouth, Keyes's money shot becomes an authenticating device, evidence that Lisa's fantasy has finally been fulfilled.[21] Yet unlike *Behind the Green Door*, which rendered its climactic scene in psychedelic oranges, yellows, and greens—a colorful celebration of fellatio which visually effaced the protagonists' races—*Sexworld*'s money shot in this scene explicitly emphasizes the color contrast between Lisa's white hand which holds Keyes's black penis as he ejaculates (echoing the Jill and Roger money shot, which also calls attention to the color contrast between the bodies) (figures 3.11 and 3.12). In so doing, Lisa's pleasure in enacting *Behind the Green Door*'s climactic fellatio scene *and* her pleasure in engaging in racially transgressive sex is rendered visible.

Reading the Lisa and Keyes scene against the Roger and Jill scene demonstrates the panoply of ways that black bodies can be represented vis-à-vis racialized pleasures, even in the same film. The most striking difference between the interracial scenes is the presence (or invisibility) of the black body in the visual field; while Keyes is largely *absent* from his scene, appearing only instrumentally, Jill is emphatically present in the Jill and Roger scene. The Lisa and Keyes scene is marked by Keyes's silence. In fact, the spectator never hears his voice or even an aural register of his

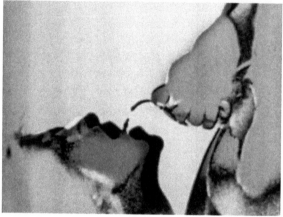

3.11 Johnnie Keyes's money shot in *Sexworld*
3.12 Johnnie Keyes's money shot in *Behind the Green Door*

pleasure in the form of groans, moans, or whimpers.[22] Instead, the viewer hears Lisa's moans and whimpers, proof of *her* pleasure. Keyes's relegation to silence renders his body his only real presence in the scene, and since it is clad in a white leotard that calls attention to his ever-erect penis, he *becomes* the mythic big, black penis (or, as Williams calls it, "a pornographic version of the African savage").[23] In contrast, Jill is insistently present in the Roger and Jill scene; in fact, their engagement is structured by constant verbal sparring. While Roger initially shares his disgust at Jill's body, and at black women's bodies more generally, Jill responds to his every assertion, insisting on her body's sexual virtues, which she imagines as particular to black female sexuality. As the scene progresses, Jill explicitly pokes fun at the racial fictions that give the encounter its erotic charge, playing with the conception of black women's sexual alterity and even locating pleasure in it.

Moreover, Jill's and Keyes's respective bodies are treated differently by the camera. Though both are costumed in white, presumably to provide a visual contrast between their skin and their clothing, and though both wear outfits that showcase their genitalia, Jill's body is present in its entirety throughout the Roger and Jill scene. Even as Jill encourages Roger to sample her "honey pot" or to touch her "jugs," the viewer sees her whole body; it is never reduced to its constituent parts. By contrast, Keyes's body is consistently reduced to his penis, which his costume accentuates. The viewer rarely sees images of Keyes's entire body, instead seeing close shots of the mythical black phallus and its effect on Lisa.

Ultimately, the two scenes display the black body in very different relationships to pleasure. While Jill is depicted as a pleasurable black body—she provides pleasure for Roger and takes pleasure in her own body—Keyes is reduced to exclusively an *instrument* of pleasure. For example, while Jill urges Roger to "dip into the valley, dally into the valley for a while," she is not merely attempting to tantalize him with her imagined difference; in celebrating her "valley," Jill shows the pleasures she takes in her own blackness, flaunting and effectively celebrating the sites that are so often thought of as deviant. Moreover, when she declares, "Now don't these thighs make your peter rise? . . . Ain't this a class ass?," Jill takes up imagined difference as a site of pleasure, as a rhetorical strategy that permits

3.13 Lisa in pleasure

her to proudly display her body. In sharp contrast, Keyes functions merely as an instrument of pleasure for Lisa. The camera zooms in on Keyes's tongue performing cunnilingus, his penis penetrating her, and finally, his penis inserted into her mouth, inviting the spectator to either enjoy Lisa's pleasure or to enjoy the "transgressive" pleasure of viewing interracial sex (figure 3.13).

A comparison of *Sexworld*'s representations of its two black characters shows the multitude of ways that pornographic texts can depict the interracial scene and the variety of ways that black bodies can be positioned vis-à-vis pleasure. In fact, the film shows that black protagonists' relationship to pleasure can be varied not only on the pornographic screen in general, but also within a singular pornographic text. Ultimately, comparing the film's treatment of Jill and Keyes reveals that black bodies are far more than merely instruments of white pleasure. Instead, *Sexworld* represents the possibilities of pleasure *in* blackness, an erotic enjoyment of the black body which takes up racial fictions and mobilizes them for sexual delight.

Reading for Race-Pleasure

Sexworld operates as a window through which possibilities of pornographic representations of the black female body in race-pleasure can be analyzed. Of course, the idea that blacks can take pleasure in race is not altogether new. The highly contentious debates around appropriations of blackness illustrate that black subjects have long been imagined as stakeholders in the maintenance of race. Yet these scholarly treatments of black subjects' investment in blackness rarely consider the erotic hold that race has over black bodies, nor the sexual stake that black subjects might have in blackness itself. My reading of *Sexworld* responds to this scholarly absence, showing that the pornographic screen can represent black protagonists' embodied race-pleasure and that black pleasures in race far exceed possessive ownership over cultural production and in fact can be corporeal, aesthetic, and deeply erotic. Moreover, *Sexworld* suggests that stereotypes, fictions, fantasies, and hyperbole can be sites of black pleasures, offering ways of naming longings, staging sexual encounters, and locating desires. Indeed, the "controlling images" of black female sexual alterity that black feminists have long critiqued can function as sites of play, performance, and pleasure even as they injure, constrain, and wound.

In reading the racialized pornographic screen for evidence of black women's race-pleasure, I aspire to pose larger questions about the centrality of pleasure to race itself, showing that blackness can, at times, provide black subjects with a lexicon for speaking about pleasure, along with a set of legible (and stereotypical) scripts that black subjects can enact and perform for their own pleasures. Scholars have long documented the various forms of violent injuries that race inflicts on the black body—ranging from hyper-imprisonment to segregation to the infliction of biopolitical reproductive restrictions—and studied the pleasures, privileges, and power that race confers on white subjects. Indeed, the pleasures that race confers on white subjects have long been understood to stand at the heart of race's tenacity. But race can also confer a set of pleasures—particularly sexual pleasures—on black subjects, pleasures which are far more complex than problematically seductive pleasures in humiliation.[24]

The mythologies that have shaped dominant sexual imaginations have also shaped black imaginations, and the very fictions that limit black female sexual subjectivities—the myth of the black female excessive sexual appetite, for example—can also function as performed, embodied pleasures. Indeed, Jill's performance of the hypersexual black women becomes both a sign of how "controlling images" limit black sexualities and a testament to the ways that race can provide an essential lexicon of desire. Of course, pleasure is a complicated site; it can mask inequality, it can render hierarchy invisible. And yet it is also, as Michel Foucault notes, a locus of "possibility for creative lives."[25] One of the great insights of antipornography feminism has been to encourage critical engagement with the very nature of pleasure, interrogating the host of ways that what excites or arouses might oppress. My analysis of race-pleasure is privy to all of these concerns and does not argue for the normative desirability or inherent transgressiveness of race-pleasure. Rather, I place black pleasures in racialization into the center of scholarly conversations about how it is that race maintains its hold on all of our individual and collective imaginations, and I displace the prevailing black feminist idea that racial pleasures are the property of white subjects engendered by their visual consumption of black female bodies.

A consideration of race-pleasure suggests the possibility of critical theoretical and political shifts within the parameters of black feminism, gesturing to the importance of generating new vocabularies that black female subjects can use to articulate their pleasures-in-the-flesh. Indeed, the labor of black feminism has long been focused on destabilizing "controlling images" and exposing the historical underpinnings of contemporary representations of black women's bodies. While this strategy has uncovered the injuries that representation can confer on bodies, it is time to begin the labor of imagining a diversity of images of black female bodies. Unlike earlier black feminist scholars, I am not interested in imagining or in generating "positive images" which black women can inhabit, perform, and use to describe their pleasures; instead, I point to the production and circulation of a panoply of images, which provides black women with an array of ways of articulating and naming desires and pleasures. If race can provide a language for naming and claiming pleasures, then more varied representations of black female bodies in race-pleasure can act as a platform for new cultural space for envisioning the black female body in ecstasy.

4 | LAUGHING MATTERS

Race-Humor on the Pornographic Screen

The Silver Age pornographic film *Black Taboo* (dir. Drea, 1984) begins incongruously with a close-up of a stained-glass window. Solemn organ music is interrupted by a man's voice bellowing, "It's like a dream come true, after ten long years, Sonny Boy is finally coming home!" A woman's voice responds, "Praise the Lord! Praise the Lord!" It is only when the camera zooms out that the man and woman are shown to be having sex in their dimly lit bedroom. The organ's low hum is then transformed into rhythmical music punctuated by the woman's moans, and her periodic exclamation of "Praise the Lord!" The viewer learns that the couple, Cleotus and Veranda Richardson, is having sex to celebrate their son's long-awaited homecoming from military service. Veranda's "Praise the Lord!" marks both her sexual pleasure and her excitement at seeing her son again. *Black Taboo*'s opening moments—where a seemingly sanctified space becomes the backdrop for the film's first sexual scene—reveal that the film is committed to embedding all-black hard-core sexual scenes in an absurdly comical narrative.

Though pornography is often described as "masturbation material," it is also laughter material.[1] In fact, pornography's parody-laden titles, absurd storylines, mechanical music, low-end sets, and clumsy dialogue have made pornography and comedy appear to be intimately related genres, even as pornography's insistence on a kind of documentary realism runs contrary to comedy's interest in the absurd.[2] Laura Kipnis argues that pornography is a genre whose representational and political labor is to transgress boundaries; its "favorite terrain is the tender spots where the individual psyche collides with the historical process of molding social subjects."[3] Humor acts as a device that allows pornography to touch—or perhaps to probe—cultural "tender spots."[4]

If porn humor has been a staple of the hard-core, it has taken on different forms in distinctive technological and historical epochs. Stag porn humor, for example, ameliorated the homoerotics of collective arousal, with communal laughter hiding the fact of "men getting hard pretending not to watch men get hard watching images of men getting hard watching or fucking women."[5] Its insistently low-brow humor also allowed audiences to poke fun at middle-class mores, norms, and traditions.[6] Golden Age humor was often embedded in narrative twists. For example, *Deep Throat's* female protagonist, Linda, discovered she could not achieve orgasm because her clitoris was located in her throat; her sexual fulfillment thus conveniently (and absurdly) required her to perform fellatio.[7] In both the stag and Golden Age eras, porn humor was fundamentally connected to collective viewing arrangements; the experience of viewing the film together permitted the experience of laughing together (and perhaps laughing was designed, at least in part, to allow spectators to forget that they were viewing pornographic films together).

For the first time in pornography's history, Silver Age films were consumed privately and domestically, accessed through videocassettes and cable television.[8] Silver Age humor, many scholars have argued, was tailored to a moment when spectators were screening films alone; porn humor's purpose was therefore not to alleviate the potential awkwardness (or eroticism) of viewing explicit material together. Instead, Silver Age porn humor often consisted of pornographic films poking fun at their mainstream counterparts, most notably by riffing on mainstream film titles.[9] Lehman suggests that this brand of Silver Age humor often "consists of isolated, single jokes" where titles with playful puns become the locus of the joke.[10] For Lehman, these wisecracks are not "integrated into the film that follows"; they merely bracket the film, rather than becoming part of its narrative fabric.[11] If Silver Age humor rhetorically porned mainstream texts, the proliferation of amateur videos and the low production standards for pornographic videos flooded the market with "trashy" low-brow films.[12] As "producers threw off the 'quality' trappings of the golden era to start manufacturing product for the rapidly expanding V C R market," the hard-core genre was infused with "militantly stupid, class-iconoclastic, below-the-belt humor."[13] Silver Age films (not unlike stag films) contained a kind of anti-institutional humor: cracking snide jokes about mainstream texts and poking fun at the mores of an imagined middle-class American life.

Drawing on scholarly work analyzing the primacy of humor in pornography, I argue that humor was central to pornographic meaning-making during the Silver Age in ways that existing scholarship has not taken up: this era—with its newly visible all-black and interracial genres—often depended on a particular form of humor, one which I call *race-humor*. By *race-humor*, I refer not to narrative strategies which make black pornographic protagonists the subjects of the films' jokes, but to the host of ways that black pornographic protagonists engage in strategies that render racial fictions—the very mythologies that make legible the Silver Age's black and interracial markets—visible. Oftentimes the labor of making racial fictions discernible comes through narrative vehicles that are politically troubling; indeed, this labor is a kind of representational and political tightrope that threatens to entrench precisely what it aspires to uproot.[14] Yet black pornographic protagonists, particularly black female pornographic protagonists, manage to navigate these tightropes, traversing complex representational and political terrain, and, at times, falling prey to pernicious racial fictions.

Current scholarly work on race and humor often examines how humor is a strategy that permits black subjects to expose the persistent pain of racial wounds.[15] For example, Glenda Carpio's *Laughing Fit to Kill* analyzes contemporary black performance that explicitly references slavery and its continuing effects on the present. Carpio treats black performance broadly, ranging from Dave Chappelle's comedy to Kara Walker's haunting cut silhouettes, and concludes that black performers "oscillate between the past and the present, linking, for instance, police brutality or the taboo against miscegenation to analogous practices during slavery."[16] In so doing, they theorize temporality in a new way, drawing critical continuities between past and present. This "black time," to riff on Judith Halberstam's concept of "queer time," upsets linear, positivist narratives of historical progress and exposes the "seething" presence of the past in everyday life.[17] My analysis of pornographic race-humor does not study the strategies that pornographers or pornographic protagonists use to reference the still-open wounds of slavery and Jim Crow, or the ongoing wounds that contemporary regimes of neo-Jim Crow and racial inequality (both institutional and quotidian) inflict on black bodies.[18] Instead, I use race-humor to refer to the comical strategies that black pornographic protagonists—particularly black female protagonists—deploy to articulate and even amplify racial fictions within the parameters of a genre that both depends on those fictions and hinges on those fictions remaining unnamed. Race-humor captures how pornographic protagonists make visible the fictions that underpin the genre, a strategy akin to showing a garment's seams, exposing the stitches that hold it together. In showing the genre's underpinnings, black pornographic protagonists make the racial fictions that lend the films their erotic charge the subject of the joke.

Black female protagonists are fundamental to the at-times transgressive representational labor of Silver Age race-humor. As *Black Taboo* demonstrates, black female pornographic protagonists not only were at the center of naming the racial mythologies that underpinned the genre, but often labored to make both black male protagonists and male spectators (black and white alike) the subject of the films' jokes. Indeed, black female protagonists unsettle the very premise of the Silver Age all-black film when they name racial fictions in the context of a genre that depends on those fictions and relies on their status as "public secrets."[19]

My focus on black female pornographic protagonists' deployment of race-humor challenges certain presumptions that lie at the heart of the black feminist theoretical archive. Black feminism has never attended to the comic (and sometimes absurdly comical) dimensions of racialized representation; instead, it has read racialized representation as presumptively problematic because it is imagined to entrench and eroticize mythologies of the black female hyperlibido and to secure notions of black female alterity. As is revealed by attending to the comical nature of racialized pornography's representations of race, racial fictions can be toyed with and disrupted on the pornographic screen, even in films that hinge on racial fictions. The very ideologies that "control" black women can be adopted by black female protagonists to expose their construction, as well as to make the spectator, rather than the black female protagonist, the object of scrutiny. Playing with racial mythologies in the context of a film that depends on those mythologies is a powerful form of critique that black feminist interpretative work should take seriously.

In foregrounding Silver Age pornography's race-humor, I do not suggest that what makes us laugh is unproblematic. Hierarchy often cloaks itself in humor, in much the same ways that it disguises itself in pleasure. Nonetheless, I turn attention toward race-humor to uncover the intimate relationship among race, gender, pleasure, and humor on the pornographic screen. By turning to the comical dimensions of race, I underscore the at-times performative and pleasurable aspects of race for black pornographic protagonists, upending the prevailing black feminist tradition, which insists on race as a wound inflicted again and again on black flesh. Moreover, I show that race-humor acted as a powerful and fraught tool, capable of both imploding racial fictions and entrenching them, sometimes simultaneously.

The Invention of the Silver Age

The dawning of the Silver Age coincided with the federal government's commitment to exposing pornography's harms. The year that Black Taboo was released, 1984, President Reagan signed the Child Protection Act, noting, "We've seen news reports of cases involving child pornography and child abuse on a large scale. We've seen reports suggesting a link between child molesting and pornography. And academics' studies have suggested a link between pornography and sexual violence toward women."[20] He used the signing of the act as an opportunity to announce his establishment of a commission, headed by Attorney General Edwin Meese, to study pornography's effects. The Meese Report, as the commission's findings came to be known, was, as Linda Williams notes, a "curious hybrid of empirical and moral arguments against pornography culled from social scientists, new-right 'moral majority' and anti-pornography feminists" who called attention to pornography's dangers.[21] The Meese Report relied on the antipornography activist work of feminists, including Catharine MacKinnon and Andrea Dworkin, so much so that it has been argued that Meese's "co-opt[ation of] feminist rhetoric" masked the report's "conservative Christian perspectives on pornography and sexuality."[22] It is unclear if the commission intentionally co-opted antipornography rhetoric or simply found a convenient alliance with radical feminism; what is clear is that many feminists outside of antipornography circles found Meese and MacKinnon and Dworkin to be "strange bedfellows."[23]

If pornography was under siege from the state, it was also in the midst of a radical transformation because of technological shifts. The early 1980s were marked by the birth of the videocassette, an innovation that allowed pornographers to produce films faster and cheaper than ever before.[24] The pornographic market was flooded with an endless variety of representations of bodies, a plethora of pornographies. Pornographers' new commitment to a "wider variety of pornographies" required the emergence of the niche market, which functioned as an organizing principle that allowed pornographers to market their films to new audiences and enabled spectators to find films that spoke sex to their specific fantasies and desires.

Drea, the director of *Black Taboo*, played a significant role in the formation of the Silver Age's newly legible black market, one of the many niche markets created in the mid-1980s, as the pornographic marketplace was inundated with cheaply made films. Though many consumers assumed Drea was black because of her imagined commitment to directing all-black films, she was a white woman who recognized a gap in the pornographic marketplace and seized an opportunity to profit from filling that gap.[25] She directed many of the era's most significant all-black films, including *Hot Chocolate* (1984) (and its sequels, *Hotter Chocolate* and *Hottest Chocolate*), *Black Jail Bait* (1984), *Brown Sugar* (1984), and *Black Taboo*, all of which made 1984 a landmark year for the formation of a distinctive and commercially successful black market, one which promised to present all-black casts to pornographic spectators.[26]

While the Silver Age enabled viewers to watch films that were clearly racially marked, it also changed how consumers screened those films. New viewing technologies like the VCR and cable television allowed spectators to screen pornography on television sets in the confines of their own homes, rather than with the company of an audience in urban movie theaters. The erosion of public, collective pornographic consumption also changed the forms of pleasures that spectators garnered from pornography. Nina Martin argues that solitary viewing seemed designed exclusively to encourage masturbation, unlike communal viewing arrangements which invited spectators to interact while screening films. Martin notes, "Now that the viewing situation is often private (in the home) and frequently individual (by oneself), the purposes of hardcore are more masturbatory and also highly interactive as the spectator has control over the watching and manipulation of specific scenes."[27] Certainly the shift toward individual, private consumption of pornography altered—and perhaps foreclosed—some of the communal pleasures that screening pornography could engender. If some pleasures were effaced by technology, others were encouraged; Silver Age spectators were often armed with remote controls and could view films in whatever order they chose, ignoring particular scenes and viewing others repeatedly, imposing their own narrative structure onto films.

Dirty Jokes

Black Taboo chronicles a family's excitement about the return of their eldest child, Sonny, who has been missing since his military service in the Vietnam War. Sonny's return is often eagerly discussed in scenes which culminate in sex: between Sonny's parents (Cleotus and Veranda), between his sisters (Valdesta and Theodora), and between Sonny's mother and her brother-in-law (Elton). While Sonny is not present in any of these scenes, the film suggests that the collective excitement surrounding his homecoming has produced the family's intense sexual longings. Though Sonny's family celebrates his arrival, Sonny returns with a deep sense of ambivalence about his now unfamiliar domestic life. As he unpacks his small duffel bag, he confesses to Jodi—an inflatable doll who served as his sole companion during his years in Vietnam—that family life is now strange. He turns to her and says, "It's been so long, I don't even remember these people. They're like strangers. I guess it doesn't matter, I'm home."

To ease Sonny's transition into familial life, Veranda, Valdesta, and Theodora, one by one, have sex with him. Sonny's father is, of course, wholly absent from these incestuous sex acts because male-male sexual interaction violates the implicit homophobic promise that undergirds the heterosexual pornographic screen: male bodies must never pleasure each other.[28] In quintessentially domestic scenes—Veranda delivering milk and cookies to her son, Valdesta practicing her cheerleading routine for Sonny, Theodora reading excerpts from her biology textbook to her brother—the innocent, asexual relationships between family members are quickly

4.1 Valdesta cheering

transformed into "taboo" sexual relationships (the word *taboo* is also used to mark the pornographic category of films that represents incest or the illusion of incest).[29]

Black Taboo's humor works, at least in part, by pairing chaste domestic life with unchaste sexual perversions. In *Black Taboo*, as is often the case with incongruity humor, "the essence of amusement [is] in our enjoyment of experiencing something which clashes with our conceptual systems, our understanding of 'how things are supposed to be.'"[30] The film situates the family's taboo sexual longings in precisely the spaces and relationships that are supposed to be safely asexual. Familiar spaces such as the kitchen and the family room become hotbeds of sexual deviance, and asexual relationships—between siblings, in-laws, and uncles and nieces—develop a sexual charge. This humorous juxtaposition is evident in the film's second sexual scene, where Valdesta visits Sonny's bedroom to show off her new cheerleading routine. Valdesta's outfit—bright red socks, yellow pom-poms—signals her innocence (figure 4.1). As she performs her cheer, Sonny lies naked on his bed, excitedly watching her. In this context, Sonny's nudity, rather than being a sign of taboo incestuous desire for Valdesta, functions as a sign of their relatedness; their relationship is so asexual that his nakedness is rendered chaste. The seemingly benign cheer quickly turns into a sexual encounter after Sonny asks Valdesta if she can perform a split. Valdesta reclines on the bed, spreads

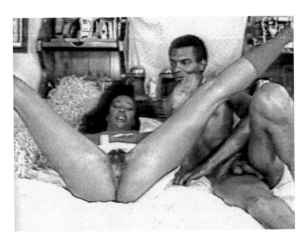

4.2 Valdesta showing her split

her legs in front of Sonny, and emphatically says, "I can do a split!" (figure 4.2). As Sonny looks down Valdesta's spread legs, Valdesta conveniently spreads her labia, exposing her vagina to her brother (and to the spectator); the asexual interaction between siblings transforms into a scene marked by intrafamilial longings and desires, and the asexual domestic space of Sonny's bedroom becomes steeped in perversion.

After Sonny's welcome-home dinner, the domestic space of the family room similarly becomes a site of perversion. As the sisters Valdesta and Theodora lounge on the family-room sofa after the celebratory meal, Uncle Elton pokes his head into the room and asks Valdesta for a favor. Elton mentions that he has a bet on an upcoming football game, then asks Valdesta if she would consider trying to alter the outcome of the game by "fuck[ing] the quarterback to exhaustion the night before the game." Theodora is offended that Elton presumes that her sister would be more efficient at sexually incapacitating the quarterback than she would. The sisters begin to squabble as to who would be most skilled at throwing the results of the game, at which point Valdesta suggests that they have a "fuck off" to determine who is better suited to aid Uncle Elton in winning his bet. Inviting Elton to assess their respective sexual skills, the two simultaneously perform fellatio on him, then take turns having sex with him. The scene concludes with Elton ejaculating on Theodora's breasts while Valdesta strokes his penis. The sisters demand to know the result of the competition, and Elton smiles mischievously, declaring "I can't decide. You both do it." This scene shows that seemingly desexualized moments—a conversation between an uncle and his nieces—can become rife with sexual innuendo and intrafamilial desire. Moreover, the film indicates that even seemingly normative familial relationships, like sibling rivalry, can become imbued with sexual longings. While Valdesta's and Theodora's competition for their uncle's attention is easily legible as a component of normative familial relations, its easy slippage into a moment of intrafamilial sex suggests a flimsy boundary between the taboo and the normative.

In addition to comically locating the perverse *within* black domesticity, the film consistently bleeds the boundaries between the deviant and the sacred, humorously layering images of religion and of sexual perversity. In so doing, *Black Taboo* implies that for black subjects, the boundary between the religious and the profane is easily effaced. More than that, *Black Taboo* suggests that religious belief *enhances* sexual pleasure for the film's protagonists, with the trappings of religious rhetoric deepening protagonists' enjoyment of sexual encounters. At the very beginning, *Black Taboo* tricks the viewer into interpreting a sexual scene as a religious scene, then reveals that the sounds of fervent religiosity are actually the pleasurable sounds of sexual intercourse. While Cleotus and Veranda seem to be praising God for their son's safe return, the camera slowly reveals that their celebration is sexual. Of course, sex between a married couple is neither taboo nor necessarily transgressive; yet the scene is peculiar in the constant referencing of God as Cleotus and Veranda have sex. The aural landscape of the scene is transformed from a set of moans and whimpers—the normal soundtrack of the pornographic film—into a set of "praise the Lords," a refrain which makes God present in precisely the moment when the viewer might expect God to be most absent.[31]

Similarly, the layering of religion and perversity is visible in a scene in which Veranda prepares a celebratory meal in honor of her son's return. When Elton, her brother-in-law, enters the kitchen and playfully sticks his fingers into the bowl of icing she has prepared, she gets visibly frustrated. He encourages her to chastise him, taking pleasure in her irritation, and she refuses to give in, pronouncing, "I won't say it, I'm a Christian woman!" Despite her proclaimed Christianity, minutes later, when Elton places his hands on her breasts, she sighs and says, "We shouldn't

4.3 Elton and Veranda in the kitchen

be doing this. What if Cleotus comes in?" Elton replies, "I'll just tell him you spilled some icing on yourself and I'm cleaning it up." He then covers her breasts in icing and begins to lick them clean. Her visible pleasure at sex with her brother-in-law is clearly at odds with her "Christian woman" status, as is the blowjob she eventually performs on Elton (figure 4.3).

The film's humorous use of juxtapositions—the domestic and the perverse, the religious and the profane—is designed to comically rationalize the black family's deviance. It is precisely the Richardsons' inability to understand the domestic as asexual, or the religious as sacred, that explains their inability to distinguish the familial from the sexual. This flimsy boundary between the normative and the taboo, between the domestic and the sexual, is explained by the characters' blackness; blackness permits, and possibly even encourages, taboo. The work of race-humor in this context, then, is to foreground the comical connections between blackness and taboo, showing the myriad ways that black bodies fail to comply with the demands of the normative.[32] If blackness explains taboo, or if blackness is, in and of itself, a kind of taboo, then race-humor can be understood as an ethnographic enterprise. The film's comical juxtapositions provide insight into the perversities of black domestic life, perversities that enable a family to transgress a fundamental taboo and turn to each other in sexual delight. *Black Taboo* offers the spectator uninterrupted voyeuristic access to precisely how the black family is a perverse formation, one that is unregulated by the foundational taboos that order social life, including the incest taboo. Yet race-humor, which can so easily be read as violently ethnographic—as allowing the spectator to chuckle at the imagined perversity of black domestic life—can serve a different purpose on the Silver Age all-black screen, often with quite transgressive results.

Punch Lines

If *Black Taboo* allows the spectator to laugh at its black protagonists, it is also a film invested in pulling the rug out from under the spectator. Nowhere is this more visible than in the film's climax, which begins when Veranda brings Sonny a quintessentially domestic bedtime snack: a plate of chocolate chip cookies and a glass of milk. As Sonny begins to eat, Veranda compliments him on his appearance and asks to inspect his "hard muscles." Moments later, Sonny is lying down as his mother massages his back and shoulders (figure 4.4). Encouraging Sonny to relax, Veranda places a pillow underneath his head and removes his underwear, gently placing his penis in her mouth. When Veranda begins to perform fellatio on Sonny, he confesses that he remembers her "just vaguely." As if her body might jar his memory, he climbs on top of her and begins to perform cunnilingus on her, and she whispers, "I missed my Sonny." Then Veranda notices that Sonny's identifying birthmark is missing, and they engage in a breathy, barely audible conversation that concludes with the revelation that Sonny is not, in fact, her son.

> *Veranda:* Where's your birthmark, Sonny boy?
> *Sonny:* Birthmark? What birthmark?
> *Veranda:* The birthmark that used to be on your right shoulder.
> *Sonny:* I never had a birthmark on my right shoulder!
> *Veranda:* Poor thing! They must have given you a painful operation that confused you.
> *Sonny:* No, no operations. I'm not confused. I never had a birthmark. Wait a minute! Now that you mention it, my mother used to have small titties, you have big titties, unless *you* had an operation.
> *Veranda:* No! But I *am* your mother!
> *Sonny:* You are? Mama's titties were never big.

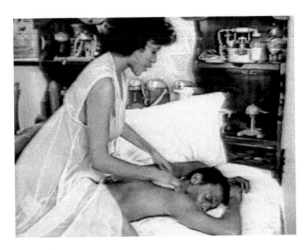

4.4 Mother-son massage

Veranda: Yes, my chest has *always* been big! [Pause] Well, I guess we made a mistake. Well, you know what they say: we all look alike!

Sonny: I guess so, baby, I guess so.

The film's conclusion divulges that the Richardson family "made a mistake" in thinking that Sonny was their missing relative: the seemingly incestuous sex between family members was, indeed, sex between strangers.[33] In this light, the taboo of the film is effectively deflated, as is the racial mythology that lent the film its erotic charge: that black desires are sufficiently perverse and deviant to enable incestuous sex. But how do we make sense of a final scene that uses a prevailing racial fiction—that black people "all look alike"—to undo the film's narrative promise (even if that racial fiction is delivered in an almost inaudible moment)? And what do we make of the fact that it is a black female character who amplifies the racial fiction of black bodies' fungibility?

Some scholars have read Veranda's articulation of the mythology that black bodies all look alike as a validation of the fiction of black subjects' inflated sexual appetite. Black bodies are imagined to be so hypersexual that black subjects overlook or wholly ignore the fundamental taboos that order the social world, including the incest taboo. Mireille Miller-Young captures this position, asserting that the film's appeal to racial mythology "reiterates the conception of black hypersexuality as so vast and urgent, that it does not discriminate, even amongst the most intimate familial relations."[34] In reading the film's final scene as foregrounding the black feminine hyperlibido, Miller-Young argues that *Black Taboo* allows—indeed, encourages—the spectator to cast an ethnographic gaze at the peculiarities of the black family. Yet it is possible to read "against the grain" and ask if the invocation of racial mythology at the end of the film, particularly as it is amplified by a black female protagonist, might do more (or different) work than simply objectifying black female flesh and entrenching racial fictions.

The film's final moment offers a profound indictment of race as a visual regime, showing that racial mythologies operate by allowing black subjects to fall prey to precisely the racial fantasies that ensnare them. "We all look alike" gestures to the idea that racial fictions pervert black subjects' capacities to see themselves and each other, an eerie reminder of the continued power of race to shape the parameters of the visible even for black subjects.[35] Moreover, "we all look alike" acts as a condemnation of the spectator's viewing practices; Veranda's remark suggests that spectators' belief in racial fictions—including the mythology that black bodies are interchangeable—enables them to disregard the obvious visual differences between the characters on-screen, dissimilarities which would necessarily call into question the presumed relatedness of Sonny, Veranda, Valdesta, and Theodora. Implicating the spectator's (mis)reading of the film's visual evidence hints that spectators' desire to believe in the fantasy of racial difference permits them to overlook the lack of any visual evidence of sameness. Miller-Young offers this possible reading, asserting that "we all look alike" shows that "under the dominant, exploitative, and consumptive gaze, black bodies are fractured and interchangeable."[36] Yet it is crucial that "we all look alike" implicates the *spectator's* gaze.

If the film's conclusion gestures to how race alters the visual field, literally coloring what can (and can't) be seen, how we can read it as a comical invitation to reread the film, and the Silver Age all-black genre more generally? The final scene is particularly significant because Veranda's comment comically places spectators' knowledge of racial mythologies at the center of the pornographic narrative. In concluding by poking fun at a predominant racial fiction—that black bodies are interchangeable—*Black Taboo* places spectators in the uncomfortable position of recognizing their knowledge of (though perhaps not their belief in) the mythologies that underpin the all-black Silver Age film. After all, it is the very idea that black spectators are fungible, that any one black body could fulfill the "black" portion of "black taboo," that undergirds the film's very structure, and the all-black marketplace.

Racialized pornography often allows spectators to take pleasure in their knowledge of familiar racial stereotype, regardless of their actual belief in the validity of the stereotype. Linda Williams writes,

> Pornographic and erotic fantasies of interracial lust rely on all viewers, male and female, black and white, *knowing* these stereotypes. Although nothing necessarily rules out their also *believing* them—that is, they can certainly be interpreted in a racist manner—the pleasure taken in pornographic depictions of interracial lust does not depend on believing them.[37]

By alluding to commonly known racial stereotypes, racialized pornography produces both an erotic and a political charge. The pleasure of the racialized scene, then, is that it flirts with collectively held racial fictions without ever explicitly engaging questions of race. While it seems obvious that pornography does not question the workings of racial domination—after all, how arousing would an investigation of racial formation be?—racialized pornography incessantly and necessarily alludes to collective racial "knowledge." In the racialized pornographic scene, race is both ubiquitous *and* absent; it is the background informing the narrative, yet its importance to the pornographic narrative is never explicitly addressed. Veranda's articulation of the myth of black fungibility effectively challenges the pornographic convention of relying on racial fictions but leaving them unnamed. Instead, her character spotlights the very mythologies on which the Silver Age's all-black film rested, moving racial fiction from the film's background to its foreground. In so doing, Veranda problematizes something that lies at the very heart of the Silver Age's all-black market: that the on-screen black protagonists can stand in for *all* black subjects, that the Richardsons' pleasures are emblematic of *all* black pleasures.[38] With its explicit racialized title promising to showcase black pleasures, the all-black film treats black bodies as the ultimate metonymy, with a few black bodies standing for the totality, offering proof that "we all look alike." More than that, Veranda's claim that "we all look alike" operates as a way of naming a "public secret," forcing viewers to "confront, rather than avoid" the "legacy [of stereotypes] by exploring their theatricality and their appeal across differences of race, class, and gender."[39] By humorously naming the presumption that undergirds the film, Veranda's utterance "sets stereotype in disturbing motion" by making it hypervisible, and implicates the spectator in this "disturbing motion" by foregrounding the viewer's knowledge of the stereotypes that animate the all-black market.[40]

Deviant Men, Resistant Women

If *Black Taboo's* humor is double-edged, allowing spectators to laugh at the protagonists and inviting them to laugh, however uncomfortably, at their knowledge of racial stereotypes, then black female protagonists are essential conduits of the film's humorous messages. While Veranda serves as the most explicit mouthpiece for *Black Taboo's* jabs at the spectator, the film's other black female protagonists play an essential role in making the film's black male protagonist and the film's viewers, rather than *Black Taboo's* black female protagonists, the butt-end of the movie's joke. Ultimately, the film's black female protagonists are foundational in turning the film's potentially ethnographic racialized humor on its head, making the film's imagined spectator, rather than the Richardson family, the subject of the joke.

If one considers identification to be one of cinema's primary pleasures, *Black Taboo's* female protagonists actively trouble the spectator's desire to identify with the film's black male protagonist, Sonny.[41] While Sonny is a celebrated war hero, he is also depicted as someone who has been damaged by the war, a fact that the film's black female protagonists routinely foreground.[42] For example, an early scene featuring Sonny and his sister Theodora is marked by questions about Sonny's failure to become aroused by Theodora's insistent flirtation. When Theodora enters Sonny's room with her biology textbook, she tells Sonny that she wants to test the rule of visual stimulation: "If I flash my tits, you get hard." When Theodora does, in fact, "flash her tits," Sonny does not become hard (figure 4.5). After asking whether that could be because she is not "stimulating enough," she elects to use "physical stimulation" to arouse Sonny. While Sonny is eventually aroused by Theodora, and the scene culminates in visual evidence of Sonny's pleasure, the encounter is framed by Sonny's phallic un-

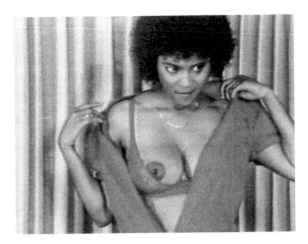

4.5 Theodora testing her "brother"

responsiveness, his inability to be stimulated by the visual. This unresponsiveness shrouds the scene in doubt, enabling the spectator to question Sonny's virility and, ultimately, the authenticity of his masculinity.

Whereas Theodora fails to immediately arouse Sonny, Sonny's inflatable companion, Jodi, consistently excites him. Jodi is originally presented as a kind of security blanket, a figure that helped Sonny alleviate his loneliness during his long years of military service. When Sonny first returns to the Richardson house, he seems to take comfort in her presence. But as the film progresses, it becomes clear that Jodi is more than a source of emotional comfort for Sonny. During Sonny's military service, Jodi also functioned as a masturbatory device, one which he continues to secretly use over the course of the film. Though Jodi confers sexual pleasure on Sonny, he is keenly aware that she is to be kept secret; whenever "real" family members enter his room, he quickly tucks Jodi away. When Sonny and Jodi are together, he consistently remarks that he is pleased to finally have time alone with her and that the pleasures she confers on him are preferable to those that "real" women provide. In fact, in one scene, Sonny inflates Jodi with his mouth and then tells her, "Wow, it's been so long Jodi. I can't for the life of me remember having no sister [referring to Valdesta], not that I'm not glad to have her. She's a real good piece of ass, but I wouldn't have made it through these last ten years if it wasn't for you, Jodi." This scene demonstrates that Jodi is more real to Sonny, emotionally

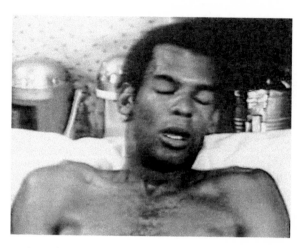

4.6 Sonny in pleasure

and physically, than his family is, and that he prefers intimacy with her to the sexual intimacy he experiences with real women, including Valdesta, Theodora, and Veranda. Jodi's presence in the film humorously calls into question Sonny's ostensibly normative heteromasculinity. By representing his desire for an inanimate woman as more profound than his desire for the real women who populate the pornographic screen, *Black Taboo* pokes fun at Sonny's masculinity, implying that a kind of queer desire underpins his heteromasculinity. Jodi's on-screen presence also troubles whatever identificatory pleasures the spectator might take in watching the film's black male protagonist. Indeed, a male pornographic protagonist who cannot be aroused by the film's real women or who prefers the company of inflatable women is an unlikely pornographic protagonist, one whose desires cast questions on the very premise of the hard-core.

While Sonny's sexual interest in Jodi might disrupt the spectator's identificatory pleasures, Jodi's presence in the film also calls into question spectators' desires, comically inviting them to interrogate how their own arousal is bound up in seeing Sonny pleasured by Jodi. For example, in the moments leading up to the film's climactic sexual number between Veranda and Sonny, the viewer sees only Sonny sitting in his bed. The camera slowly zooms in on his face in pleasure, and the aural landscape is punctuated by his moans (figure 4.6). The viewer is invited to imagine that Sonny's pleasure is garnered either from masturbation or from someone

4.7 Sonny and Jodi

performing fellatio on him. As the camera slowly pans down, the viewer's anticipation builds. Yet when the camera finally arrives at Sonny's penis, it is revealed that Jodi's mouth is placed over it and that he is using her as a masturbatory device (figure 4.7). He says, "Jodi, it's awfully nice to finally be alone with you. I thought it was hard hiding from the guards in the prison, this family is ten times as noisy and I still can't remember them!"

In this scene, Jodi becomes integral to playing a joke on the spectator. Much as in the film's earlier scenes, the framing of this scene is designed to trick the spectator. Sonny's open mouth and his rolled-back eyes indicate that he is in the midst of intense pleasure. And, in fact, they are signs of pleasure—yet that pleasure has come not from the female protagonists' bodies, but from an inanimate object. The fact of the spectator's potential enjoyment of the scene implicates the spectator in the joke-making that lies at the center of Black Taboo. If the spectator locates pleasure in Sonny's interaction with Jodi, or even if the spectator misreads Sonny's moans and groans as proof of actual fellatio and becomes aroused, only to find that Sonny is pleasuring himself with an inflatable doll, the spectator's own pleasures and desires become the subject of the film's joke. By replacing a real woman with Jodi in scenes where the spectator expects to see documentary evidence of bodies in pleasure, the film calls into question the spectator's own longings. What does it mean if the spectator takes pleasure in seeing Jodi pleasure Sonny? What does it mean if representations of "fake" black women pleasuring black men are as pleasurable as representations of "real" black women pleasuring black men, particularly in a genre which hinges on documentary realism, on an insistence on showing "real" bodies in pleasure?

Jodi's presence in the film is significant because she, alongside the host of real women who populate the pornographic screen in *Black Taboo*, is emphatically black. Her body is explicitly racialized, from its brown hue (identical to Sonny's) to her imagined "black hair." Even her breasts are a deep shade of brown (capped with white nipples, in this way joining pornography's long history of emphasizing color contrasts in racialized films). The film's incessant racialization of Jodi is notable because her body, like the black bodies of Valdesta, Theodora, and Veranda, is emphatically marked, yet it resists the ethnographic impulse of race-humor. While Jodi could easily be the subject of the joke—an inflatable doll could certainly serve as the film's punch line—it is Sonny's *use* of Jodi, his pleasuring of himself with her body, that becomes integral to the film's humor. Like the film's other black female characters, Jodi comically casts doubt on Sonny's masculinity. In this way, it is Sonny's desires and pleasures—and perhaps the desires and pleasures of the film's spectators—rather than Jodi's black body, which become the subject of the film's jokes.

Laughing at Them, Laughing at Me

The birth of the Silver Age all-black market hinged on a simple idea: that a few black bodies could stand in for black bodies. Films like *Hot Chocolate*, *Blacks Have More Fun*, and, of course, *Black Taboo* offered some black bodies as representative of black bodies more generally. These films' explicitly racialized titles, often absurd plots, and comical narratives allowed the spectator to laugh at the all-black cast while also taking pleasure in the black bodies that populated the pornographic screen. Yet *Black Taboo* shows that race-humor operated in a host of ways on the Silver Age screen, including ways that disrupt the potentially ethnographic aspects of pornographic race-humor. *Black Taboo* is a film that is animated by tricks: its opening sequence seems religious, but isn't; it promises to show what is most taboo, but doesn't. The film's black female protagonists are an integral part of this trick-making as they incessantly poke fun at both the film's black male protagonist, whose heteromasculinity is ultimately the subject of at least one of the film's jokes, and at the spectator who longs to see proof that blackness enables taboo.

Ultimately, my emphasis on Silver Age race-humor aspires to engender a few shifts within black feminist interpretive work. First, I underscore the importance of humor generally, and race-humor particularly, to analyses of the racialized pornographic screen—as much as Black Taboo aspires to arouse, it also aspires to amuse. I suggest humor's place in scholarly understandings of the pleasures pornography engenders, and emphasize the humorous (and sometimes absurd) work that race often performs on the pornographic screen. In so doing, I show that race's eroticism is often linked to its hyperbolic absurdity, and that racial fictions can be both comical and alluring simultaneously (even as they are also painful). My focus on the humorous work that black bodies can produce on-screen shows that black bodies often poke fun at the very fictions that undergird the films they star in. Second, I point to the pleasures (political, sexual, and aesthetic) that the film's black female protagonists take in mobilizing and exaggerating racial fiction, only to deflate it. Their version of race-humor shows that the racialized pornographic screen can be a site where painful racial fictions are played with, exaggerated, rendered absurd, deflated, and even rendered exciting and sexy. Finally, I trace moments of failure in Black Taboo; while the film's title and very construction promise to showcase the ways in which "taboo" is racialized, it is the very racial fictions that undergird the genre that undo the film's promise.

Black Taboo effectively takes the very idea at the heart of the all-black Silver Age film—that black bodies are fungible—and explicitly makes it the subject of the film's joke. By naming the fiction that "we all look alike," and by revealing how the fiction of black interchangeability generates the film's erotic charge, black female protagonists effectively release themselves from being the subjects of ethnographic race-humor and instead turn an uncomfortable comic gaze on the spectator. The labor of race-humor becomes one of naming the racial fantasies that hinge on their unspokenness. Once named, the fictions that provide the film their racial charge are exposed, rendered absurd, and made laugh-able.

5 / ON REFUSAL

Racial Promises and the Silver Age Screen

The narrative promise of *Black Throat* (dir. Gregory Dark, 1985) is made explicit on the videocassette case: an image of two black women displayed alongside text reading "deep throating with an ethnic flavor" reveals the film's commitment to displaying black women's particular (and particularly "ethnic") practices of fellatio. The film's opening song—with the refrain "You will see some black chicks sucking on some white dicks. They wrap their lips around you, you cum unbelievably"—makes *Black Throat*'s promise of racial difference even clearer. The first moments of the film, which feature its white male protagonist, Roscoe, digging through his trash, finding some leftover chicken, and exclaiming, "It's white meat, and *you know* you and I both like white meat," only entrench the idea that the film intends to "speak race" and "speak sex" simultaneously. Roscoe's mention of "white meat," like Roger's evocation of "white meat" in *Sexworld*, provides a highly racialized vocabulary for articulating sexual "preference" and for naming desires. This opening scene also prepares the viewer for the narrative tension that will underpin the film: though Roscoe voices a penchant for "white meat"—that is, sex with white women—he will be introduced to the ostensibly different way that black women perform fellatio.[1]

Black Throat's director, Gregory Dark (born Gregory Hippolyte Brown), was half of the Dark Brothers production team that built a career out of controversial displays of imagined racial difference.[2] Brown was a film-school graduate shooting a documentary about the pornography industry when Walter Gernert offered him a partnership to make pornographic films. A few years later, New Wave Hookers (1985) and Between the Cheeks (1985) were released, and the films quickly established the Dark Brothers, a white male duo, as "the most influential force in X," and as creators of distinctive films featuring "satirical storylines, avant-garde sets, contemporary music."[3]

While their films enjoyed commercial success and critical acclaim— Black Throat was celebrated as the X-Rated Critics Organization (XRCO) 1985 Video of the Year and later inducted into the XRCO hall of fame— their work was also the subject of controversy, even outside of X. Black Throat found itself at the center of a federal investigation when authorities discovered that one of the film's actresses, Traci Lords, was underage at the time of the filming.[4] While the extent of the Dark Brothers' knowledge of Lords's age will never be satisfactorily determined, what is clear is that Lords was only sixteen years old when she starred in an array of pornographic videos, including Black Throat. In response to the investigation, the Dark Brothers removed all scenes that included Lords.[5]

While the Lords underage pornography scandal was resolved by editing Black Throat (and the host of other films in which she appeared), the Dark Brothers faced other challenges that would be even more damning. In 1985, they produced Let Me Tell Ya 'bout Black Chicks.[6] Like its companion film, Let Me Tell Ya 'bout White Chicks (1984), Black Chicks trafficked in offensive racial stereotype; yet the film went much further, making racial violence the centerpiece of its narrative. The film included an interracial scene featuring two white men wearing Klan robes having sex with one of the film's black female protagonists.[7] In an era where hard-core pornography was at the center of political debates about obscenity, Black Chicks's Klan scene became emblematic of pornography's sexualized and racialized harms. In 1985, United States Attorney General Edwin Meese appointed members to a commission to "determine the nature, extent, and impact on society of pornography in the United States, and to make specific recommendations . . . concerning more effective ways in which the spread of pornography could be contained."[8] The Meese Commission's final report, released in 1986, concluded that pornography was increasingly violent and that even nonviolent pornography contained images which "depict people, usually women, as existing solely for the sexual satisfaction of others, usually men, [and] . . . in decidedly subordinate roles in their sexual relations with others."[9] As the Meese Commission insisted on pornography's social dangers, antipornography feminists proposed legislation to ban it, and the Department of Justice formed the National Obscenity Enforcement Unit to curb obscenity (the same team which helped federal prosecutors pursue the Traci Lords case).[10] It was in this moment—one where pornography and obscenity were part of a national debate—that *Black Chicks* was banned. As Linda Williams notes, "[*Black Chicks*] was selected for indictment during the Reagan era, resulting in the disappearance of *Black Chicks* from all shelves. Even the writer [of the film] claims not to be able to obtain a copy."[11] In the wake of the scandal, the film's distributor, VCA, removed *Black Chicks* from circulation.[12] Even in a moment when pornography was an object of federal scrutiny, pornographers like the Dark Brothers relentlessly staked claims to the cultural mainstream by attempting to speak sex to more consumers than ever and by creating niche markets which captivated new audiences by representing myriad bodies in pleasure. Silver Age films like *Black Throat* used "black"—and the promise of black bodies—to modify, or perhaps even to intensify, a film's promised pleasures, to capture a new audience, and to display black bodies in and for pleasure.

Though it is generally agreed that racialized pornography's erotic charge emerges from its commitment to displaying imagined racial difference, and that Silver Age pornography, with its interracial and all-black markets, is particularly animated by a promise of making racial difference visible, there has been considerable scholarly debate as to how to interpret that promise. Some scholars treat the hard-core as a quintessentially ethnographic project, one preoccupied by both promising and displaying difference.[13] These scholars, including Brian Wallis, Christian Hansen, Catherine Needham, and Bill Nichols, treat pornography and ethnography as "teleological cognates" because both share a commitment to realistically displaying bodies and their workings, and because both "strive for the achievement of epistemological utopias where the 'Other' and knowledge of the 'Other' can be mastered and contained."[14] Underpinning both genres' investment in documentary realism is what Hansen, Needham, and Nichols term a "discourse of domination": "the desire to know and possess, to 'know' by possessing and possess by knowing. . . . Each discourse, then, constantly produces and reproduces a 'reality' (a manifestation of power and a system of constraints) while at the same time disavowing its own complicity with a tradition it appears to contest."[15] Ethnography and pornography share a desire to know the "truth" of other/Other's bodies and a commitment to crafting a representational universe which contains the Other.

Moreover, these scholars argue that pleasure occupies a central place in both ethnographic and pornographic work. Both genres share an interest in displaying the Other's body for the excitement of the viewer: whether the racial, ethnic, or "native" Other, as in the case of ethnography, or the sexed Other, as in the case of pornography.[16] Hansen, Needham, and Nichols argue, "Difference is constantly discovered and placed in the service of pleasure. The desirability of the Other is stressed; Others avail themselves for desire. It is a world in which We *have* Them, a world of lust unbound."[17] This theory of pleasure presumes that the spectator is differentially situated—in terms of race, ethnicity, or gender—than the subjects who appear on-screen, and that pleasure is generated from the titillation of screening "different" bodies and witnessing the "truth" of their bodies' workings. This conception of pornography's pleasures has also been amplified by feminist porn studies scholar Linda Williams who, as I explained earlier, argues that pornography can best be understood as a *scientia sexualis*. As Williams explains, hard-core is a documentary genre animated by a "drive for knowledge through confession."[18] Pornography uses particular genre conventions to showcase its commitment to realism: "close-ups of body parts over other shots; overlight[ing] easily obscured genitals; select[ing] sexual positions that show the most of bodies and organs; and . . . creat[ing] generic conventions, such as the variety of sexual 'numbers' of the externally ejaculating penis—so important to the 1970s feature-length manifestations of the genre."[19] Pornography's visual conventions, then, have been developed to confirm the genre's documentary impulse, and to allow the genre to insistently make bodies, particularly female bodies, and their imagined difference known and knowable.

Proponents of the ethnopornography perspective point to the rich historical archive documenting moments when ethnography and pornography acted as "cognates" conferring a similar set of viewing pleasures on spectators. For example, Brian Wallis's examination of Louis Agassiz's slave daguerreotypes—fifteen nude photographs of enslaved men and women taken in 1850—argues that the images had both ethnographic and pornographic underpinnings.[20] While the photographs sought to expose the differences between whites and blacks, and to use those differences to secure prevailing conceptions of white superiority, they were also designed to titillate their white viewers. Wallis writes, "It is perhaps not coincidental that by their unprecedented nudity, the slave daguerreotypes intersect with pornography. . . . The vaguely eroticized nature of the slave daguerreotypes derives from the unwavering, voyeuristic manner with which they indiscriminately survey the bodies of the Africans, irrespective of the subjects' lives."[21] Wallis's investigation of Agassiz's daguerreotypes (not unlike scholarly work on the Hottentot Venus) suggests that the visual display of black bodies both secured white privilege and conferred sexual pleasure on white spectators.

Recently, Celine Parreñas Shimizu's groundbreaking archival work has contested the ethnopornographic tradition, offering a distinct interpretation of pornography's racialized promises: pornography often promises difference, but actually culminates in a universalizing sex act which overcomes difference.[22] Her analysis shows that Asian (or ostensibly Asian) women's bodies were central to marking the racialized stag film in an era where "race [had to] be identifiable through the [film] titles in order to solicit purchase of the sexual product. The film marketers offer the [racialized] classifications to both create and fulfill specific desires for viewers who need to know if they are getting what they want—the 'something different' that race fulfills."[23] While the racialized stag film insistently gestured toward "something different" and explicitly mobilized race to market itself, racial difference was effaced in the film's climax, where "sex itself universalizes all the difference produced by the end of the films."[24] Ultimately, Shimizu is quite critical of the move toward universalization through sex: "Racial difference is subsumed in a narrative that uses it only for its sexual titillation. It works as a utopic formation without reference to the havoc it represents in contemporaneous society. So, ultimately, transgressive and transformative meanings of the role of race in sex have no place in the stag. . . . The stags contain the threat of racial difference and translate it towards different ends."[25] The stag film's inattention to race's material and social consequences negates the "havoc [race] represents in contemporary society" and effectively treats race merely as a pornographic category rather than as a violent site of inequality. Pornography's fantasies thus include not simply the visualization of racial difference but also the "assimilation of the racial Other."[26]

Though these two accounts offer distinctive accounts of the viewer's pleasure in screening racialized pornography and focus on different moments in pornography's history, both view the racialized pornographic encounter as fundamentally structured by difference: either pornography exploits or effaces difference. I treat Black Throat as a challenge to both scholarly traditions' conceptions of the pornographic promises of racial differences. While the film promises its viewer that black women's sexual differences—namely, black women's distinctive practices of fellatio—will be exposed, it never fulfills the pact it makes with its viewer. Black women's bodies are rhetorically and visually offered as sites of racial-sexual difference and refuse to provide the very evidence that they are supposed to, ultimately frustrating the basic promise of the film. In so doing, black female protagonists problematize, and perhaps even destabilize, the foundation of the all-black and interracial Silver Age markets: that black female bodies "do it differently."

Promises of Black Throats

If the Dark Brothers were famous for their absurdly comical pornographic plotlines, Black Throat remains true to their narrative commitments. The film begins when Roscoe, a white, unemployed garbageman, finds a business card for Madame Mambo's "House of Divine Inspiration Thru Fellatio" in the trash.[27] As Roscoe struggles to pronounce *fellatio*, he tells his trusted companion, a pet rat named Mr. Bob, that he has no idea what *fellatio* means.[28] When Mr. Bob explains that fellatio is "cocksucking, blow job, head, skull, going down, knob licking, getting your head done" and Roscoe remains confused, Mr. Bob decides to help Roscoe discover the pleasures of oral sex. Mr. Bob enlists Jamal, a young, black, self-described "urban professional pimp," to help Roscoe locate Madame Mambo and her "divine" fellatio practice.[29]

Black Throat unfolds as a pornographic take on an interracial buddy film, as Roscoe and Jamal travel door-to-door in Roscoe's apartment building,

5.1 Mambo's ceremony

searching for Madame Mambo.[30] As they enter one apartment after another, they stumble on bodies in the midst of distinctive pleasures, including interracial sex, ménage à trois, and sadomasochistic sex—yet the duo sadly returns to Roscoe's apartment at the end of the film with their dream of finding Mambo unfulfilled. On returning to Roscoe's decrepit apartment, they are surprised to find Mambo has inhabited it and transformed it into the site for a ritual ceremony. She throws her nearly naked body over a skeleton and chants while an audience of naked white men covered in black capes watches and silently masturbates (figure 5.1). One by one, each man penetrates Mambo while the others excitedly watch. As the orgy reaches a frenetic climax, Roscoe is initiated into the pleasures of fellatio as Mambo performs fellatio on him, and the crowd collectively chants, "Mambo!" The film then ends precisely as it began, with Roscoe digging through the trash, discovering Madame Mambo's card, mispronouncing fellatio, and, finally, belching.[31]

Though the film presents itself as a difference narrative—one which will conclude with definitive evidence of the distinctive practices of the "black throat"—I argue that Mambo refuses to offer the evidence that the film promises, causing the film to reorient its narrative in two significant ways. First, the film reveals itself to be an initiation narrative masquerading as a difference narrative. As an initiation narrative, *Black Throat* concludes in a peculiar way: rather than making visible the black female fellatio practitioner's distinctive practice (which is, after all, what the film has promised), the film's climax showcases Roscoe's induction into the pleasures of fellatio. Second, the film's difference-seeking impulses, which cannot be satisfied by Mambo's "throat," get relocated onto male bodies; Roscoe's and Jamal's interracial friendship, rather than Mambo's throat, becomes the site where the film explores imagined racial-sexual difference.

My reading of the film and its narrative masquerade is informed by Linda Williams's method for analyzing pornographic films.[32] Williams argues that the hard-core is a genre like the musical, that it is likewise structured by aesthetic principles and traditions; where the musical is constituted by "musical numbers," the pornographic film is formed by "sexual numbers." Pornography's climactic scene, like the musical's dramatic finale, consists of the moment when the "numbers" reach their visual and aural climax. In the case of pornography, the climax is usually marked by a "multiplication of depictions of graphic sexual acts," or what Williams terms a "frenzy of the visible."[33] If we consider every scene in a pornographic film as a sexual number leading to a climax, then *Black Throat* should consist of a series of scenes that leads to a celebration of "bodies and pleasures," *and* conclude with documentary evidence of the distinctive black throat. Yet, while the film's scenes intensify in the pleasures they represent, and while the final scene showcases an "out-of-control confession of pleasure," the film leaves wholly invisible what it is that makes black throats distinctive.[34] Instead, what structures the final scene is Roscoe's pleasure in finally partaking in, rather than simply observing, fellatio.

The film's first sexual number commences when Roscoe, Jamal, and Mr. Bob stumble into an apartment where two black women are performing fellatio on a white man (figure 5.2). The trio stands on the periphery of the scene and quietly observes the sexual action. Curiously, this scene contains many of the elements one might expect from the film's climax: an interracial encounter featuring a white man and black women, and fellatio performed by multiple black throats. Yet its placement at the very beginning of the film suggests that the film's climax will contain something *more*, a "frenzy of the visible" which will exceed and deepen the pleasures that begin the film. As the scene unfolds, Jamal uses the trio's position as voyeurs as an opportunity for instructing Roscoe on the practice

5.2 *Black Throat's* first sexual number

of fellatio, whispering, "She's deep throating his balls. Such a tiny mouth sucking on such a big dick, oh man, she's got a tight little mouth man. A mouth like that makes you forget all about pussy." Clearly, Jamal's analysis of fellatio's technical aspects is designed to offer Roscoe an education in pleasure and to prepare him for a later initiation into the particular delight of fellatio. Despite their proximity to the action, Jamal and Roscoe go completely unnoticed until completion of the sex act, at which point they ask the women if they know Madame Mambo. The women insist that Mambo is not in their apartment, and Jamal and Roscoe stumble into a second apartment, and into the film's second sexual number.

The second number, like the first, features ménage à trois, this time with a different racial and sexual configuration of bodies: a white woman and two white men. The number begins with the white woman, alone, masturbating, and Roscoe whispers, "Looks like we're just in time for chicken" (figure 5.3). A few moments later, the two white men join the scene, and the number culminates in fellatio, then anal sex. Yet the racial configuration—and its difference from that of the film's first number— remains unmentioned by Roscoe, and Jamal's instructive commentary on bodies and their pleasures remains consistent between the scenes, as if the differences between the white throat and the black throat are insignificant. His only interest seems to be in preparing Roscoe for his first experience of fellatio. As Roscoe and Jamal again stand on the sidelines, the

5.3 *Black Throat*'s second sexual number

bodies in action serve as a kind of instruction manual, demonstrating the range of the sexually possible to the uninitiated Roscoe.

The film's third sexual number is a parody of a heterosexual sadomasochism scene: a white woman wearing a leather bustier and holding a whip verbally berates a white man whose body is fastened to the bed by handcuffs and wears a comically oversized white cuff around his neck (figure 5.4). Despite the pretenses of a sadomasochistic scene, the number culminates with the woman unshackling the man, and the two having vaginal sex. The scene is thus significant precisely for what isn't represented: even though the film is preoccupied with fellatio, the fabled sex act is unexpectedly absent from the encounter. Roscoe's own frustration with this absence becomes apparent when he turns to Jamal and exclaims, "I have to find the secret of fellatio."

What is striking about the numbers that precede the pornographic climax is that in all three, bodies—male and female, black and white—function as displays for Roscoe and Jamal, who cast their gazes on bodies in pleasure while searching for the "truth" of fellatio. In each scene, the two men stand on the sidelines, with Jamal educating Roscoe and pointing out the remarkable features of each sexual act. While bodies provide evidence of the wide range of pleasures that sexual practices can confer, the race of those bodies remains unimportant to both men. As the scenes progress, it becomes clear that Roscoe's search is not for the pleasures of

5.4 *Black Throat*'s third sexual number

the black throat, but for his own authentic, unmediated experience of fellatio. It is his longing to become privy to this "secret" (to use the word he deploys at the end of the third number) that reveals that his journey will end only when he becomes the recipient of this fabled sexual practice.

What makes the film's climax a "frenzy of the visible"? In the film's final scene, Mambo performs a ceremony in Roscoe's apartment, as a crowd of white voyeurs silently masturbates. The white audience members take turns penetrating Mambo, then continue to masturbate when their turn is complete. What distinguishes the film's final scene from its earlier ones is the sheer number of bodies populating the screen; unlike the small sexual numbers that precede the climax, the film's finale is a veritable orgy. Moreover, unlike the film's earlier numbers, the final scene seems to garner its erotic charge from race, with Mambo's body being literally cloaked in signifiers of difference: she wears a colorful wig, her wrists are adorned with silver bangles, and she is in the midst of an ambiguous but clearly racialized ceremony. These accoutrements are designed to mark her body—and her sexuality—as somehow exotic, as different from the other female bodies the film has represented.

The biggest difference between the film's earlier numbers and the finale is that Roscoe is no longer simply a voyeur watching other men enjoy fellatio. For the first time, he experiences the pleasures of the sex act the film mythologizes. Yet the fellatio that Mambo performs on Roscoe is visually identical to the fellatio performed on the men who populate the film's earlier sexual numbers; moreover, the kind of evidence that the viewer sees—Roscoe's erection and the conclusive money shot—are identical to the markers of pleasure that structure the film's earlier numbers. What distinguishes the film's climax from its earlier scenes is therefore not the presence of fellatio or even the presence of a black female body performing fellatio; instead, it is that Roscoe finally gets initiated. Jamal no longer needs to decipher or interpret oral sex for Roscoe; instead, Roscoe, now armed with ample information on the workings of oral sex, is ready to experience the pleasure of unmediated fellatio.

Reading Black Throat as a series of sexual numbers whose climax is the male protagonist's enjoyment of fellatio rather than the revelation of the "black throat's" difference demonstrates that the film is, indeed, an initiation narrative veiled as a difference narrative, and reveals the film's tenuous claim to the truth of "deep throating with ethnic flavor." Rather than displaying the distinctiveness of black women's sexual practices, the film's climax ushers Roscoe into the pleasures of pornography's "most photogenic" act.[35] The promise of the truth of the black throat is left unfulfilled, and the viewer is left to locate pleasure in the culmination of Roscoe's sexual odyssey.

However, the film's incessant difference-seeking impulse does not stop simply because Mambo's throat refuses to provide the evidence the film promises. Since the film is unable to showcase black female difference, the film's interracial male buddy partnership becomes a significant platform for investigating and representing racial difference (figure 5.5).[36] Male bodies, rather than black female bodies, serve as the film's vehicle for exploring racial fictions and projecting racial mythologies. From the film's beginning, Roscoe is marked as "white trash," a subject who stands outside of normative whiteness precisely because he is racially marked.[37] To entrench the spectator's association of Roscoe with white trash, the film begins with Roscoe literally picking through the trash in his dilapidated apartment, searching for food when he stumbles on Mambo's card. The spectator is then encouraged to associate Roscoe's white-trash position with his job as a trash collector, his silly clothes, his plastic sunglasses, his pet rat sidekick, and, most important, his lack of sexual knowledge.

Jamal, Roscoe's hyperstylized (and hyperstylish) black sidekick, is presented as Roscoe's polar opposite. If Roscoe is, in Mr. Bob's words, a

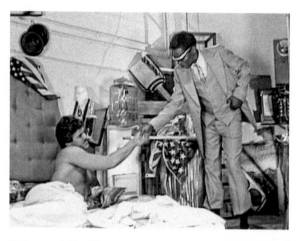

5.5 Interracial buddies

"honky," Jamal is "the best pimp in the world, he can throw bitches out
of the grave and make them do some shit." Where Roscoe lacks sexual
knowledge, Jamal is an expert; where Roscoe wears casual beach clothes,
Jamal wears a suit; where Roscoe characterizes himself as an unemployed
garbageman, Jamal calls himself an "urban pimp"; where Roscoe is white,
Jamal is black; and where Roscoe is decidedly outside of the trappings of
bourgeois culture, Jamal describes himself as a

> whole new breed of pimp, a young urban professional pimp. I prefer
> to be called a flesh broker. I traded in my pink El Dorado and got my-
> self a BMW 321, I ditched my leather suit and got myself these Brooks
> Brothers threads, I quit taking drugs and joined the health club, I quit
> eating fried chicken and got hooked on nouvelle cuisine, I put down
> my Thunderbird and picked up Dom Perignon, I took my money out of
> my mattress and put it in a Merrill Lynch mutual money fund market.

Jamal's fast-talking self-fashioning foregrounds his knowledge: about
finances, about nutrition, about fashion, and, most important, about sex.
And his quick introduction foregrounds the visible proof of the difference
between black male bodies and white male bodies that the film offers:
Jamal's slick clothes, fashionable sunglasses, and quick staccato speech
are all directly opposed to Roscoe. Ultimately, the interracial partnership
between Roscoe and Jamal depends on their differences: their respective

5.6 Roscoe's climax

positions vis-à-vis sexual knowledge and their respectively (and differently) raced bodies.

While Jamal's knowledge is essential to Roscoe's initiation, the film's climax suggests that Jamal's sexual knowledge must ultimately be cabined to secure Roscoe's pleasure (figure 5.6). In the film's final scene, Roscoe and Jamal initially stand on the sidelines, much as they have in earlier sexual numbers, peering in on spectacles of bodies in pleasure. Unlike earlier scenes, though, both men masturbate as they observe Mambo's ceremony. While Roscoe's penis is hypervisible, the camera lingering over shots of his hand rubbing his penis, Jamal's penis is virtually invisible, hidden by the flap of his pants. While the relative absence of Jamal's penis—and his pleasure—from the scene is striking, what is more striking is that while the white male audience members take turns penetrating Mambo, Jamal remains on the periphery of the scene, never touching her. Instead, he performs the role of a faithful and selfless sidekick, silently pleasuring himself and cheering as Roscoe experiences his first blowjob (figure 5.7).

Of course, Jamal's relegation to the visual periphery might, in part, be explained by the film's very construction as an initiation narrative. The climax of the film displays Roscoe's initiation into the pleasure of fellatio, and thus it is logical that the concluding "frenzy of the visible" would center on Roscoe's pleasures, rather than on Roscoe's and Jamal's shared

5.7 Jamal watching from afar

pleasures. Yet if so many of the men populating the screen in the final scene enjoy Mambo's body, why is Jamal relegated to the visual margins? Why doesn't Jamal also have his few moments of pleasure with Mambo?

Jamal's relative absence from the film's climax might be explained by the imagined (and imaginative) power of the black phallus—yet another racial difference that the film explores through its male protagonists. Linda Williams argues that the presence of the black male phallus, imagined as always erect, always larger than life, stands as a threat to white masculinity, potentially signaling the inauthenticity or effeminacy of white male sexuality.[38] She notes, "White men, for their part, have historically feared black male prowess, even while (and as a means of) exercising sexual sovereignty over black women. White male fear of the black man's sexual threat to white women has been the ostensible reason . . . for countless acts of violence against black men."[39] If Jamal's black penis signifies "sexual sovereignty" and "male prowess," in the same way that his presence in the film signifies sexual knowledge, then his penis must be excised from the climax to allow Roscoe access to the pleasures of fellatio. And so Jamal's almost invisible penis ensures that the black male hyperphallus does not overshadow inexperienced Roscoe's white penis.

Moreover, in a visual economy where same-race partners are imagined to be suited for each other, Jamal might be presumed to be Mambo's "appropriate" partner. Indeed, given that Mambo and Jamal are the only two black bodies populating the film's climactic scene, a spectator could easily presume that a coupling of the two would be "natural." Williams's work suggests that a kind of triangulation underpins the interracial pornographic scene; even when the same-race partner is visually absent, his presence is palpable and lends the scene an erotic charge. She notes,

> Different interracial permutations ... contain a nonpresent third term that haunts the scene. This is the putatively "proper," same-race partner whom the spectacle of interracial lust can be said to betray. When the black woman and the white man recognize and desire one another across their differences, this recognition is nevertheless haunted and erotically animated by the missing figure of the black man, who finds his very masculinity and virility jeopardized by his exclusion.[40]

While Williams's analysis uncovers the triad that undergirds the interracial pornographic scene (one which presumes a certain configuration of race and gender), *Black Throat* presents alternative interpretations of the specter of the same-race partner. Jamal's blackness in fact enables the interracial scene: his sexual knowledge (ostensibly linked to his blackness) introduces Roscoe to fellatio, and his relative absence from the final scene allows Roscoe to enjoy Mambo's body. Yet Jamal must be visually absent from the climax to fully allow for Roscoe—and the other white men on-screen—to access Mambo's body. White male access to Mambo's black body thus requires the absence of the black male phallus, even though it is the film's black male protagonist who enables the white male protagonist's "discovery" of Mambo.

On Refusal

Rather than using the racially marked female subject's difference—either its insistent presence or its insistent absence—as the prevailing analytic for studying racialized pornography, my reading of *Black Throat* suggests that reading for failures, for inconsistencies, for ruptures, and for refusals might provide rich entry points into theorizing racialized pornography's insecure narrative promises. Indeed, my reading of *Black Throat* underscores a paradox that marked the birth of the Silver Age all-black and interracial markets: even as these genres relied on difference to mark their parameters, their claims to revealing difference were always tenuous. Ultimately, *Black Throat* demonstrates neither that difference is ethnographically displayed nor that difference is elided; instead, difference is a frustrating problem on the Silver Age pornographic screen precisely because it cannot be captured, made legible. The Dark Brothers' film finds a way to solve the "problem" of its black female protagonist's refusal to make her difference knowable: they instead locate racial difference on the film's male bodies and transform the film's narrative from a focus on black women's racial difference into an interracial buddy film where male bodies' racial difference allows the white male protagonist's initiation into the pleasures of fellatio.

In underscoring *Black Throat*'s peculiar investment in locating sexual difference in male bodies, I am not suggesting that there is anything inherently transgressive about a narrative that posits white male bodies as innocent and black male bodies as lustful and inherently sexual, nor is there anything particularly resistant about a narrative where black bodies usher white bodies into "the dark side," introducing them to the possibilities of new bodily pleasures. For my purposes, what makes *Black Throat* distinctive—and significant—is the narrative labor it has to perform in light of Mambo's refusal to produce the difference that rhetorically undergirds the film. When black female protagonists' bodies refuse to provide the difference that is promised, the fantasy apparatus of the film's narrative instead looks for difference in male bodies.

If the film's representation of Roscoe's and Jamal's racial difference only shores up prevailing racial fantasies, Mambo's frustration of the film's promise makes a transgressive claim about the fundamental sameness of bodies even as that claim is packaged, quite literally, in the promise of difference. Rather than exposing that "black women do it differently," the film shows that sexual practices are identical across the imagined color line, that the black throat and the white throat are, in fact, equivalent. In so doing, the film gestures to a larger productive tension in the Silver Age all-black and interracial markets. While racialized pornographic films like the ones that proliferated during the Silver Age implicitly suggest that "race *counts* as a different sexual practice," the failure of the genre to ever effectively capture this difference calls into question not only the racial fictions that underpinned the Silver Age's racialized markets but the very idea of racial difference itself.[41] If the black throat resembles the white throat, and if racialized pornography can never capture imagined racial-sexual difference, the difference narrative is always necessarily unstable, and can be unmade and undone in any moment. Indeed, *Black Throat* reveals that black female protagonists are instrumental in exposing that bodies *are* bodies, that throats *are* throats, that the imagined "them" is always already quite similar, if not identical, to the imagined "us."

CONCLUSION

Reading Ecstasy

From the "sex wars" of the 1980s to debates about the "pornification" of popular culture, pornography has been one of the most contentious sites in feminist theory and politics.[1] Conversations about pornography have functioned as rich sites of debate about the role of the state in safeguarding women's bodily integrity, the nature of sexual freedom and agency, the social consequences of representation, and the ubiquity of sexual violence. Yet the vibrancy of these debates has been substantially diminished when feminists turn their attention to racialized pornography; indeed, feminist scholarship on racialized pornography—regardless of the politics of the scholarship—has been more *normative* than *analytical*, informed by what Loïc Wacquant terms the "logic of the trial," an impulse to diagnose and condemn rather than to closely examine pornography's historically and technologically specific meanings.[2] Far too often, the word *black* in front of the word *pornography* is treated as an intensifier, as something that produces political anxiety rather than as something that engenders theoretical energy and analytical sophistication.[3]

For black feminism, the rich and vibrant tradition I locate as my intellectual "home place," critiques of racialized pornography are part of a larger critical assessment of dominant representation.[4] In this volume, I argue that the heterogeneous texts that constitute the black feminist theoretical archive have produced a singular theory of representation that presumes the violence of the visual field even as it locates the origins and nature of that violence differently, and even as it envisions possibilities of resistance differently. This archive emphasizes how dominant visual culture perpetuates "controlling images," entrenches the idea of the black feminine hyperlibido, reenacts the violence of the past including slavery and ethnographic exhibitions of black female bodies, reduces black women to fetishized body parts—particularly breasts and buttocks—or to icons, and incessantly sutures black femininity to ideas of excess, deviance, and alterity. If dominant representation injures, resistance and recovery are possible only when black women act as authors of their own images, taking the site of violence—the visual field—and making it a space for performing their wholeness.

This volume uses racial iconography as a hermeneutic that both ruptures this prevailing black feminist narrative and opens up new black feminist attention to ecstasy. Racial iconography allows me to trace the panoply of technologically and historically embedded pleasures that racialized pornography can produce for black female bodies, including pleasures in performing blackness, pleasures in race-humor, pleasures in upending the conventions of the racialized pornographic film, pleasures in being watched, and pleasures in watching. My contention, of course, is not that these complex pleasures exculpate racialized pornography from the moments when it traffics in racial brutality and violence, or to suggest that race is merely an instrument of pleasure that can be decontextualized from the practices, quotidian and institutional, of inequality.

Rather, I am attracted to the pornographic texts I analyze here because they are sites where one would not expect to locate political possibility; these are texts where black women's bodies have been represented not to engender political shifts, but to generate new profits. Yet it is in this surprising location—the pornographic archive—that I find black pleasures articulated, amplified, and practiced. The political freedoms that I argue are embedded in these texts are the basis of the shift that I hope to engender within black feminist theory: moving the black feminist theoretical archive beyond a rehearsal of black women's troubled relationship with representation, toward a consideration of the fraught pleasures that come in and through blackness, and in and through performances of racial fictions.

While I have been particularly interested in the racialized pornographic archive, one that I think black feminism has been far too quick to condemn and dismiss, the book's theoretical and political investment in foregrounding ecstasy as a reprieve from injury and recovery has implications well beyond the specific visual site I interrogate here. Indeed, my investment in making space for black women's pleasures is an intervention into a long scholarly tradition of reciting the discursive absence of black women's pleasures, both on the pornographic screen, and in visual culture generally. Linda Williams concludes her essay "Skin Flicks on the Racial Border" with a commentary on the impossibility of black women's pornographic pleasures: "The pleasures of sexual-racial difference once available to white masters alone are now more available to all, though not equally to all. Black female viewing pleasure, it would seem, is the least well served by these newly racialized, noisy confessions of pleasure."[5] Williams's assumption—that black women's desires are the "least well served" by the pornographic marketplace—is a common scholarly refrain. If black women's viewing pleasures are not regularly anticipated by pornography, black women are also, as Mireille Miller-Young notes, "systemically positioned in spaces and roles of lesser importance to white women, who are valued as the most prized commodities in the sexual marketplace of hardcore."[6] Both Williams and Miller-Young underscore that black women's pleasures—as protagonists and spectators—are ignored or effaced by pornography.

This sentiment dovetails with a lengthy tradition of black feminist work that highlights the discursive and representational invisibility of black women's pleasures: Hortense Spillers notes, "Black women are the beached whales of the sexual universe, unvoiced, misseen, not doing, awaiting their verb"; Evelynn Hammonds uses the term "problematic of silence" to describe a moment where "we know more about the elision of sexuality by black women then we do about the possible varieties of expression of sexual desire"; Darlene Clark Hine's "culture of dissemblance" is often used as a transhistorical catch-all that describes the "behavior and attitudes of Black women that created the appearance of openness and disclosure but actually shielded the truth of their inner lives and selves from their oppressors"; and Evelyn Brooks Higginbotham's "politics of respectability" describes an ideology that "equated public behavior with individual self-respect and with the advancement of African Americans as a group. . . . 'Respectable' behavior in public would earn their people a measure of esteem from white America."[7] Taken together, these scholars document the strategic rationales for black female sexual silence and uncover a larger cultural silence surrounding black female pleasures.

By capturing the regulations that constrain black female sexuality and the silences that black women have strategically deployed to avoid cultural scrutiny, these texts often reproduce the very sexual silences they critique. Indeed, while black feminists have labored to document representation's violence, too often our work has reproduced another kind of violence, effectively rendering black female pleasures invisible and making impossible the conceptualization of black female pleasures from *within* black feminism. Despite calls by scholars like Hammonds to study black women's "pleasure, exploration, and agency," there remains, as Lisa Thompson notes, a "dearth of theoretical interventions around black female sexuality."[8]

Of course, as long as black feminists have documented the strategic silences that black women adopt to protect their bodies from scrutiny, there have been some black feminists breaking that silence. Tricia Rose's *Longing to Tell*, Shayne Lee's *Erotic Revolutionaries*, LaMonda Horton Stallings's *Mutha' Is Half a Word*, and Thompson's *Beyond the Black Lady* are examples of scholarly texts that have produced critical ruptures in this silence. These texts theorize "radical Black female sexual subjectivity," celebrate black female "erotic revolutionaries," revel in "Black women who laugh out loud, curse, sit with their legs open, and selfishly act on their desires," and reveal that black women have long crafted space to be "bawdy, explicit, and downright shameless in their expressions of sexual desires, despite reprimands they may have received."[9] Rather than reproducing silence, these books emphatically speak sex, documenting black women's embodied erotic experiences. My book shares this scholarship's commitment to locating radical theories of black women's sexual pleasure within black feminism, though I extend this body of scholarship in significant ways.

First, I analytically separate ecstasy from pleasure, and endeavor to produce a black feminist theoretical archive that is oriented toward ecstasy. For me, ecstasy marks the fraught nature of racial-sexual pleasure, and underscores what is unnerving and complicated about the pleasures that I trace in this volume. My use of the term ecstasy signals that this work is not an unabashedly pro-pornography project. I do not imagine

Hopkinson!

pleasure as existing outside of inequality, violence, or pain, nor do I imagine pleasure to circulate outside of the systems of domination which constrain us. My readings of black female pornographic protagonists' pleasures have emphasized that pleasure is often shot through with pain, that desire is often fraught and complicated terrain, and that "speaking sex" is always shaped by the conditions of profound racial inequality that shape the unfolding present.

In pushing black feminism toward ecstasy rather than pleasure, I ask how race can become a site of naming longings, and underscore that the persistence of race as a social, cultural, and economic project is fundamentally related to its hold on all of our erotic imaginations. Indeed, this kind of black feminist archive would recognize that race is an erotic project, not simply because it pleasures majoritarian subjects, but because it shapes minoritarian desires and pleasures as well, constituting how minoritarian subjects imagine their bodies, longings, and desires. In short, a black feminist archive oriented toward ecstasy foregrounds how race acts both to limit our sexual imaginations, and to provide us with powerful vocabularies for naming what we desire; it recognizes that the very structures we critique and seek to dismantle can also thrill.

Secondly, in arguing for a black feminist theoretical archive oriented toward ecstasy, I center fantasy in the political life of black feminism. Black feminism has long exposed the dangers of fantasies of black women's difference; the fictions that allowed Saartjie Baartman's nineteenth-century display, many black feminists have argued, continue to animate the dominant visual field, reducing black women to "excess flesh."[10] But black feminism has yet to turn to the productive elements of racial fantasies, particularly the relationship between fantasy and freedom for black female subjects for whom there are far too few representations of black bodies in pleasure. What if the black feminist theoretical archive were to imagine fantasy as a productive space of subject formation, a site where subjects (white and black alike) articulate longings, perform pleasures, and name desires in ways that both traffic in racial stereotype and transcend stereotype (and sometimes both simultaneously)? What if the labor of the black feminist theoretical archive were to be, at least in part, to expand the fantastical structures available to subjects, to strive for heterogeneous representational economies which make space for varied black pleasures? What if fantasy were articulated as both a right and a freedom,

as absolutely central to black feminist political work?[11] A black femin
theoretical archive centered on ecstasy recognizes the fundamental ii
portance of fantasy, not simply as a violent technology which proliferates
hyperbolic images of black female sexuality, but as a tool of imagination,
as a space of freedom, and as a critical locus of play and performance for
minoritarian subjects.

Finally, my investment in ecstasy calls for a black feminist reconsideration of the very meaning of blackness. Blackness, I have argued, is not simply an embodied wound inflicted on black flesh repeatedly for white pleasure, nor is it exclusively a locus of historically rooted trauma. Most importantly, pleasures in blackness are not manifestations of false consciousness, or elaborate acts of self-delusion. My close readings of racialized pornographic films capture how blackness electrifies, excites, titillates, arouses, and generates intensities, some of which might make us politically uncomfortable even as they make us sexually excited. Indeed, in the films I examine, blackness is a site of pain and a locus of pleasure (and, I argue, blackness may serve as a critical site in examining how pain and pleasure are bound up in significant ways, never entirely freed from each other). My engagement with racialized pornography reveals that blackness must be understood as a complex circuit of desires and pleasures that constrains and violates while pleasuring and titillating, and as a construction that can produce embodied delight.

Ultimately, if speaking race is an integral part of speaking sex, a strategy that I have shown black pornographic protagonists and spectators use to name, claim, and locate pleasure—and to expose prevailing racial fictions—then the labor of black feminism must be to carve out imaginative and cultural space for black subjects, particularly black female subjects, to speak sex in as many tongues as possible. Indeed, our political work could constantly expand lexicons of desire, so that prevailing fictions need not be the only avenue for black subjects to speak sex. The possibility of ecstasy—and the freedoms that ecstasy can bring—hinges on it.

NOTES

Introduction

1   I am imagining black feminism as an evolving intellectual, theoretical, and political tradition that has been committed to examining the variety, heterogeneity, and complexity of black women's lived experiences. My understanding of black feminism is informed by Patricia Hill Collins's seminal text *Black Feminist Thought*, which posits black feminism as a "critical social theory" that "encompasses bodies of knowledge and sets of institutional practices that actively grapple with the central questions facing U.S. Black women as a collectivity. . . . Black feminist thought's identity as a 'critical' social theory lies in its commitment to justice, both for U.S. Black women as a collectivity and for that of other similarly oppressed groups" (9). It is important to note that black feminism is increasingly invested in de-centering American blackness, and in recognizing the host of ways that blackness is performed, articulated, and transformed globally. My understanding of black feminism is mindful of the transnational black feminist turn(s). See, for example, Mirza, *Black British Feminism*; Samantrai, *Alter-Natives*; Wing, ed., *Global Critical Race Feminism*.

2   My understanding of representation as a wounding project is informed by Carol E. Henderson's *Scarring the Black Body: Race and Representation in African American Literature*.

3   Shimizu, *The Hypersexuality of Race*, 140.

4   Butler, "Endangered/Endangering: Schematic Racism and White Paranoia," 20.

5 See, for example, Irigaray, *This Sex Which Is Not One*; Kristeva, *Revolution in Poetic Language*.

6 Muñoz, *Cruising Utopia*, 187; Wilson, "One Way or Another," 24.

7 Muñoz, *Cruising Utopia*, 186.

8 My interest in black feminism's "protectionist" tendencies is informed by Shayne Lee's work. See Lee, *Erotic Revolutionaries*.

9 See Wacquant, "For an Analytic of Racial Domination"; Omi and Winant, *Racial Formation in the United States*; Telles, *Race in Another America*; Butler, "Endangered/Endangering," 20; Fleetwood, *Troubling Vision*; Patricia Hill Collins, *Black Feminist Thought*; Abel, *Signs of the Times*.

10 See Lipsitz, *The Possessive Investment in Whiteness*; Cheryl Harris, "Whiteness as Property"; Farley, "The Black Body as Fetish Object."

11 Reed, "Introduction," 170.

12 Jafa, "69," 253.

13 See E. Patrick Johnson, *Appropriating Blackness*; Shimizu, *The Hypersexuality of Race*; Shimizu, "Sex for Sale"; Robin Bernstein, "Dances with Things"; Harvey Young, *Embodying Black Experience*.

14 Butler, *Gender Trouble*, 179.

15 Lisa Collins, "Economies of the Flesh," 99.

16 For more on the "negative" and "positive" images debate, see Michele Wallace, *Invisibility Blues*. Also see Shimizu, "The Bind of Representation."

17 Shimizu, *The Hypersexuality of Race*, 26.

18 My idea of the "tightrope" is drawn from Glenda Carpio's work. See Carpio, *Laughing Fit to Kill*, 71.

19 Shimizu, *The Hypersexuality of Race*, 54.

20 Walker, *You Can't Keep a Good Woman Down*, 42.

21 Alice Walker notes, "The more ancient roots of modern pornography are to be found in the almost always pornographic treatment of black women, who, from the moment they entered slavery . . . were subjected to rape as the 'logical' convergence of sex and violence. Conquest, in short" (*You Can't Keep a Good Woman Down*, 42).

22 MacKinnon, *Feminism Unmodified*, 8.

23 Walker, *You Can't Keep a Good Woman Down*, 52.

24 Patricia J. Williams, *The Alchemy of Race and Rights*, 10. Avery Gordon's *Ghostly Matters* insightfully draws on Williams's acknowledgment. For more on the political work that black women (or black feminists) are so often called on to perform for mainstream feminism, see Ann duCille's *Skin Trade*, in which she argues, "Today there is so much interest in black women that I have begun to think of myself as a sacred text. . . . Within the modern academy, racial and gender alterity has become a hot commodity that has claimed black women as its principal signifier.

I am alternately pleased and perturbed by this, by the alterity that is perpetually thrust upon African American women, by the production of black women as infinitely deconstructable 'othered' matter. Why are black women always other? . . . Why have black women become the subjected subjects of so much contemporary scholarly investigation, the peasants under glass of intellectual inquiry in the 1990s?" (81).

25 "Loving critique" is a term Tricia Rose used to describe her scholarly engagement with hip-hop at the panel discussion "Is Hip-hop Good for the Black Community?" held on 19 February 2008 at Harvard's Kennedy School of Government. Thanks to Sarah Howard for bringing this term to my attention.

26 For histories of the sex wars, see Duggan and Hunter, *Sex Wars*.

27 Jakobsen, "Introduction."

28 Catharine MacKinnon articulates the idea that pornography is an act, and not expression, in *Only Words*.

29 MacKinnon, *Feminism Unmodified*, 171.

30 MacKinnon, *Women's Lives, Men's Laws*, 301.

31 Leidholdt, "When Women Defend Pornography," 129.

32 Angela Harris poignantly captures antipornography feminism's use of black women as "black women are white women, only more so" ("Race and Essentialism in Feminist Legal Theory," 592).

33 Leidholdt, "Where Pornography Meets Fascism," 20.

34 Angela Harris, "Race and Essentialism in Feminist Legal Theory," 596.

35 MacKinnon, *Women's Lives, Men's Laws*, 301–2.

36 Teish, "A Quiet Subversion," 117.

37 Angela Harris terms this antipornography tendency "nuance theory," which she defines as the practice of offering generalizations about women as a class while offering "qualifying statements, often in footnotes, [which] supplement the general account with the subtle nuances of experience that 'different' women add to the mix" ("Race and Essentialism in Feminist Legal Theory," 595). Harris critiques this antipornography rhetorical strategy for its reification of whiteness as the norm and its implicit suggestion that black female subjectivity is different (deviant?). It seems equally problematic that this theoretical configuration ignores the complex simultaneity of privilege and oppression for both white and black subjects, ignoring the ways in which positions of marginality (and privilege) are always far more complex than the simple idea that "black women have it worse." In ignoring the ways in which questions of sexuality and class, among many others, mediate black women's subject positions, MacKinnon assumes the inherent subordination of black female subjects without fully interrogating or exploring the complexity of black female—in fact, of all—subjectivity.

38 MacKinnon and Dworkin, *In Harm's Way*, 5.

39 MacKinnon and Dworkin, *In Harm's Way*, 117.

40 MacKinnon, *Feminism Unmodified*, 175.

41 The MacKinnon-Dworkin ordinance was passed by the Minneapolis city council in 1983, but vetoed by Mayor Donald Fraser. The modified ordinance was passed in Indianapolis, and signed into law by Mayor William Hudnut. The ordinance was also on the ballot in Cambridge, Massachusetts, in 1985, and in Bellingham, Washington, in 1988.

42 See *American Booksellers v. Hudnut*, 771 F.2d 323 (7th Cir. 1985).

43 Doherty and Dines, "Living in a Porn Culture."

44 Doherty and Dines, "Living in a Porn Culture."

45 For more on sexual hierarchies, see Rubin's "Thinking Sex: Notes for a Radical Theory of the Politics of Sexuality." The critique of sexual hierarchy emerging from Rubin's "Thinking Sex" would form the basis for an emerging queer theory.

46 For more on unexpected feminist alliances, see Duggan and Hunter, *Sex Wars*, 67.

47 Quoted in Duggan and Hunter, *Sex Wars*, 235.

48 Naomi Wolf coined the particularly problematic term "victim feminism," in *Fire with Fire*.

49 Abrams, "Sex Wars Redux," 305.

50 Paglia, *Vamps and Tramps*, 66.

51 Paglia, *Vamps and Tramps*, 66.

52 For more on third-wave feminism, see Snyder, "What Is Third-Wave Feminism?"

53 Lee, *Erotic Revolutionaries*, xvii. For more on these texts, see Nash, "New Directions in Black Feminist Studies."

54 In this way, sex-radical feminism anticipated sex-positive feminism, which emerged in the mid- to late 1990s.

55 Hollibaugh, "Desire for the Future," 409.

56 Cornell, *The Imaginary Domain*, 104.

57 See Nagle, *Whores and Other Feminists*; Chapkis, *Live Sex Acts*; R. Danielle Egan, *Dancing for Dollars and Paying for Love*; Delacoste and Alexander, *Sex Work*.

58 Linda Williams, *Hard Core*, 282.

59 Linda Williams, *Porn Studies*, 2.

60 *Hard Core* focused on heterosexual pornography because, as Linda Williams noted, "as a heterosexual woman I do not feel that I should be the first one to address questions raised by a body of films [queer pornography] not aimed primarily at me. I acknowledge that this did not stop me from presuming, as a woman, to interpret pornographic texts aimed primarily at men; but since heterosexual, predominantly male oriented sexuality is the dominant sexual identity of our culture, such analysis is justifiable. . . . Because lesbian and gay pornography do not address me personally, their initial mapping as genres properly belongs to those who can read them better" (*Hard Core*, 6–7).

A few years later, in an essay in *More Dirty Looks*, Williams revisited her decision to focus on heterosexual pornography, noting that "I was unable to see then that what I was learning from the book [*Hard Core*] was actually how easy it was to identify with diverse subject positions and to desire diverse objects. Indeed, how polymorphously perverse the genre of pornography could be. . . . I had far too rigid a sense of the proper audience for each sub-genre" ("Second Thoughts on *Hard Core*," 171).

61 Linda Williams, *Hard Core*, 49.

62 Luce Irigaray's work has theorized female sexuality as an inherently disruptive economy, one where female pleasure exceeds the phallocentric economy which privileges legibility and quantifiability. See Irigaray, *This Sex Which Is Not One*. While mainstream heterosexual pornography appears frustrated by its constant desire to see female pleasure and its climactic money shot, which showcases only male pleasure, female pleasures are, in fact, showcased on the pornographic screen, though in different registers than male pleasures. John Corbett and Terri Kapsalis argue that the sounds of female pleasure—moans, whimpers, and groans—punctuate pornography such that "sound becomes the proof of female pleasure in the absence of its clear visual demonstration. The quantitative evaluation of male sexual pleasure by means of the money shot . . . may, for female sexual pleasure, be represented in the quality and volume of the female vocalizations" ("Aural Sex," 103).

63 Linda Williams, *Porn Studies*, 8.

64 Linda Williams, "'White Slavery' versus the Ethnography of 'Sexworkers,'" 124.

65 The transformation of rape scenes into pleasurable scenes is itself a kind of pornographic trope, one which I write more about in chapters 2 and 3.

66 Linda Williams, "'White Slavery' versus the Ethnography of 'Sexworkers,'" 126.

67 Angela Harris, "Race and Essentialism in Feminist Legal Theory," 596. In the same piece Harris notes, "In MacKinnon's writing, the word 'black,' applied to women, is an intensifier: If things are bad for everybody (meaning white women), then they're even worse for black women. Silent and suffering, we are trotted onto the page (mostly in footnotes) as the ultimate example of how bad things are" (596).

68 Kipnis, *Bound and Gagged*, 162.

69 Champagne, "'Stop Reading Films!,'" 77.

70 Rich Cante and Angelo Restivo argue that queer pornographies stand in a complex relationship to space because filmed queer sex is always already in conversation with an imagined public, even when its filmed setting is private. They write, "Despite all the gains made in public acceptance and increased visibility, homosexual acts—as well as their witnessing—still force the subject to situate itself in relation to publicity, one way or another: 'I'm gay'; 'I needed money'; 'I was

drunk and horny and didn't know what I was doing but I'm really not gay.' . . .
Each of these phrases aspires to performing this mapping function relative to
the public sphere or some section of it, though each one does it differently"
("The Cultural-Aesthetic Specificities of All-Male Moving-Image Pornography,"
142–43).

71 Catharine MacKinnon epitomizes this position, noting that "pornography is
masturbation material. It is used as sex. It therefore is sex. Men know this. . . .
With pornography, men masturbate to women being exposed, humiliated, violated, degraded, mutilated, dismembered, bound, gagged, tortured, and killed.
In the visual materials, they experience this *being done* by watching it *being
done*. . . . Men come doing this" (*Only Words*, 17, emphasis in original).

72 Wicke, "Through a Glass Darkly," 70.

73 Wicke, "Through a Glass Darkly," 70.

74 MacKinnon, *Only Words*, 17.

75 Kipnis, *Bound and Gagged*, 177, emphasis in original.

76 See, for example, Delany, *Times Square Red, Times Square Blue*.

77 Freeman, *Time Binds*, xvii.

78 Mulvey, "Visual Pleasure and Narrative Cinema," 22. I discuss Laura Mulvey's
work in greater detail in chapter 2.

79 Snow, "Theorizing the Male Gaze: Some Problems," 30. Various scholars have
reconceptualized the male gaze, problematizing the assumptions that undergird feminist film theory. See Gaines, "White Privilege and Looking Relations";
hooks, *Black Looks*; Kaplan, "Is the Gaze Male?"

80 For some of the rich debate regarding the role of images in porn studies scholarship, see *Cinema Journal* 46.4 (2007).

81 Linda Williams, *Hard Core*, 33.

82 Linda Williams, *Hard Core*, 33. Williams later criticized her decision not to illustrate *Hard Core*: "If we are going to do scholarship about pornography, and if we
are going to teach pornography, then it seems self-evident that there are times
when it is necessary to show the images of which we speak and to run the risk
that the images will do what they aim to do: arouse, disgust, amuse, and even
malign" ("'Frenzy of the Visible,' Indeed!," 107).

83 See Wiegman, *Object Lessons*.

84 Hemmings, *Why Stories Matter*, 2.

1. *Archives of Pain*

1 For a sampling of work of scholarly work on Baartman, see Elizabeth Alexander,
The Venus Hottentot; Parks, *Venus*; Sharpley-Whiting, *Black Venus*; Skelly, *No Strangers
to Beauty*; Hobson, *Venus in the Dark*; Strother, "Display of the Body Hottentot";

Fausto-Sterling, "Gender, Race, and Nation"; Magubane, "Which Bodies Matter?"; Holmes, *African Queen*; Blanchard et al., *Human Zoos*; Crais and Scully, *Sara Baartman and the Hottentot Venus*; Willis, *Black Venus*.

2 Anne Fausto-Sterling's work underscores the complexity of categorizing Baartman. She argues that Dutch colonists called colonial subjects on the Cape of Good Hope "Hottentots" despite the fact that the inhabitants called themselves "Khoikhoi." To that end, Fausto-Sterling demonstrates the fundamental instability of categories like Hottentot, Khoikhoi, and Bushmen, and suggests the importance of examining the politics of classification. The fact that Baartman's story has been taken as a political parable about black American bodies is also of interest to me, as it suggests that categories of nation and ethnicity have not yet informed analyses of Baartman's history.

Zine Magubane is particularly attentive to the differences between these audiences. Magubane notes that it is important to consider "Baartman's relatively weak interpellation into British medical and scientific discourses as compared to French. . . . It is important to note that at the time of Baartmann's exhibition in London, medical science was no less developed or commercialized than in France. There were many large medical hospitals and 'theaters of anatomy' wherein the nongentlemanly members of the British scientific community earned their livelihoods" (Magubane, "Which Bodies Matter?," 826–27). Magubane concludes that a rigorous understanding of Baartman's distinctive treatment in London and Paris requires an understanding of political debates circulating in both places. She argues, "A substantial portion of the British public actually saw her as representing much more. When many people looked at Baartmann, they saw not only racial and sexual alterity but also a personification of current debates about the right to liberty versus the right to property. For many, Baartmann's captivity encapsulated the conflict between individual freedom and the interests of capital" (Magubane, "Which Bodies Matter?," 827–28).

3 On colonialism, see Stoler, *Carnal Knowledge*; McClintock, *Imperial Leather*. On Baartman's body as a "master text," see Sharpley-Whiting, *Black Venus*, 17. As Zine Magubane also notes, Baartman was also central to debates about the abolition of slavery. Sadiah Qureshi argues, "Baartman's exhibition aroused intense public interest when abolitionists objected to her display on humanitarian grounds. . . . The abolitionist interest prompted a court case: Baartman's self-appointed protectors argued that the exhibit was both indecent and, crucially, that Baartman was being held against her will. In conjunction with the African Association, the abolitionists also arranged for Baartman's repatriation to her native Cape. Ultimately, the court found in favor of the defendant, Cezar, upon the presentation of a contract between Baartman and [Alexander] Dunlop. Although it is highly probably the contract was drawn up hastily in the light of the court case, and

that Baartman may not even have seen it, the judge felt it inappropriate to press charges and the show continued" ("Displaying Sara Baartman," 238–39).

4 Anne Fausto-Sterling notes, "The term *steatopygia* (from the roots for fat and buttocks) was used as early as 1822 in a traveler's account of South Africa, but the observer said the 'condition' was not characteristic of all Hottentots nor was it, for that matter, characteristic of any particular people. Later in the century, what had been essentially a curiosity found its way into medical textbooks as an abnormality. According to Gilman, by the middle of the nineteenth century the buttocks had become a clear symbol of female sexuality; and the intense interest in the backside, a displacement for fascination with the genitalia" (Fausto-Sterling, "Gender, Race, and Nation," 78). Fausto-Sterling notes that "scientists" were not able to examine Baartman's genitals until after her death. For more on the "scientific" debate surrounding Baartman's labia, see Fausto-Sterling, "Gender, Race, and Nation," 81–82.

5 Singer, "Reclaiming Venus," 89.

6 For more on the racialized practices of photography, see Wallis, "Black Bodies, White Science"; Hight and Sampson, *Colonialist Photography*; Ryan, *Picturing Empire*; Rogers and Blight, *Delia's Tears*; Shawn Michelle Smith, *Photography on the Color Line*.

7 I refer to the "Hottentot Venus story" (rather than to the "Saartjie Baartman story") to be mindful of the ways that retellings of the story often elide Baartman's biography, the complex ways that Baartman's racial identity was interpreted in different sites, and even the fact that the term *Hottentot Venus* was used to describe multiple people. As Kianga Ford notes, after Baartman's death, another "Hottentot Venus" was popular with European audiences: "This second Venus, whose name is not so readily available in the annals of history as is Baartman's, would be followed by a host of figurative successors for whom the designation Hottentot Venus would operate not as a reference to the particularity of an individual, but to a category and criteria of (e)valuation" ("Playing with Venus," 100).

8 Hershini Young notes, "Her gaze does not allow for modesty or for shame at her nakedness but instead directly challenges the viewer—look at me, look at my body, and look at the imperial specters that have dictated how I have traditionally been viewed" (*Haunting Capital*, 5).

9 "After Hot-En-Tot: A Conversation with Artist Renee Cox," Spelman College Museum of Fine Art, 22 October 2009. Accessed 13 June 2013. http://www.youtube.com/watch?v=IzcNulmKf6o.

10 Hobson, *Venus in the Dark*, 69.

11 Hobson, *Venus in the Dark*, 69.

12 Ford, "Playing with Venus," 100.

13 Henderson, *Scarring the Black Body*, 7. On protectionism, see Lee, *Erotic Revolutionaries*, xii.

14 Gopinath, *Impossible Desires*, 15–16.

15 See, for example, Christian, "The Race for Theory"; duCille, *Skin Trade*; Patricia J. Williams, *Alchemy of Race and Rights*.

16 Christian, "The Race for Theory," 336.

17 Patricia Hill Collins, *Black Feminist Thought*, 8, 13. For more on the centrality of *Black Feminist Thought* to black feminism's formation as an institutionalized field, see Nash, "'Home Truths' on Intersectionality." Collins elaborates on her interest in standpoint epistemology in her now seminal article "Learning from the Outsider Within."

18 Patricia Hill Collins, *Black Feminist Thought*, 2d ed., 3.

19 See King, "Multiple Jeopardy, Multiple Consciousness," 42–72.

20 Patricia Hill Collins, *Black Feminist Thought*, 70.

21 Patricia Hill Collins, *Black Feminist Thought*, 69.

22 See hooks, *Black Looks*; Patricia Hill Collins, *Black Feminist Thought*, 93.

23 Patricia Hill Collins, *Black Feminist Thought*, 93.

24 Patricia Hill Collins, *Black Feminist Thought*, 96.

25 Collins's pages on pornography have been anthologized in a number of anti-pornography anthologies including *Making Violence Sexy, Gender Violence: Interdisciplinary Perspectives*, and *Violence against Women: The Bloody Footprints*.

26 See Gilman, "Black Bodies, White Bodies."

27 T. Denean Sharpley-Whiting notes that "it was this riveting attribute, 'large as a cauldron pot,' as one bawdy English ballad attests, that Europeans paid to see" (*Black Venus*, 18). Crais and Scully, *Sara Baartman and the Hottentot Venus*, 73.

28 To avoid the continued circulation of this image, I have chosen not to reproduce this comic. Readers who are interested in seeing this image will find that it is widely available. See, for example, Hobson, *Venus in the Dark*, 38.

29 Sharpley-Whiting, *Black Venus*, 21.

30 Gilman, "Black Bodies, White Bodies," 219.

31 In an underexplored portion of Gilman's article, he argues that connections were also drawn between black female sexuality and lesbian sexuality. Gilman's analysis of gynecological textbooks from the 1870s—particularly Billroth's *Handbook of Gynecological Diseases*—suggests that the Hottentot was presumed to have an overdeveloped clitoris, often leading to sexual excesses, including lesbianism. He writes, "The concupiscence of the black is thus associated also with the sexuality of the lesbian" (Gilman, "Black Bodies, White Bodies," 218). Gilman goes on to argue that the same "physical anomalies" which permitted scientists to link the Hottentot to lesbianism also allowed them to link the Hottentot to prostitution. "Both [lesbians and prostitutes] are seen as possessing the physical

signs which set them apart from the normal" (Gilman, "Black Bodies, White Bodies," 226). Thanks to Emily Owens, whose work insightfully draws out these connections.

32 Qureshi, "Displaying Sara Baartman," 241.

33 Fausto-Sterling, "Gender, Race, and Nation," 224.

34 Qureshi, "Displaying Sara Baartman," 242.

35 Sharpley-Whiting, Black Venus, 29.

36 Baartman's remains were returned to South Africa in 2002.

37 Gilman, "Black Bodies, White Bodies," 206.

38 Zine Magubane points to this when she describes the "veritable theoretical industry" that has emerged around Baartman ("Whose Bodies Matter?," 817.)

39 Patricia Hill Collins, Black Feminist Thought, 137.

40 Patricia Hill Collins, Black Feminist Thought, 136.

41 Patricia Hill Collins, Black Feminist Thought, 138.

42 Patricia Hill Collins, Black Feminist Thought, 138.

43 Patricia Hill Collins, Black Feminist Thought, 137.

44 Patricia Hill Collins, Black Feminist Thought, 141.

45 Patricia Hill Collins, Black Feminist Thought, 140, 136.

46 Patricia Hill Collins, Black Feminist Thought, 142.

47 See MacKinnon, Only Words.

48 Patricia Hill Collins, Black Feminist Thought, 136–37.

49 See MacKinnon, Only Words.

50 Spillers et al., "'Whatcha Gonna Do?,'" 300.

51 I talk more about the Barnard Conference in the introduction. The conference papers are now anthologized in Pleasure and Danger: Exploring Female Sexuality.

52 Spillers et al., "'Whatcha Gonna Do?,'" 301.

53 Sharpe, Monstrous Intimacies, 4.

54 Spillers, "Mama's Baby, Papa's Maybe," 206.

55 Spillers, "Mama's Baby, Papa's Maybe," 206.

56 Spillers, "Interstices," 155.

57 Spillers, "Mama's Baby, Papa's Maybe," 206.

58 This echoes Anthony Paul Farley's work, which I discuss in greater detail in chapter 3.

59 Spillers, "Interstices," 155.

60 Chaney, Fugitive Vision, 63.

61 Spillers, "Interstices," 165.

62 Spillers, "Interstices," 166, emphasis in original.

63 Hobson, Venus in the Dark, 2.

64 Hobson, Venus in the Dark, 1.

65 Hobson, Venus in the Dark, 57.

66 Hobson, *Venus in the Dark*, 1.

67 Hobson, *Venus in the Dark*, 13.

68 Hobson, *Venus in the Dark*, 15.

69 Fleetwood, *Troubling Vision*, 13.

70 Fleetwood, *Troubling Vision*, 3.

71 Fleetwood, *Troubling Vision*, 2.

72 Fleetwood, *Troubling Vision*, 118.

73 Fleetwood, *Troubling Vision*, 109.

74 I discuss the black feminist commitment to recovery, a fourth black feminist interpretative strategy, later in this chapter.

75 Fleetwood, *Troubling Vision*, 106.

76 Fleetwood, *Troubling Vision*, 112.

77 See, respectively, Hobson, *Venus in the Dark*, 15; Powell, *Cutting a Figure*, 221; Singer, "Reclaiming Venus," 94.

78 Bennett and Dickerson, *Recovering the Black Female Body*, 13.

79 Fleetwood, *Troubling Vision*, 109.

80 The art historian Richard J. Powell suggest that the image's title is significant in translation. Powell reveals that the image's title translates from German as "Go, in Death," revealing the haunting conclusion of Baartman's short life. The variety of meanings embedded even in Cox's title suggest the complex connections the image draws between the historical past and the present.

81 Magubane, "Which Bodies Matter?," 822.

82 Magubane, "Which Bodies Matter?," 822.

83 Magubane, "Which Bodies Matter?," 823.

84 Carrie Mae Weems employs similar strategies in her *Here I Saw What Happened and I Cried* series. Celeste-Marie Bernier describes Weems's work: "Weems' haunting late twentieth-century images of naked and scarred black women and men have their origins in a series of 'slave daguerreotypes' produced over one hundred and fifty years ago. . . . In these prints, Weems confronts this shocking and abusive history by drenching the bodies of Jack, Drana, Renty and Delia [the names of the enslaved subjects represented] in an ethereal blood-red glow, at the same time she inscribes white slogans across their chests. She thwarts voyeuristic inspections of her enslaved subjects by typing 'AN ANTHROPOLOGICAL DEBATE' over Jack's body, just as she inserts '& A PHOTOGRAPHIC SUBJECT' over the body of his daughter, Drana. . . . By juxtaposing text and image, she shows how a twentieth-century African American female artist can subvert, destabilise and negate nineteenth-century white male racist iconography" (Bernier, *African American Visual Arts*, 14–15).

85 Singer, "Reclaming Venus," 89.

86 Hershini Young, *Haunting Capital*, 5.

87 Singer, "Reclaming Venus," 89.

88 For examples of celebrations of Cox's work, see Ford, "Playing with Venus"; Fleetwood, *Troubling Vision*; Qureshi, "Displaying Sara Baartman." Readings of the Cox/Harris collaboration are quite different; Powell refers to Cox as Harris's "mannequin for (and procurer of) manufacuted breasts and buttocks" (Powell, *Cutting a Figure*, 198) and Priscilla Netto refers to the image as "revel[ing] in the authored and affirmative display of the Black body in all its sexual, racial and gender particularities" (Netto, "Reclaiming the Body of the 'Hottentot,'" 157).

89 Lisa Collins, "Economies of the Flesh," 100.

90 Lisa Collins, "Economies of the Flesh," 122, 103.

91 Lorde, *Sister Outsider*, 54.

92 Lorde, *Sister Outsider*, 55.

93 Shawn Michelle Smith, "Taking Another Look at Race," 7.

94 "Visible seam" is Nicole Fleetwood's term, which she uses to describe a "technique and a discursive intervention to address narrative erasure and to insert a troubling presence in dominant racializing structures" (*Troubling Vision*, 9).

95 Carla Williams, "Naked, Neutered, or Noble," 197.

2. Speaking Sex/Speaking Race

1 Light in the Attic Records and Productions, distributor of Bernard "Pretty" Purdie's *Lialeh* soundtrack, referred to Lialeh as the "black deep throat," analogizing it to the Golden Age classic film *Deep Throat* (dirs. Jim and Artie Mitchell, 1972). The film's cover describes *Lialeh* as "the first black XXX film ever made! Soulful Sounds! Soulful Sista's [sic]! Soulful sex! No holds barred . . . super sexy black action!" When scholars and critics refer to *Lialeh* as an all-black film, they are not ignoring the presence of white characters in the film. Instead, they are noting that all of the film's major characters are black.

2 Linda Williams, *Hard Core*, 2.

3 Constance Penley describes the Golden Age as a moment of "big-budget, theatrically released, feature-length narrative films like *Behind the Green Door* (dir. Mitchell Bros., 1972), *The Opening of Misty Beethoven* (dir. Radley Metzger, 1975), *The Resurrection of Eve* (dir. Mitchell Bros., 1973), and *The Story of Joanna* (dir. Gerard Damiano, 1975). In an era in which the makers of adult films were trying to respond at once to the sexual revolution, women's lib, and the possibility of expanding their demographics beyond the raincoat brigade and fraternal lodge members, the narratives began to center, albeit very anxiously, around the woman and her sexual odyssey" ("Crackers and Whackers," 320). For more on the place of narrative in hard-core pornography, see Linda Williams, *Hard Core*, 120–52.

4 For more on blaxploitation, see Sieving, *Soul Searching*; Koven, *Blaxploitation Films*; Lawrence, *Blaxploitation Films of the 1970s*; Grant, *Post-Soul Black Cinema*; Darius James, *That's Blaxploitation!*; Martinez, Martinez, and Chavez, *What It Is . . . What It Was!*; Howard, *Blaxploitation Cinema*; Guerrero, *Framing Blackness*; Massood, *Black City Cinema*.

5 Linda Williams, "Why I Did Not Want to Write This Essay," 1264. The issue of *Signs* that includes Williams's essay is dedicated to feminist media scholarship that moves beyond the gaze.

6 See Diawara, "Black Spectatorship"; hooks, *Black Looks*; Bobo, "Reading through the Text," 272. Janell Hobson envisions hooks's concept of the oppositional gaze as a way of seeing that "probes, revises, and inspires to see differently. It hints at the possibilities of interpreting the world, and in this context, the world of cinema—as white identified and male oriented as it often is—through an empowered sense of pleasure and looking" ("Viewing in the Dark," 54). Hobson and hooks are not alone in making these claims. Manthia Diawara draws on Mulvey's work to argue that black bodies are rendered "to-be-looked-at" objects by the cinema, requiring black spectators to actively reinterpret cinema to take pleasure in looking. It is precisely because black subjects exist in the visual field for "the pleasure of White spectators" that blacks develop positions of resistant spectatorship where they "transform . . . the problem of passive identification into active criticism which both informs and interrelates with contemporary oppositional filmmaking" (Diawara, "Black Spectatorship," 219).

The "oppositional" black spectator has also been theorized in texts which are not explicitly engaged in a feminist analysis. For example, Anna Everett's historical analysis of black film criticism argues that "it is a little known fact that at least from 1909 onward, African Americans regularly returned the motion picture camera's often distorting gaze by scrutinizing the medium closely, vigilantly, and forcefully, and by publishing their criticisms and observations in the extensive network of publications that make up the black press" (*Returning the Gaze*, 1).

7 hooks, *Black Looks*, 126. "Eating the other" is the term bell hooks used to describe white subjects' consumption of racially marked others.

8 hooks, *Black Looks*, 118.

9 Patricia Hill Collins, *Black Feminist Thought*, 93. I call these "dominant" texts to differentiate them from texts authored by black women.

10 Bobo, "Reading through the Text," 272.

11 Bobo, "Reading through the Text," 272.

12 Bobo, "Reading through the Text," 273.

13 Bobo, "Reading through the Text," 285.

14 Bobo, "Reading through the Text," 286.

15 For more on stag films, see Di Lauro and Rabkin, *Dirty Movies*; Linda Williams, "'White Slavery' versus the Ethnography of 'Sexworkers'"; Waugh, "Homosociality in the Classical American Stag Film."

16 While I emphasize the legal shifts that enabled the Golden Age, other scholars underscore technological changes. See Schaefer, "Gauging a Revolution."

17 Miller-Young, "A Taste for Brown Sugar," 117.

18 See, for example, Delany, *Times Square Red, Times Square Blue*.

19 Linda Williams, *Screening Sex*, 132.

20 I borrow the phrase "education of desire" from Ann Laura Stoler's work. *Deep Throat* particularly contained "education" about fellatio. As Linda Williams notes, "Fellatio was certainly not invented by the generation of the seventies but, hard as it might be to recall this in the post-Monica Lewinsky era, neither was it a sex act that before *Deep Throat* and the era of porno chic had much mainstream public recognition" (*Screening Sex*, 137).

21 Linda Williams, *Screening Sex*, 127.

22 Linda Williams, *Screening Sex*, 127.

23 Bogle, *Blacks in American Film and Television*, 185.

24 Blaxploitation also drew on the exploitation film tradition. For more on exploitation films, see Quarles, *Down and Dirty*; Jaworzyn, *Shock*; Clark, *At a Theater or Drive-in Near You*. The singer Curtis Mayfield's work on the *Super Fly* soundtrack and Isaac Hayes's version of *Shaft*'s theme song demonstrate blaxploitation's interest in crafting catchy, engaging soundtracks. As blaxploitation developed, it also featured black heroines. For more on the blaxploitation heroine, see Sims, *Women of Blaxploitation*; Dunn, "Baad Bitches" and *Sassy Supermamas*; Brody, "The Returns of 'Cleopatra Jones'"; Smith-Shomade, "Rock-a-Bye, Baby!"

25 While theorizing blaxploitation as a cinematic formation with particular genre conventions, I am also attentive to the variety within the genre. While many scholars have imagined blaxploitation films as commercial, mainstream cinematic formations, Tommy Lott's work underscores the fact that many blaxploitation films "were not commercially oriented" and that some were "very worthwhile from a social and political standpoint. To reduce them all to the hero formula . . . is to overlook their many differences in style, audience orientation, and political content" ("A No-Theory Theory of Contemporary Black Cinema," 86).

26 This was echoed by the film's dedication to "all of the black brothers and sisters who have had enough of The Man."

27 Koven, *Blaxploitation Films*, 14–15.

28 Junius Griffin, quoted in Guerrero, *Framing Blackness*, 101.

29 Mireille Miller-Young notes that this opening sequence "places it [*Lialeh*] squarely within the black film movement of the early 1970s in the way that it references

scenes like Curtis Mayfield's performance of 'Pusher Man' on the stage in the club scene in *Super Fly*" ("A Taste for Brown Sugar," 136). While Miller-Young underscores the resonance between *Lialeh* and *Super Fly*, *Lialeh*'s lengthy opening score, coupled with the introduction to the male protagonist through the urban landscape, suggests that *Lialeh* also explicitly references *Shaft* to secure its status as a blaxploitation film. Also significant about this opening scene is that it alerts the spectator, particularly the contemporary spectator, to the technical limitations of the film. The grainy quality makes it difficult to see the urban landscape with any great detail, and the muffled and often muted sound can render it difficult to discern what the actors are saying.

30 According to Linda Williams, "maximum visibility" has "operated in different ways at different stages of the genre's history: to privilege close-ups of body parts over other shots, to overlight easily obscured genitals; to select sexual positions that show the most of bodies and organs; and, later, to create generic conventions, such as the variety of sexual 'numbers' or the externally ejaculating penis—so important to the 1970s feature-length manifestation of the genre" (*Hard Core*, 48–49).

31 Part of the appeal (and controversy) surrounding *Behind the Green Door* was that actress Marilyn Chambers had been a model for Procter & Gamble and had appeared as the Ivory Soap spokeswoman. Once the movie was released, Procter & Gamble recalled all of their products that contained her image. For more on *Behind the Green Door*, see Williams, *Hard Core*, 156–60.

32 The unnamed black man in *Behind the Green Door* is the actor Johnnie Keyes, whom I discuss in greater detail in chapter 3.

33 Linda Williams notes that the interracial scene in *Behind the Green Door* is "the first American feature-length hard-core film to include a major interracial sex scene" ("Skin Flicks on the Racial Border," 299).

34 Linda Williams, *Hard Core*, 48–49.

35 Bogle, *Blacks in American Film and Television*, 133.

36 Miller-Young, "A Taste for Brown Sugar," 142.

37 Linda Williams, *Screening Sex*, 341 n. 54.

38 See Davis, *Women, Race, and Class.*

39 Linda Williams, *Hard Core*, 93.

40 Wlodarz, "Beyond the Black Macho," 10.

41 This is epitomized by the figure of the femme fatale.

42 For more on the complexity of identification, see Wilcox, "Cross-Gender Identification in Commercial Pornographic Films."

43 Miller-Young, "A Taste for Brown Sugar," 139.

44 Miller-Young, "A Taste for Brown Sugar," 139.

45 There has been extensive feminist debate about the dildo and whether it is merely

a phallic substitute or a "sex toy . . . [with] an authentic place in the history of lesbian subculture" (Findlay, "Freud's 'Fetishism' and the Lesbian Dildo Debates," 564). Findlay's essay offers an excellent articulation of the history of this debate.

3. Race-Pleasures

1 Anthony Spinelli was Samuel Weinstein's pseudonym; Spinelli is part of a pornographic film family (his son is Mitchell Spinelli, who has directed several films, including *Taped College Confessions*). Anthony Spinelli was inducted into the AVN Hall of Fame in 1986, and won AVN awards for best director in 1985 and 1993.

2 *Sexworld*'s premise was familiar to its late 1970s viewer because it was explicitly based on *Westworld* (dir. Michael Crichton, 1973), a commercially successful Hollywood film. In Crichton's *Westworld*, tourists travel to historical fantasy lands—Medieval World, Roman World, or West World—and experience the pleasure of inhabiting mythologized versions of times past. These fantastical pasts are populated by robots, machines that lack the capacity to feel pain and pleasure, and are thus the perfect companions for human tourists, who can inflict their desires and wishes on these human replicas. However, the very machines that enable guests to enjoy the pleasure of inhabiting the past become the source of the film's dramatic tension when the robots populating the fantastical West World begin to malfunction, culminating in a duel between a robot and two tourists who mistake the battle for a continuation of their historical fantasy.

3 Linda Williams is one of the first scholars to read *Behind the Green Door* as an interracial film. See Williams, *Hard Core*.

4 When scholars have written about interracial pornography, they have tended to focus on the black male–white female configuration, implicitly reifying the idea that "interracialism" requires a particular gendered configuration of bodies. See, for example, Linda Williams, "Skin Flicks on the Racial Border."

5 Farley, "The Black Body as Fetish Object," 506, emphasis in original.

6 MacKinnon, *Feminism Unmodified*, 8.

7 The idea of productive shame has permeated scholarship emerging out of queer theory for decades. Emblematic of this approach is Leo Bersani's canonical essay "Is the Rectum a Grave?," which advocates reading "shameful" queer sex acts as sites for a radical casting off of the self. Bersani, writing at the height of the AIDS epidemic, argues that much in the way nineteenth-century prostitutes were imagined to be carriers of illness (syphilis), twentieth-century gay men were also imagined to be carriers of illness (AIDS). Yet, instead of rejecting the shaming of the queer sex act, Bersani seeks to locate the redemptive potential of queer sex, seeing in queer sex the possibility of overcoming the self. To that

end, he writes: "Gay men's 'obsession' with sex, far from being denied, should be celebrated. . . . Male homosexuality advertises the risk of the sexual itself as the risk of self-dismissal, of *losing sight* of the self, and in so doing it proposes and dangerously represents jouissannce as a mode of ascesis" ("Is the Rectum a Grave?," 222). Similarly, Douglas Crimp actively reclaims the "shameful" practice of "promiscuity," casting it as a kind of queer ethic, a creative remaking of sex in response to AIDS. Crimp writes, "Gay people invented safe sex. We knew that the alternatives—monogamy and abstinence—were unsafe. . . . Our promiscuity taught us many things, not only about the pleasures of sex, but about the great multiplicity of those pleasures" ("How to Have Promiscuity in an Epidemic," 64). Other scholars have been quite critical of the role of "shame" in queer politics. Patrick Moore, for example, argues that "gay shame" has obscured gay history, disconnecting the (post)modern queer subject from his queer predecessors. Moore notes: "We are a community of shame. Shame defines our view of a sexual past that segued into AIDS, confirming to us our worst fears about ourselves and lending the condemnation of bigots a truthful echo. Shame motivates our forward movement as we fearfully suppress images of gay people as sexual beings, encouraging instead non-threatening roles (parent, homeowner, or campy friend) that prove 'we're just like you.' In our community of shame, we believe that by actively forgetting the past we can erase it, and many important parts of our legacy are now being lost or willfully abandoned" (*Beyond Shame*, xxi–xxii). Other critics of the "gay shame" scholarship have suggested that it focuses on a queer white male subject. Judith Halberstam notes: "Shame for women and shame for people of color plays out in different ways and creates different modes of abjection, marginalization, and self-abnegation; it also leads to very different political strategies. While female shame can be countered by feminism and racialized shame can be countered by what Rod Ferguson calls 'queer of color critique,' it is white gay male shame that has proposed 'pride' as the appropriate remedy and that focuses its libidinal and other energies on simply rebuilding the self that shame dismantled rather than taking apart the social processes that project shame onto queer subjects in the first place" ("Shame and White Gay Masculinity," 223–24).

8 Stockton, *Beautiful Bottom, Beautiful Shame*, 24.

9 Stockton, *Beautiful Bottom, Beautiful Shame*, 104, 2.

10 Darieck Scott, *Extravagant Abjection*, 9.

11 Weiss, *Techniques of Pleasure*, 200–201.

12 Omi and Winant, *Racial Formations in the United States*, 60.

13 Butler, "Performative Acts and Gender Constitution," 531.

14 Butler, "Endangered/Endangering: Schematic Racism and White Paranoia," 20.

15 I addressed the relationship between speaking sex and speaking race in more

detail in chapter 2. My thinking about the relationship between race and pleasure here is informed by Shimizu, *The Hypersexuality of Race*.

16 Miller-Young, "A Taste for Brown Sugar," 146–47.

17 Miller-Young, "A Taste for Brown Sugar," 146.

18 Miller-Young, "A Taste for Brown Sugar," 146.

19 See Shimizu's *Hypersexuality of Race* for more on the trope of racialized bodies' "hypersexuality."

20 I discuss the interracial scene in *Behind the Green Door* in greater detail in chapter 2.

21 This fetishization of the money shot is, of course, not something found only in *Behind the Green Door*. Linda Williams notes that *Deep Throat*, the film which comically located the female protagonist's clitoris in her throat, was instrumental in making fellatio "the privileged figure for the expression of climax and satisfaction (reaching, in fact, a kind of apotheosis in *Behind the Green Door*, made later that same year)" (*Hard Core*, 111).

22 My thinking on aural pornographic pleasures is informed by Corbett and Kapsalis, "Aural Sex."

23 Linda Williams, "Skin Flicks on the Racial Border," 300.

24 In critiquing the tendency to pathologize black pleasures, I am inspired by Daryl Scott's work on "damage imagery," in *Contempt and Pity*.

25 Foucault, "The Ethic of Care for the Self as a Practice of Freedom," 113.

4. Laughing Matters

1 MacKinnon, *Only Words*, 17.

2 While I view pornography and comedy as intimately related genres, other scholars have mapped out their relationship differently. Linda Williams famously analyzed the similar genre conventions of three seemingly "low" sites of cultural production: pornography, melodrama, and horror. Williams terms these three "body genres," as all represent the body—usually the female body—"in the grip of intense sensation or emotion" or depict the body as " 'beside itself' with sexual pleasure, fear and terror, or overpowering sadness" ("Film Bodies," 269). Moreover, body genres seek to extract a physical response from their spectators: ejaculate (in the case of pornography), tears (in the case of the melodrama, or "weepie"), and screams (in the case of the horror). Since comedy also seeks to extract a physical response—laughter—from its spectator, and often displays the body "beside itself"—either in laughter or in absurd gesture—comedy is surprisingly absent from Williams's formulation of body genres. Williams defends the exclusion of comedy by arguing that body genres are marked by "the perception that the body of the spectator is caught up in an almost involuntary mimicry of the emotions or sensation of the body on the screen along with the

fact that the body displayed is female" ("Film Bodies," 270). However, if body genres are defined by the body-as-spectacle and by the genre's desire to elicit something—ejaculate, tears, screams, or laughter—from the body of the spectator, then perhaps comedy is also a body genre, one where the spectator and protagonist are in an uneasy alliance. For more on pornography and humor, see Lehman, "Twin Cheeks, Twin Peaks, and Twin Freaks." For examples of porn parodies, see *Pulp Friction* (dir. Anthony Spinelli, 1994), *Twin Cheeks* (dir. Henri Pachard, 1990), *Beaverly Hills Cop* (dir. Adam, 1985), *The Flintbones* (dir. Mad Dad Don, 1992), *White Men Can Hump* (dir. Anthony Spinelli, 1992), and *The Sheets of San Francisco* (dir. Scotty Fox, 1986).

3 Kipnis, *Bound and Gagged*, 167.

4 For both Kipnis and Constance Penley, porn humor is fundamentally connected to the genre's unrelenting affection for the low.

5 Waugh, "Homosociality in the Classical American Stag Film," 32.

6 See Constance Penley's work for more on this.

7 Waugh, "Homosociality in the Classical American Stag Film," 32. Linda Williams's *Screening Sex* offers an in-depth reading of *Deep Throat*'s narrative twists.

8 For more on the relationship between pornography and cable television, see Juffer, *At Home with Pornography*.

9 Peter Lehman's work offers a vivid example of this: the pornographic film *Twin Cheeks*, for example, explicitly references David Lynch's and Mark Frost's non-pornographic television series *Twin Peaks*. See Lehman, "Twin Cheeks, Twin Peaks, and Twin Freaks."

10 Lehman, "Twin Cheeks, Twin Peaks, and Twin Freaks," 90.

11 Lehman, "Twin Cheeks, Twin Peaks, and Twin Freaks," 90.

12 Penley, "Crackers and Whackers," 320.

13 Penley, "Crackers and Whackers," 324.

14 Carpio talks about this tightrope, in *Laughing Fit to Kill*, 71.

15 Here I am thinking of Carpio, *Laughing Fit to Kill*, and Haggins, *Laughing Mad*.

16 Carpio, *Laughing Fit to Kill*, 12.

17 Gordon, *Ghostly Matters*, 195. "Queer time" is borrowed from Judith Halberstam's work, which argues that "queer uses of time and space develop, at least in part, in opposition to the institutions of family, heterosexuality, and reproduction. They also develop according to other logics of location, movement, and identification" (*In a Queer Time and Place*, 1). My thinking on race and temporality is also informed by David Eng's *The Feeling of Kinship*.

18 My thinking is informed by Anthony Paul Farley's brilliant insight: "Slavery is white-over-black to white-over-black to white-over-black, and that continually. Whether white-over-black appears before us as slavery or as segregation or as neosegregation is not at all important. All three haunts, slavery, segregation and

neosegregation, present us with the same death, white-over-black, that we have all already died" ("When the Stars Begin to Fall," 226).

19 Taussig argues that "the most important social knowledge" is often constituted by a "public secret," that which we "know . . . not to know" (*Defacement*, 2).

20 Ronald Reagan, "Remarks on Signing the Child Protection Act of 1984," University of Texas, Austin, Ronald Reagan Presidential Library, accessed 26 January 2012, www.reagan.utexas.edu/archives/speeches/1984/52184b.htm.

21 Linda Williams, *Hard Core*, 15–16.

22 Strub, *Perversion for Profit*, 180.

23 Strossen, *Defending Pornography*, 19.

24 I do not view the Silver Age as a plotless era, as others do. Eric Schaefer, for example, argues that "what has become increasingly evident is that the feature-length hardcore narrative [of the Golden Age] was merely an entr'acte between reels of essentially plotless underground stag movies . . . and the similarly plotless ruttings of porn in the video age" ("Gauging a Revolution," 4). Instead, I view the Silver Age as an era in which the tremendous preoccupation with narrative coherency (and with crafting films that resembled mainstream feature films) declined; that is, what Silver Age films feature are less elaborately designed plots.

25 Susie Bright, "Inter-racial and Black Videos," 1986, *Susie Bright's Journal* (blog), accessed 25 February 2011, www.susiebright.blogs.com/Inter-RacialandBlack Videos.pdf.

26 See Susie Bright, "Inter-racial and Black Videos," 1986, *Susie Bright's Journal* (blog), accessed 25 February 2011, www.susiebright.blogs.com/Inter-RacialandBlack Videos.pdf.

27 Martin, "Never Laugh at a Man with His Pants Down," 192.

28 For more on this, see my discussion of male-male pleasure in *Lialeh* in chapter 2. Stephen Ziplow's checklist of sexual acts that a hard-core film should include advocates ménage à trois, but he notes, "It seems to go without saying that while two female members of such a configuration may involve themselves with each other, it is taboo for two men to do so in heterosexual hard core" (qtd. in Linda Williams, *Hard Core*, 127).

29 While *Black Taboo*'s narrative investment in representing incest, a genre which pornographers call taboo, a host of literary scholars have examined the long tradition of pairing representations of incest and representations of miscegenation. See Sollors, *Neither Black nor White yet Both*; Bauman, "'Incestuous Sheets' and 'Adulterate Beasts.'"

Claude Lévi-Strauss describes the incest taboo as a social prohibition designed to promote exogamy: "Exchange . . . provides the means of binding men together, and of superimposing upon the natural links of kinship the henceforth artificial links—artificial in the sense that they are removed form chance encounters or the promiscuity of family life—of alliance governed by rule" (*The Elementary Structures of Kinship*, 480). Feminist rewritings of the incest taboo have envisioned this prohibition on endogamy as a deeply gendered one that relies on the exchange of women. Gayle Rubin argues that the exchange of women between unrelated families through marriage enables partnerships between unrelated people, conferring on men the "quasi-mystical power of social linkage" ("Thinking Sex," 174).

30 Morreall, "The Rejection of Humor in Western Thought," 243.

31 See Corbett and Kapsalis, "Aural Sex." They argue, "Where male sexual pleasure is accompanied by what Williams calls the 'frenzy of the visible,' female sexual pleasure is better thought of in terms of a 'frenzy of the audible.' Sound becomes the proof of female pleasure in the absence of its clear visual determination" (103).

32 Of course, we all fail to comply with the normative—see Michael Warner, *Trouble with Normal*—yet "normalcy" and normativity continue to maintain a hold. In representing black bodies' failure to comply with the normative, *Black Taboo* made light of black bodies' imagined deviance in a moment, like many others, where blackness was already culturally constructed as a sexually taboo formation. In 1984, Health and Human Services Secretary Margaret Heckler announced the "discovery" of HIV, and assured the public of the availability of an HIV vaccine within two to three years. With the "discovery" of HIV, and given omnipresent concerns about the virus's geographical and cultural origins, the "4-Hs"—"homosexuals, heroin addicts, hemophiliacs, and Haitians"—were singled out as disease vectors. Black bodies, along with a host of other bodies, were thus marked as deviant, as subjects whose nonnormative, taboo sexual practices posed a larger public danger.

Cathy Cohen echoes this notion: "Undoubtedly, the lack of action [in response to AIDS] from the general public on down to the president, was and is directly tied to the conception of AIDS as a disease of white gay men, black and Latino/a drug users, and other marginal people engaged in 'immoral behavior'" (*Boundaries of Blackness*, 20). Sander Gilman discusses the so-called 4-Hs in his article "AIDS and Syphilis."

33 *Black Taboo* ostensibly invites its spectator to reread the film's earlier scenes; however, this rereading happens in a confusing context, as the film's final lines are breathy and, at times, inaudible, which could allow willing spectators to continue to believe in the film's incest narrative. I contend that the film's final lines only partially allow the film to circumvent incest, but Bill Margold, Drea's assistant director, insists that *Black Taboo* circumvents incest entirely. In fact, Margold claims that sex between sisters does not constitute incest (he does not comment

on sex between in-laws or between uncles and nieces). Bill Margold, personal interview, 16 October 2007. My reading of Margold's claim is that he further amplifies the flirtation with incest that the film enacts: the boundaries of what constitutes incest are unclear in his film, leaving space for the film to act both as an incest film and as a nearly incest film simultaneously, depending on how a spectator interprets the final sexual number.

34 Miller-Young, "A Taste for Brown Sugar," 210.

35 My understanding of the relationship between race and visibility is indebted to Judith Butler's "Endangered/Endangering."

36 Miller-Young, "A Taste for Brown Sugar," 210.

37 Linda Williams, "Skin Flicks on the Racial Border," 286.

38 In some ways, this reflects the problem of metonymy that I describe in chapter 1.

39 Carpio, Laughing Fit to Kill, 13.

40 Carpio, Laughing Fit to Kill, 13.

41 Laura Mulvey's early intervention in feminist film theory, "Visual Pleasure and Narrative Cinema" (1992), placed identification at the heart of cinema's imagined pleasures. In the years following publication of that essay, identification has been taken up by a number of scholars, including Hansen, "Pleasure, Ambivalence, Identification"; Briefel, "Monster Pains"; Manlove, "Visual 'Drive' and Cinematic Narrative."

42 Some of this might be attributed, at least in part, to prevailing anxieties about America's failure in Vietnam. Jerry Lembcke notes that "the loss of the war is experienced as a loss of masculinity, leading the male imagination to visualize the enemy that defeated him as his gendered 'other'" ("Post-Vietnam Masculinity," 621).

5. On Refusal

1 The film's promise of black women, rather than black men, is implicit in the title. While queer pornographic films are usually rhetorically marked by the explicit promise of queer sex in the title of the film, the fact that Black Throat promises black women's throats, however, does not foreclose the possibility that the film was (and still is) consumed and enjoyed by queer consumers, female consumers, and nonwhite male consumers.

2 The collaborators Gregory Dark and Walter Dark (Walter Gernert's pseudonym), together known as the Dark Brothers, directed a number of successful pornographic films in the 1980s, including New Wave Hookers (1985), Between the Cheeks (1985), and Deep Inside Vanessa del Rio (1986). Since then, Gregory Dark has become a mainstream music video director for artists including Britney Spears and Snoop Dogg. He also directed the mainstream films See No Evil (2006) and Little

Fish, Strange Pond (2008). Though I have purposefully downplayed biographies of pornographic film producers in this volume, I introduce the Dark Brothers here because the controversy surrounding their work, particularly their racialized pornographic films, is central to understanding the particularities (and peculiarities) of the Silver Age racialized market.

3 Petkovich, *The X Factory*, 43. For more information on the Dark Brothers, see Tom Junod, "The Devil in Greg Dark," *Esquire*, 1 February 2001, accessed 20 January 2012, www.esquire.com/ESQ0201-FEB_Greg_Dark_rev.

4 In 1986, federal authorities learned that Traci Lords, who had claimed to be twenty-two years old, had in fact only been sixteen when she appeared in a number of X-rated videos.

5 For more on the Traci Lords case, see *United States v. X-Citement Video, Inc.* 513 US 64 (1994), and Strub, *Perversion for Profit*.

6 For more on the plot of *Let Me Tell Ya 'bout Black Chicks*, see Miller-Young, "Let Me Tell Ya 'bout Black Chicks."

7 The Klan scene in *Let Me Tell Ya 'bout Black Chicks* is not without historical precedent. Linda Williams's work on the stag film archive at the Kinsey Institute, which I reference in the book's introduction, reveals the presence of at least one other Klan film, *KKK Night Riders* (circa 1930s), which "portrays a corpulent white Klansmen in full dress, including hood, who invades the cabin of a black woman and forces her to have sex at knife point" ("'White Slavery' versus the Ethnography of 'Sexworkers,'" 125). What seems to distinguish *Let Me Tell Ya 'bout Black Chicks* is that its black female protagonist, as is the quintessential pornographic fantasy, locates pleasure in the interaction with the hooded Klansmen.

8 Attorney General's Commission on Pornography: Final Report, July 1986, part 2, chapter 1, "The Commission and Its Mandate," accessed 19 February 2011, www.porn-report.com/contents.htm. It is noteworthy how much the language the Meese Report adopts resonates with the language of the antipornography ordinance that MacKinnon and Dworkin proposed.

9 Attorney General's Commission on Pornography: Final Report, July 1986, part 2, chapter 5, section 5.2.1, "Sexually Violent Material" and section 5.2.2, "Nonviolent Materials Depicting Degradation, Domination, Subordination, or Humiliation," accessed 19 February 2011, www.porn-report.com/contents.htm. Linda Williams notes, "The 1986 commission . . . appointed by Ronald Reagan and dominated by moral majority conservatives, came to the overwhelming conclusion that hard-core pornography is violence" (*Hard Core*, 16).

10 See chapter 1 for more on proposed antipornography legislation.

11 Linda Williams, *Porn Studies*, 304 n. 7.

12 Russell Hampshire, president of VCA, later spent time in jail on obscenity charges. As a testament to how technology changes pornography's circulation

and reception, with the advent of the Internet, one can easily access copies of *Black Chicks* online.

13 Other scholars have also worked on racialized pornography's interest in exploring black men's difference. See, for example, Dines, "The White Man's Burden."

14 Muñoz, *Disidentifications*, 80.

15 Hansen, Needham, and Nichols, "Pornography, Ethnography, and the Discourses of Power," 209–10.

16 Hansen, Needham, and Nichols, "Pornography, Ethnography, and the Discourses of Power," 211. A number of scholars have been particularly interested in linking ethnopornography to Saartjie Baartmann. Janell Hobson notes that "such 'educational' display of black bodies, linked to pornography, spawned an underground market for this racialized desire and an erotically suppressed reading of such nudity. . . . When this colonial historic imagery combines with the more familiar American popular iconography of desexualized, fully clothed mammy images and celebratory imagery of white female beauty, we may be able to more fully comprehend interstices between race and gender that shape our uneasy responses to sexualized visual representations of black women" (*Venus in the Dark*, 119). Similarly, Brian Wallis notes, "The case of the Hottentot Venus marked the collapse of scientific investigation of the racial other into the realm of the pornographic" ("Black Bodies, White Science," 54).

17 Hansen, Needham, and Nichols, "Pornography, Ethnography, and the Discourses of Power," 212.

18 Linda Williams, *Hard Core*, 48.

19 Linda Williams, *Hard Core*, 49.

20 The artist Carrie Mae Weems's work includes images from Agassiz's daguerreotypes. As Wallis notes, "She did not alter or transform the images; she only selected, enlarged, and recontextualized them. By placing them beside pictures of remnants of the African culture the Gulla brought to America, Weems viewed their lives empathetically from a black point of view. She saw these men and women not as representatives of some typology but as living, breathing ancestors. She made them portraits" ("Black Bodies, White Science," 59).

21 Wallis, "Black Bodies, White Science," 54.

22 Interestingly, Shimizu also problematizes some of her investment in pornography's sameness narrative: "Since the facticity of racial difference may not register as visibly reliable, pornography finds ways to establish its titillation through production design and narrativization, such as in its intertitle texts or dialogue. These elements work to establish racial difference as the erotic meat of pornography" ("Making Woman Asian," 148).

23 Shimizu, "Making Woman Asian," 131. Shimizu notes that ostensibly Asian actresses were often actually white actresses in "yellowface." Shimizu's work

seems informed by a Foucauldian engagement with pornography. To that end, Shimizu imagines stag films as underpinned by a requirement that they show the truth of "the Asian woman." She notes that stag films must incessantly display the female Asian body because "it will not be enough to see her genitals—we must know that he [the male protagonist] is fucking an Asian woman whose body is different. And her body must be as whole as possible, almost totally included in the shot" ("Making Woman Asian," 141).

24 Shimizu, "Making Woman Asian," 164.

25 Shimizu, "Making Woman Asian," 164–65. Many queer scholars make similar claims about the pornographic "containment" of difference. Dwight McBride argues that queer pornography displays "virtual blackness," which he describes as "contained blackness," as "always there in different forms—including gay porn, as I have been discussing—for the taking, the watching, the pleasuring when one wants it. But because it is contained and virtual, there is no danger of it speaking back, objecting, calling you out, making demands, or not giving you exactly what you have come to expect from it—your fetishistic fulfillment" (Why I Hate Abercrombie and Fitch, 105).

26 Shimizu, The Hypersexuality of Race, 135.

27 The original version of Black Throat had a different beginning than the version I screened. According to The X-Rated Videotape Guide, in the film's original version, when Bob discovers that Roscoe has never received oral sex, Bob procures a woman (the actress Traci Lords) from a strip club to perform fellatio on Roscoe. After this initial fellatio scene, Roscoe and Jamal meet to find Mambo and her fabled fellatio. The early version of the film underscores the discovery of "inspirational fellatio" as central to the narrative of the film.

28 It is significant that Roscoe cannot pronounce fellatio (he calls it "fill-a-tee-o"), a detail that has the effect of introducing comedy to the narrative and of linking Roscoe's position as a working-class white man to a kind of sexual ignorance.

29 Fellatio has long held a privileged representational position in moving-image hard-core pornography. Golden Age films like Deep Throat and Behind the Green Door made use of "the most photogenic of all sexual practices" as a technical solution to the "problem" of how to best visually capture male pleasure (Linda Williams, Hard Core, 111). Representing fellatio solved this problem by making male ejaculation hypervisible, often as it streamed out of the female protagonist's mouth or covered her face. Black Throat drew on the long tradition of representing fellatio and coupled it with the pornographic obsession with representing racial difference, explicitly endeavoring to show Mambo's distinctively black, "divinely inspired" fellatio.

30 See Donalson, Masculinity in the Interracial Buddy Film; Brian Locke, Racial Stigma on the Hollywood Screen from World War II to the Present.

31 I do not talk extensively about the film's peculiar circularity here, but my understanding of it is informed by Judith Halberstam's work, which reads the film *Dude, Where's My Car?* and its circularity as "a useful tool for jamming the smooth operations of the normal and the ordinary. . . . Forgetfulness becomes a rupture with the eternally self-generating present, a break with a self-authorizing past, and an opportunity for a non-hetero-reproductive future" (*The Queer Art of Failure*, 70).

32 See Linda Williams, *Hard Core*.

33 Linda Williams, *Hard Core*, 151.

34 Linda Williams, *Hard Core*, 50.

35 Linda Williams, *Hard Core*, 111.

36 Donalson offers a striking interpretation of the interracial buddy film, noting that such films satisfy four conditions: first, they imply that "conflicts can find resolutions," that race can be undone through friendship; second, they "suggest that democracy and equal treatment have been obtained because it exists on the big screen"; third, they show that "the American capitalist system nurtures humanity and tolerance"; and fourth, they reveal that "men of all races share positions in the dominant power scheme" (*Masculinity in the Interracial Buddy Film*, 11).

37 Matt Wray and Annalee Newitz call "white trash" the "most visible and clearly marked form of whiteness" (*White Trash*, 4).

38 I discuss the notion that black masculinity is authentic and that white masculinity is effeminate and inauthentic in greater detail in chapter 2.

39 Linda Williams, "Skin Flicks on the Racial Border," 286–87.

40 Linda Williams, "Skin Flicks on the Racial Border," 297. Underpinning Williams's conception of the erotics of the interracial scene is a claim about the role of taboo in sexual desire and pleasure: "It is fear—the fear once generated by white masters to keep white women and black men apart—that gives erotic tension to interracial sex acts which in 'ordinary,' nonracialized pornography often become rote" ("Skin Flicks on the Racial Border," 275). Further research might consider problematizing the unstated premise that taboo is the backbone of the erotic, as unexplored in Williams's framework is whether sameness might also function as a source of erotic desire and sexual pleasure.

41 Muñoz, *Disidentifications*, 88.

Conclusion

1 See Paul, *Pornified*.

2 See Wacquant, "For an Analytic of Racial Domination."

3 Angela Harris, "Race and Essentialism in Feminist Legal Theory," 596.

4 See hooks, *Belonging*.

5 Linda Williams, "Skin Flicks on the Racial Border," 302–3.

6 Miller-Young, "Putting Hypersexuality to Work," 2.

7 Spillers, *Black, White, and in Color*, 153, emphasis in original; Hammonds, "Toward a Genealogy of Black Female Sexuality," 170, 177; Hine, "Rape and the Inner Lives of Black Women in the Middle West," 912; Higginbotham, *Righteous Discontent*, 14. It is important to note that Hine was writing about a specific historical moment—migration in the early twentieth century—which she argues was animated by sexual violence and the threat of sexual violence: "Many Black women quit the South out of a desire to achieve personal autonomy and to escape both from sexual exploitation from inside and outside of their families and from the rape and threat of rape by white as well as Black males" ("Rape and the Inner Lives of Black Women in the Middle West," 914). I emphasize the historical context Hine writes about because "culture of dissemblance" is now regularly treated as a transhistorical, transspatial condition of the black female subject.

8 Hammonds, "Toward a Genealogy of Black Female Sexuality," 177; Thompson, *Beyond the Black Lady*, 8.

9 See, respectively, Stallings, *Mutha' Is Half a Word*, 2; Lee, *Erotic Revolutionaries*; Stallings, *Mutha' Is Half a Word*, 1, 5.

10 See Fleetwood, *Troubling Vision*.

11 Here, I am inspired by Patricia J. Williams's breathtakingly broad (and stunning) articulation of rights: "Instead, society must *give* [rights] away. Unlock them from reification by giving them to slaves. Give them to trees. Give them to cows. Give them to history. Give them to rivers and rocks. Give to all of society's objects and untouchables the rights of privacy, integrity, and self-assertion; give them distance and respect. Flood them with the animating spirit that rights mythology fires in this country's most oppressed psyches, and wash away the shrouds of inanimate-object status, so that we may say not that we own gold but that a luminous golden spirit owns us" (*Alchemy of Race and Rights*, 165). Similarly, I am inspired by Stallings's claim that "discourses of desire [can] lead to languages of sexual rights that Black females need to know and embrace for their own sake" (*Mutha' Is Half a Word*, 293).

BIBLIOGRAPHY

Primary Sources

American Booksellers v. Hudnut, 771 F.2d 323 (7th Cir. 1985).

Borcovichy, Barron, dir. *Lialeh*. New York: BT Production Company / Kenneth Elliot Productions, 1973.

Crichton, Michael, dir. *Westworld*. Beverly Hills, CA: MGM, 1973.

Damiano, Gerard, dir. *Deep Throat*. Los Angeles: Gerard Damiano Film Productions, 1972.

Dark Brothers, dirs. *Black Throat*. Los Angeles: Dark Brothers Entertainment, 1985.

———, dirs. *Let Me Tell Ya 'bout Black Chicks*. Los Angeles: Dark Brothers Production / VCA Pictures, 1984.

———, dirs. *Let Me Tell Ya 'bout White Chicks*. Los Angeles: Dark Brothers Production, 1984.

Davis, Ossie, dir. *Cotton Comes to Harlem*. New York: Formosa Productions, 1970.

Drea, dir. *Black Jail Bait*. Los Angeles: LA Video, 1984.

———, dir. *Blacks Have More Fun*. Los Angeles: AVC Video, 1985.

———, dir. *Black Taboo*. Los Angeles: Taboo Entertainment, 1984.

———, dir. *Brown Sugar*. Los Angeles: VCX Entertainment, 1984.

———, dir. *Hot Chocolate*. Hollywood, CA: Essex Video/Electric Hollywood, 1984.

Gerdler, William, dir. *Sheba, Baby*. Los Angeles: American International Pictures/ Mid-America Pictures, 1975.

Hill, Jack, dir. *Foxy Brown*. Los Angeles: American International Pictures, 1974.

Miller v. California, 413 U.S. 15 (1973).

Mitchell, Artie, and Jim Mitchell, dirs. *Behind the Green Door*. Cinema 7 Film Group/ Jartech, 1972.

Osco, Bill, and Howard Ziehm, dirs. *Mona the Virgin Nymph*. Seattle, WA: Something Weird Video, 1970.

Parks, Gordon, dir. *Shaft*. Beverly Hills, CA: MGM, 1971.

———, dir. *The Learning Tree*. Los Angeles: Winger Productions, 1969.

Parks, Gordon, Jr., dir. *Super Fly*. Burbank, CA: Sig Shore Productions / Warner Brothers, 1972.

Spinelli, Anthony, dir. *Sexworld*. Hollywood, CA: Essex Pictures Company / Electric Hollywood, 1978.

Starrett, Jack, dir. *Cleopatra Jones*. Burbank, CA: Warner Brothers, 1973.

United States v. X-Citement Video, Inc., 513 U.S. 64 (1994).

Van Peebles, Melvin, dir. *Sweet Sweetback's Baadasssss Song*. Los Angeles: Cinemation Industries, 1971.

Secondary Sources

Abel, Elizabeth. *Signs of the Times: The Visual Politics of Jim Crow*. Berkeley: University of California Press, 2010.

Abel, Elizabeth, Barbara Christian, and Helene Moglen, eds. *Female Subjects in Black and White: Race, Psychoanalysis, Feminism*. Berkeley: University of California Press, 1997.

Abrahams, Yvette. "The Great Long National Insult: 'Science,' Sexuality, and the Khoisan in the Eighteenth and Early Nineteenth Century." *Agenda* 32 (1997): 34–48.

———. "Images of Sara Bartman: Sexuality, Race, and Gender in Early-Nineteenth-Century Britain." *Nation, Empire, Colony: Historicizing Gender and Race*, ed. Ruth Roach Pierson and Nupur Chadhuri, 220–36. Bloomington: Indiana University Press, 1998.

Abramovitz, Mimi. *Regulating the Lives of Women*. Boston: South End Press, 1988.

Abrams, Kathryn. "Sex Wars Redux: Agency and Coercion in Feminist Legal Theory." *Columbia Law Review* 95.2 (1995): 304–76.

Adult Video News. *The AVN Guide to the 500 Greatest Adult Films of All Time*. New York: Thunder's Mouth Press, 2005.

Alba, Richard. *Ethnic Identity: The Transformation of White America*. New Haven, CT: Yale University Press, 1992.

Alexander, Elizabeth. *The Venus Hottentot*. Charlottesville: University of Virginia Press, 1990.

Alexander, M. Jacqui, ed. *The Third Wave: Feminist Perspectives on Racism*. New York: Kitchen Table Press, 1994.

Amoah, Jewel. "Back on the Auction Block: A Discussion of Black Women and Pornography." *National Black Law Journal* 14.2 (1997): 204–21.

Antonio, Edward Phillip. "Desiring Booty and Killing the Body: Toward 'Negative' Erotics." *Loving the Body: Religious Studies and the Erotic*, ed. Anthony B. Pinn and Dwight N. Hopkins, 271–96. New York: Palgrave Macmillan, 2004.

Anzaldua, Gloria. *Borderlands/La Frontera*. San Francisco: Aunt Lute Foundation Books, 1987.

——, ed. *Making Faces, Making Soul / Haciendo Caras: Creative and Critical Perspectives by Women of Color*. San Francisco: Aunt Lute Foundation Books, 1990.

Anzaldúa, Gloria, and Cherríe Moraga, eds. *This Bridge Called My Back: Writings by Radical Women of Color*. Watertown, MA: Persephone Press, 1981.

Apter, Emily. *Feminizing the Fetish: Psychoanalysis and Narrative Obsession in Turn-of-the-Century France*. Ithaca, NY: Cornell University Press, 1991.

Apter, Emily, and William Peitz, eds. *Fetishism as Cultural Discourse*. Ithaca, NY: Cornell University Press, 1993.

Asante, M. K., Jr. *Beautiful, and Ugly Too*. New York: Africa World Press, 2005.

Austin, Regina. "Black Women, Sisterhood, and the Difference/Deviance Divide." *New England Law Review* 26.3 (1992): 877–88.

Avedon, Carol. *Nudes, Prudes, and Attitudes: Pornography and Censorship*. Cheltenham, U.K.: New Clarion Press, 1994.

Baker, Lee. *From Savage to Negro: Anthropology and the Construction of Race*. Berkeley: University of California Press, 1998.

Bal, Mieke. "The Politics of Citation." *diacritics* 21.1 (1991): 22–45.

Barker, Isabelle V. "Editing Pornography." *Feminism and Pornography*, ed. Drucilla Cornell, 643–52. Oxford: Oxford University Press, 2000.

Barrera, Magdalena. "Hottentot 2000: Jennifer Lopez and Her Butt." *Sexualities in History: A Reader*, ed. Kim Phillips and Barry Reay, 407–20. New York: Routledge, 2002.

Barron, Martin, and Michael Kimmel. "Sexual Violence in Three Pornographic Media: Towards a Sociological Explanation." *Journal of Sex Research* 37.2 (2000): 161–68.

Bauman, Kentston D. "'Incestuous Sheets' and 'Adulterate Beasts': Incest and Miscegenation in Early Modern Drama." PhD diss., University of Michigan, 2011.

Bean, Jennifer M., and Diane Negra, eds. *A Feminist Reader in Early Cinema*. Durham, NC: Duke University Press, 2002.

Bell, Laurie. *Good Girls / Bad Girls: Feminists and Sex Trade Workers Face to Face*. Toronto: Seal Press, 1987.

Bell, Shannon. "Feminist Ejaculations." *The Hysterical Male: New Feminist Theory*, ed. Arthur Kroker and Marilouise Kroker, 155–69. New York: St. Martin's, 1991.

Bennett, Michael, and Vanessa D. Dickerson, eds. *Recovering the Black Female Body: Self-Representation by African American Women*. New Brunswick, NJ: Rutgers University Press, 2001.

Benshoff, Harry M. "Blaxploitation Horror Films: Generic Reappropriation or Reinscription?" *Cinema Journal* 39.2 (2000): 31–50.

Berger, Arthur Asa. "Humor: An Introduction." *American Behavioral Scientist* 30, no. 5 (1987): 399–408.

Bergson, Henri. *Laughter: An Essay on the Meaning of the Comic*. 1911. Los Angeles: Consortium Book Sales and Distribution, 1999.

———. "Laughter." *Comedy: Meaning and Form*, ed. Robert W. Corrigan, 328–32. San Francisco: Chandler, 1965.

Berlant, Lauren. *Cruel Optimism*. Durham, NC: Duke University Press, 2011.

Bernardi, Daniel. "Cyborgs in Cyberspace: White Pride, Pedophilic Pornography, and Donna Haraway's 'Manifesto.'" *Reality Squared: Television Discourse on the Real*, ed. James Freidman, 155–84. New Brunswick, NJ: Rutgers University Press, 2002.

———. "Interracial Joysticks: Pornography's Web of Racist Attractions." *Pornography: Film and Culture*, ed. Peter Lehman, 220–43. New Brunswick, NJ: Rutgers University Press, 2006.

Bernier, Celeste-Marie. *African American Visual Arts: From Slavery to the Present*. Chapel Hill: University of North Carolina Press, 2008.

Bernstein, Elizabeth. "The Meaning of the Purchase: Desire, Demand, and the Commerce of Sex." *Ethnography* 2.3 (2001): 375–406.

———. "Sex Work for the Middle Class." *Sexualities* 10.3 (2007): 473–88.

———. *Temporarily Yours: Intimacy, Authenticity, and the Commerce of Sex*. Chicago: University of Chicago Press, 2007.

Bernstein, Robin. "Dances with Things: Material Culture and the Performance of Race." *Social Text* 27.4 (2009): 67–94.

Bersani, Leo. "Is the Rectum a Grave?" *October* 43 (1987): 197–222.

Bhabha, Homi K. "The Other Question: Difference, Discrimination and the Discourses of Colonialism." *Black British Cultural Studies*, ed. Houston A. Baker Jr., Manthia Diawara, and Ruth H. Lindeborg, 87–106. Chicago: University of Chicago Press, 1996.

Blanchard, Pierre, et al., eds. *Human Zoos: Science and Spectacle in the Age of Colonial Empires*. Liverpool: Liverpool University Press, 2008.

Bloom, Clive. "Grinding with the Bachelors: Pornography in a Machine Age." *Perspectives on Pornography: Sexuality in Film and Literature*, ed. Gary Day and Clive Bloom, 9–25. New York: St. Martin's, 1988.

Bobo, Jacqueline. "Reading through the Text: The Black Woman as Audience." *Black American Cinema*, ed. Manthia Diawara, 272–87. New York: Routledge, 1993.

———. "*The Color Purple*: Black Women as Cultural Readers." *Cultural Theory and Popular Culture*, ed. John Storey, 310–18. Essex, U.K.: Pearson, 1998.

———. " 'The Subject Is Money': Reconsidering the Black Film Audience as a Theoretical Paradigm." *Black American Literature Forum* 25.2 (1991): 421–32.

Bogdan, Robert. *Freak Show: Presenting Human Oddities for Amusement and Profit.* Chicago: University of Chicago Press, 1988.

Bogle, Donald. *Blacks in American Film and Television.* New York: Simon and Schuster, 1989.

———. *Toms, Coons, Mulattoes, Mammies, and Bucks: An Interpretative History of Blacks in American Films.* New York: Continuum, 1994.

Briefel, Aviva. "Monster Pains: Masochism, Menstruation, and Identification in the Horror Film." *Film Quarterly* 58.3 (spring 2005): 16–27.

Bright, Susie. "The Image of the Black in Adult Video." *AVN* 2.2 (1987): 64.

Brodkin, Karen. *How Jews Became White Folks and What that Says about Race in America.* New Brunswick, NJ: Rutgers University Press, 1998.

Brody, Jennifer DeVere. *Impossible Purities: Blackness, Femininity, and Victorian Culture.* Durham, NC: Duke University Press, 1998.

———. "The Returns of 'Cleopatra Jones.' " *Signs* 25.1 (1999): 91–121.

Brooks, Daphne A. *Bodies in Dissent: Spectacular Performances of Race and Freedom, 1850–1910.* Durham, NC: Duke University Press, 2006.

Brooks, Siobhan. *Unequal Desires: Race and Erotic Capital in the Stripping Industry.* Albany: State University of New York Press, 2010.

Brown, Wendy. "The Impossibility of Women's Studies." *differences* 9.3 (1997): 79–101.

———. *States of Injury.* Princeton: Princeton University Press, 1995.

Bugner, Ladislas, et al., eds. *The Image of the Black in Western Art.* Cambridge, MA: Harvard University Press, 1989.

Burger, John R. *One-Handed Histories: The Eroto-Politics of Gay Male Video Pornography.* New York: Harrington Park Press, 1995.

Burrell, Darci Elaine. "The Norplant Solution: Norplant and the Control of African-American Motherhood." *UCLA Women's Law Journal* 5.2 (1994): 401–44.

Butler, Judith. *Bodies That Matter: On the Discursive Limits of "Sex."* New York: Routledge, 1993.

———. "Endangered/Endangering: Schematic Racism and White Paranoia." *Reading Rodney King / Reading Urban Uprising*, ed. Robert Gooding-Williams, 15–22. New York: Routledge, 1993.

———. "The Force of Fantasy: Mapplethorpe, Feminism, and Discursive Excess." *differences* 2.2 (1990): 105–25.

———. *Gender Trouble: Feminism and the Subversion of Identity*. New York: Routledge, 1990.

———. "Performative Acts and Gender Constitution." *Theatre Journal* 40.4 (1988): 519–31.

Byrne, David. *Complexity Theory and the Social Sciences: An Introduction*. New York: Routledge, 1998.

Cante, Rich, and Angelo Restivo. "The Cultural-Aesthetic Specificities of All-Male Moving-Image Pornography." *Porn Studies*, ed. Linda Williams, 142–65. Durham, NC: Duke University Press, 2004.

Capino, Jose B. "Homologies of Space: Text and Spectatorship in All-Male Adult Theaters." *Cinema Journal* 45.1 (2005): 50–65.

Caraway, Nancie. *Segregated Sisterhood: Racism and the Politics of American Feminism*. Knoxville: University of Tennessee Press, 1991.

Carby, Hazel. "Policing the Black Woman's Body in the Urban Context." *Critical Inquiry* no. 18 (1992): 738–55.

———. *Race Men*. Cambridge, MA: Harvard University Press, 1998.

Cardyn, Lisa. "Sexualized Racism / Gendered Violence: Outraging the Body Politic in the Reconstruction South." *Michigan Law Review* 100.4 (2002): 675–867.

Carpio, Glenda. *Laughing Fit to Kill: Black Humor in the Fictions of Slavery*. New York: Oxford University Press, 2008.

Carson, Diane, Linda Dittmar, and Janice R. Welsch, eds. *Multiple Voices in Feminist Film Criticism*. Minneapolis: University of Minnesota Press, 1994.

Carter, Vednita, and Evelina Giobbe. "Duet: Prostitution, Racism and Feminist Discourse." *Prostitution and Pornography: Philosophical Debates about the Sex Industry*, ed. Jessica Spector, 17–39. Stanford, CA: Stanford University Press, 2006.

Cham, Mybe B., and Claire Andrade-Watkins, eds. *BlackFrames: Critical Perspectives on Black Independent Cinema*. Cambridge: Massachusetts Institute of Technology Press, 1988.

Champagne, John. "'Stop Reading Films!': Film Studies, Close Analysis, and Gay Pornography." *Cinema Journal* 36.4 (1997): 76–97.

Chaney, Michael L. *Fugitive Vision: Slave Image and Black Identity in Antebellum Narrative*. Bloomington: Indiana University Press, 2008.

Chang, Robert S., and Jerome McCristal Culp Jr. "After Intersectionality." *University of Missouri-Kansas City Law Review* 71.2 (2002): 485–92.

Chapkis, Wendy. *Live Sex Acts: Women Performing Erotic Labor*. New York: Routledge, 1997.

Cheney, Deborah. "Visual Rape." *Law and Critique* no. 9 (1993): 189–206.

Cheng, Anne Anlin. *The Melancholy of Race*. New York: Oxford University Press, 2000.

Cherny, Lynn, and Elizabeth Reba Weise. *Wired Women: Gender and New Realities in Cyberspace*. Seattle: Seal Press, 1996.

Cho, Song, ed. *Rice: Explorations into Gay Asian Culture and Politics*. Toronto: Queer Press, 1998.

Christian, Barbara. "The Race for Theory." *Making Faces, Making Soul / Haciendo Caras: Creative and Critical Perspectives by Women of Color*, ed. Gloria Anzaldúa, 335–45. San Francisco: Aunt Lute Foundation Books, 1990.

Clark, Randall. *At a Theater or Drive-in Near You: The History, Culture, and Politics of the American Exploitation Film*. New York: Garland, 1995.

Cohen, Cathy. *The Boundaries of Blackness: AIDS and the Breakdown of Black Politics*. Chicago: University of Chicago Press, 1999.

Collins, Lisa. "Economies of the Flesh: Representing the Black Female Body in Art." *Skin Deep, Spirit Strong: The Black Female Body in American Culture*, ed. Kimberly Wallace-Sanders, 99–127. Ann Arbor: University of Michigan Press, 2002.

Collins, Patricia Hill. *Black Feminist Thought: Knowledge, Consciousness, and the Politics of Empowerment*. 2d edn. New York: Routledge, 2000.

———. *Black Sexual Politics*. New York: Routledge, 2004.

———. *Fighting Words: Black Women and the Search for Justice*. Minneapolis: University of Minnesota Press, 1998.

———. "Learning from the Outsider Within: The Sociological Significance of Black Feminist Thought." *Social Problems* 33.6 (December 1986): S14–S32.

———. "Pornography and Black Women's Bodies." *Making Violence Sexy*, ed. Diana Russell, 97–104. New York: Teacher's College Press, 1993.

Columpar, Corinn. "The Gaze as Theoretical Touchstone: The Intersection of Film Studies, Feminist Theory, and Postcolonial Theory." *Women's Studies Quarterly* 30.1–2 (2002): 25–44.

Corbett, John, and Terri Kapsalis. "Aural Sex: The Female Orgasm in Popular Sound." *Drama Review* 40.3 (1996): 102–11.

Cornell, Drucilla. *At the Heart of Freedom: Feminism, Sex, and Equality*. Princeton, NJ: Princeton University Press, 1998.

———. *Beyond Accommodation: Ethical Feminism, Deconstruction, and the Law*. New York: Routledge, 1991.

———, ed. *Feminism and Pornography*. Oxford: Oxford University Press, 2000.

———. *The Imaginary Domain*. New York: Routledge, 1995.

Courtney, Susan. *Hollywood Fantasies of Miscegenation: Spectacular Narratives of Gender and Race*. Princeton, NJ: Princeton University Press, 2004.

Cowan, Gloria, and Robin Campbell. "Racism and Sexism in Interracial Pornography: A Content Analysis." *Psychology of Women Quarterly* 18 (1994): 323–38.

Crais, Clifton C., and Pamela Scully. *Sara Baartman and the Hottentot Venus: A Ghost Story and a Biography*. Princeton: Princeton University Press, 2009.

Crawford, Bridget J. "Toward a Third-Wave Feminist Legal Theory: Young Women,

Pornography and the Praxis of Pleasure." *Michigan Journal of Gender and Law* no. 14 (2007): 99–161.

Crenshaw, Kimberlé. "Beyond Racism and Misogyny: Black Feminism and 2 Live Crew." *Boston Review* 16.6 (1991): 6–32.

———. "Mapping the Margins: Intersectionality, Identity Politics, and Violence against Women of Color." *Stanford Law Review* 43.6 (1991): 1241–300.

———. "Race, Reform, and Retrenchment: Transformation and Legitimation in Antidiscrimination Law." *Harvard Law Review* 101.7 (1988): 1331–87.

———. "Whose Story Is It, Anyway?: Feminist and Antiracist Appropriations of Anita Hill." *Race-ing Justice, En-gendering Power*, ed. Toni Morrison, 402–40. New York: Pantheon, 1992.

Crenshaw, Kimberlé, et al., eds. *Critical Race Theory: The Key Writings that Formed the Movement*. New York: W. W. Norton, 1995.

Crimp, Douglas. "How to Have Promiscuity in an Epidemic." *October* 43 (1987): 237–71.

———. *Melancholia and Moralism: Essays on AIDS and Queer Politics*. Cambridge: Massachusetts Institute of Technology Press, 2002.

Cripps, Thomas. *Black Film as Genre*. Bloomington: Indiana University Press, 1978.

———. *Making Movies Black: The Hollywood Message Movie from World War II to the Civil Rights Era*. New York: Oxford University Press, 1993.

Cvetkovich, Ann. *An Archive of Feelings: Trauma, Sexuality, and Lesbian Public Cultures*. Durham, NC: Duke University Press, 2003.

Davis, Angela. *Women, Race, and Class*. New York: Random House, 1981.

Dean, Carolyn J. *The Frail Social Body: Pornography, Homosexuality, and Other Fantasies in Interwar France*. Berkeley: University of California Press, 2000.

Delacoste, Frederique, and Priscilla Alexander, eds. *Sex Work: Writings by Women in the Sex Industry*. Pittsburgh: Cleis Press, 1987.

Delany, Samuel R. *Times Square Red, Times Square Blue*. New York: New York University Press, 1999.

De Lauretis, Teresa. "Oedipus Interruptus." *Feminist Film Theory: A Reader*, ed. Sue Thornham, 83–96. New York: New York University Press, 1999.

———. *The Practice of Love: Lesbian Sexuality and Perverse Desire*. Bloomington: Indiana University Press, 1994.

Delgado, Richard, ed. *Critical Race Theory: The Cutting Edge*. Philadelphia: Temple University Press, 1995.

D'Emilio, John, and Estelle B. Freedman. *Intimate Matters: A History of Sexuality in America*. 2d edn. Chicago: University of Chicago Press, 1997.

Dennis, Kelly. "Ethno-Pornography: Veiling the Dark Continent." *History of Photography* 18 (1994): 22–28.

———. "Leave It to Beaver: The Object of Pornography." *Strategies* 6 (1991): 122–67.

Dent, Gina, ed. *Black Popular Culture*. Seattle: Bay Press, 1992.

Diamond, Irene. "Pornography and Repression: A Reconsideration." *Signs* 5.4 (1980): 686–701.

Diawara, Manthia, ed. *Black American Cinema*. New York: Routledge, 1993.

———. "Black Spectatorship: Problems of Identification and Resistance." *Screen* 29.4 (1988): 66–79.

Di Lauro, Al, and Gerald Rabkin. *Dirty Movies: An Illustrated History of the Stag Film, 1915–1970*. New York: Chelsea House, 1976.

Dines, Gail. "From Fantasy to Reality: Unmasking the Pornography Industry." *Sisterhood Is Forever*, ed. Robin Morgan, 306–14. New York: Washington Square Press, 2003.

———. "King Kong and the White Woman: *Hustler* Magazine and the Demonization of Black Masculinity." *Violence Against Women* 4.3 (1998): 291–307.

———. "The White Man's Burden: Gonzo Pornography and the Construction of Black Masculinity." *Yale Journal of Law and Feminism* 18.1 (2006): 283–97.

Doane, Mary Ann. "Aesthetics and Politics." *Signs* 30.1 (2004): 1229–35.

———. *Femme Fatales: Feminism, Film Theory, Psychoanalysis*. New York: Routledge, 1991.

———. "Film and the Masquerade: Theorizing the Female Spectator." *Writing on the Body: Female Embodiment and Feminist Theory*, ed. Katie Conboy, Nadia Medina, and Sarah Stanbury, 176–92. New York: Columbia University Press, 1997.

Doane, Mary Ann, Patricia Mellencamp, and Linda Williams, eds. *Re-vision: Essays in Feminist Film Criticism*. Los Angeles: American Film Institute, 1984.

Doherty, Alex, and Gail Dines. "Living in a Porn Culture." *New Left Project*, 15 April 2010. Accessed 30 December 2011. www.newleftproject.org/index.php/site /article_comments/living_in_a_porn_culture.

Dolan, Jill. "Desire Cloaked in a Trenchcoat." *TDR* 33.1 (1989): 59–67.

Donalson, Melvin. *Masculinity in the Interracial Buddy Film*. Jefferson, NC: McFarland, 2006.

duCille, Ann. "Othered Matters: Reconceptualizing Dominance and Difference in the History of Sexuality in America." *Journal of the History of Sexuality* 1.1 (1990): 102–27.

———. *Skin Trade*. Cambridge, MA: Harvard University Press, 1996.

Duggan, Lisa, and Nan D. Hunter. *Sex Wars: Sexual Dissent and Popular Culture*. New York: Routledge, 1995.

Dunn, Stephane. *"Baad Bitches" and Sassy Supermamas: Black Power Action Films*. Urbana: University of Illinois Press, 2008.

Dworkin, Andrea. "Against the Male Flood: Censorship, Pornography, and Equality." *Feminism and Pornography*, ed. Drucilla Cornell, 19–39. Oxford: Oxford University Press, 2000.

———. *Intercourse*. New York: Free Press, 1987.

———. *Pornography: Men Possessing Women*. New York: Putnam, 1981.

Dyer, Richard. "Gay Male Porn: Coming to Terms." *Jump Cut: A Review of Contemporary Media* 30 (1985): 27–29.

Egan, R. Danielle. *Dancing for Dollars and Paying for Love: The Relationships between Exotic Dancers and Their Regulars*. New York: Palgrave, 2006.

Egan, R. Danielle, Katherine Frank, and Merri Lisa Johnson, eds. *Flesh for Fantasy: Producing and Consuming Exotic Dance*. New York: Thunder Mouth's Press, 2006.

Elam, Harry J., and Kennell Jackson, eds. *Black Cultural Traffic: Crossroads in Global Performance and Popular Culture*. Ann Arbor: University of Michigan Press, 2005.

Elias, James, et al., eds. 1999. *Porn 101: Eroticism, Pornography, and the First Amendment*. Amherst, NY: Prometheus, 1999.

Ellis, Kate, Nan D. Hunter, Beth Jaker, Barbara O'Dair, and Abby Tallmer, eds. *Caught Looking: Feminism, Pornography, and Censorship*. New York: Caught Looking, 1986.

Emerson, Rana A. "Where My Girls At? Negotiating Black Womanhood in Music Videos." *Gender and Society* 16.1 (2002): 115–35.

Eng, David L. *The Feeling of Kinship: Queer Liberalism and the Racialization of Intimacy*. Durham, NC: Duke University Press, 2010.

———. *Racial Castration: Managing Masculinity in Asian America*. Durham, NC: Duke University Press, 2001.

English, Deirdre, Amber Hollibaugh, and Gayle Rubin. "Talking Sex: A Conversation on Sexuality and Feminism." *Feminist Review* 11 (1982): 40–52.

Erens, Patricia, ed. *Issues in Feminist Film Criticism*. Bloomington: Indiana University Press, 1991.

Escoffier, Jeffrey. "Gay-for-Pay: Straight Men and the Making of Gay Pornography." *Qualitative Sociology* 26.4 (2003): 531–55.

Everett, Anna. *Returning the Gaze: A Genealogy of Black Film Criticism, 1909–1949*. Durham, NC: Duke University Press, 2001.

Faludi, Susan. "The Money Shot." *New Yorker*, 30 October 1995, 64–87.

Fanon, Frantz. *Black Skin, White Masks*. New York: Grove Press, 1967.

Farley, Anthony Paul. 1997. "The Black Body as Fetish Object." *Oregon Law Review* 76.3 (1997): 457–536.

———. "Perfecting Slavery." *Loyola University Chicago Law Journal* 36 (2004): 225–51.

———. "The Poetics of Colorlined Space." *Crossroads, Directions, and a New Critical Race Theory*, ed. Francisco Valdes, Jerome McCristal Culp, and Angela P. Harris, 97–158. Philadelphia: Temple University Press, 2002.

———. "Sadomasochism and the Colorline: Reflections on the Million Man March." *Black Men on Race, Gender, and Sexuality: A Critical Reader*, ed. Devin Carbodo, 68–84. New York: New York University Press, 1999.

———. "When the Stars Begin to Fall: Introduction to Critical Race Theory and Marxism." *Columbia Journal of Race and Law* 1 (2012): 226–46.

Fausto-Sterling, Anne. "Gender, Race, and Nation: The Comparative Anatomy of 'Hottentot' Women in Europe, 1815–1817." *Skin Deep, Spirit Strong: The Black Female Body in American Culture*, ed. Kimberly Wallace-Sanders, 66–98. Ann Arbor: University of Michigan Press, 2002.

———. "The Five Sexes." *Sciences* (March–April 1993): 20–24.

Ferguson, Roderick A. *Aberrations in Black: Toward a Queer of Color Critique*. Minneapolis: University of Minnesota Press, 2004.

———. "Of Our Normative Strivings: African American Studies and the Histories of Sexuality." *Social Text* 23.3 (2005): 85–101.

———. "Sissies at the Picnic: The Subjugated Knowledges of a Black Rural Queer." *Feminist Waves, Feminist Generations: Life Stories from the Academy*, ed. Hokulani K. Aikau, Karla A. Erickson, and Jennifer L. Pierce, 188–96. Minneapolis: University of Minnesota Press.

Findlay, Heather. "Freud's 'Fetishism' and the Lesbian Dildo Debates." *Feminist Studies* 18.3 (1992): 563–79.

Fleetwood, Nicole. *Troubling Vision: Performance, Visuality, and Blackness*. Chicago: University of Chicago Press, 2010.

Ford, Kianga K. "Playing with Venus: Black Women Artists and the Venus Trope in Contemporary Visual Art." *Black Venus 2010: They Called Her "Hottentot,"* ed. Deborah Willis, 96–106. Philadelphia: Temple University Press, 2010.

Forna, Aminatta. "Pornography and Racism: Sexualizing Oppression and Inciting Hatred." *Pornography: Women, Violence, and Civil Liberties*, ed. Catherine Itzin, 102–12. New York: Oxford University Press, 1992.

Foster, Gwendolyn Audrey. "Third World Women's Cinema: If the Subaltern Speaks, Will We Listen?" *Interventions: Feminist Dialogues on Third World Women's Literature and Film*, ed. Bishnupriya Ghosh and Brinda Bose, 213–26. New York: Garland, 1997.

Foucault, Michel. *Discipline and Punish*. New York: Vintage, 1995.

———. "The Ethic of Care for the Self as a Practice of Freedom: An Interview with Michel Foucault." *Philosophy and Social Criticism* 12.2–3 (1987): 112–31.

———. *The History of Sexuality, Volume 1*. New York: Vintage, 1978.

Franke, Katherine M. "Putting Sex to Work." *Left Legalism / Left Critique*, ed. Wendy Brown and Janet E. Halley, 290–36. Durham, NC: Duke University Press, 2002.

———. "Theorizing Yes: An Essay on Feminism, Law, and Desire." *Columbia Law Review* 101.1 (2001): 181–208.

Frederick, Dennis. *Conquering Pornography: Overcoming the Addiction*. New York: Pleasant Word, 2007.

Freeman, Elizabeth. *Time Binds: Queer Temporalities, Queer Histories*. Durham, NC: Duke University Press, 2010.

Freud, Sigmund. *Jokes and Their Relation to the Unconscious*. New York: W. W. Norton, 1960.

Frug, Mary Joe. "A Postmodern Feminist Legal Manifesto (An Unfinished Draft)." *Harvard Law Review* 105.5 (1992): 1045–75.

Fung, Richard. "Interview with Richard Fung." *Rice: Explorations into Gay Asian Culture and Politics*, ed. Song Cho, 51–56. Toronto: Queer Press, 1998.

———. "Looking for My Penis: The Eroticized Asian in Gay Video Porn." *How Do I Look?: Queer Film and Video*, ed. Bad Object-Choices, 145–68. Seattle: Bay Press, 1991.

———. "Shortcomings: Questions about Pornography as Pedagogy." *Queer Looks: Perspectives on Lesbian and Gay Film*, ed. Martha Gever, John Greyson, and Pratibha Parmar, 355–67. New York: Routledge, 1993.

Gaines, Jane. "Competing Glances: Who Is Reading Robert Mapplethorpe's *Black Book*?" *New Formations* 16 (1992): 24–39.

———. "White Privilege and Looking Relations: Race and Gender in Feminist Film Theory." *Cultural Critique* 4 (1986): 59–79.

Gardner, Tracy A. "Racism in Pornography and the Women's Movement." *Take Back the Night: Women on Pornography*, ed. Laura Lederer, 105–14. New York: Morrow, 1980.

Gay, Claudine, and Katherine Tate. "Doubly Bound: The Impact of Gender and Race on the Politics of Black Women." *Political Psychology* 19.1 (1998): 169–84.

Geertz, Clifford. *Interpretation of Cultures*. New York: Basic Books, 1973.

George, Nelson. *Blackface: Reflections on African-Americans and the Movies*. New York: Harper Collins, 1994.

Gibson, Pamela Church, ed. *More Dirty Looks: Gender, Pornography and Power*. 2d edn. London: British Film Institute, 2004.

Giddings, Paula. *When and Where I Enter*. New York: W. Morrow, 1984.

Gilman, Sander. "AIDS and Syphilis: The Iconography of Disease." *October* 43 (winter 1987): 87–107.

———. "Black Bodies, White Bodies: Toward an Iconography of Female Sexuality in Late Nineteenth-Century Art, Medicine, and Literature." *Critical Inquiry* 12.1 (1985): 204–42.

Glassner, Barry. "Fitness and the Postmodern Self." *Journal of Health and Social Behavior* 30 (1989): 180–91.

Gledhill, Christine, ed. *Home Is Where the Heart Is: Studies in Melodrama and the Woman's Film*. London: British Film Institute, 1987.

Golden, Thelma, ed. *Black Male: Representations of Masculinity in Contemporary American Art*. New York: Whitney Museum of American Art, 1994.

Goldman, Steven L. "Images of Technology in Popular Films: Discussion and Filmography." *Science, Technology, and Human Values* 14.3 (1989): 275–301.

Gopinath, Gayatri. *Impossible Desires: Queer Diasporas and South Asian Public Cultures*. Durham, NC: Duke University Press, 2005.

Gordon, Avery. *Ghostly Matters: Haunting and the Sociological Imagination*. Minneapolis: University of Minnesota Press, 1997.

Gordon, Linda. *Woman's Body, Woman's Right: Birth Control in America*. New York: Penguin, 1976.

Gossett, Jennifer Lynn, and Sarah Byrne. " 'Click Here': A Content Analysis of Internet Rape Sites." *Gender and Society* 16.5 (2002): 689–709.

Gotanda, Neil. "Beyond Supreme Court Anti-Discrimination: An Essay on Racial Subordinations, Racial Pleasures and Commodified Race." *Columbia Journal of Race and Law* 1.3 (2012): 273–301.

Grant, W. R. *Post-Soul Black Cinema: Discontinuities, Innovations, and Breakpoints 1970–1995*. New York: Routledge, 2004.

Gray, Herman S. *Cultural Moves: African Americans and the Politics of Representation*. Berkeley: University of California Press, 2005.

Grillo, Trina. "Anti-Essentialism and Intersectionality: Tools to Dismantle the Master's House." *Berkeley Women's Law Journal* 10 (1995): 16–30.

Grillo, Trina, and Stephanie Wildman. "Obscuring the Importance of Race: The Implication of Making Comparisons between Racism and Sexism (or Other-Isms)." *Duke Law Journal* 40 (1991): 397–412.

Grosz, Elizabeth. *Jacques Lacan: A Feminist Introduction*. London: Routledge, 1990.

———. *Sexual Subversions*. St. Leonards, Australia: Allen and Unwin, 1989.

Gubar, Susan. "Representing Pornography: Feminism, Criticism, and Depictions of Female Violation." *Critical Inquiry* 13.4 (1987): 712–41.

Guerrero, Ed. *Framing Blackness: The African American Image in Film*. Philadelphia: Temple University Press, 1993.

Guillory, Monique, and Richard C. Green, eds. *Soul: Black Power, Politics, and Pleasure*. New York: New York University Press, 1998.

Gulas, Charles, and Marc G. Weinberger. *Humor in Advertising: A Comprehensive Analysis*. Armonk, NY: M. E. Sharpe, 2006.

Haggins, Bambi. *Laughing Mad: The Black Comic Persona in Post-Soul America*. New Brunswick, NJ: Rutgers University Press, 2007.

Halberstam, Judith. *Female Masculinity*. Durham, NC: Duke University Press, 1998.

———. *In a Queer Time and Place: Transgender Bodies, Subcultural Lives*. New York: New York University Press, 2005.

———. "Mackdaddy, Superfly, Rapper: Gender, Race, and Masculinity in the Drag King Scene." *Social Text* 52 (1997): 104–31.

———. *The Queer Art of Failure*. Durham, NC: Duke University Press, 2011.

———. "Shame and White Gay Masculinity." *Social Text* 23.3 (2005): 219–33.

Hall, Stuart. "What Is This Black in Black Popular Culture?" *Stuart Hall: Critical Dialogues in Cultural Studies*, ed. David Morley and Kuan-Hsing Chen, 465–75. London: Routledge, 1996.

Halley, Janet. *Split Decisions*. Princeton, NJ: Princeton University Press, 2006.

Hamamoto, Darrell Y. "The Joy Fuck Club: Prolegomenon to an Asian American Porno Practice." *Countervisions: Asian American Film Criticism*, ed. Darrell Hamamoto and Sandra Liu, 59–89. Philadelphia: Temple University Press, 2000.

Hammonds, Evelynn. "Black (W)holes and the Geometry of Black Female Sexuality." *differences* 6.2 (1994): 126–45.

———. "Race, Sex, AIDS: The Construction of 'Other.'" *Radical America* 20 (1987): 55–62.

———. "Toward a Genealogy of Black Female Sexuality: The Problematic of Silence." *Feminist Genealogies, Colonial Legacies, Democratic Futures*, ed. M. Jacqui Alexander and Chandra Talpade Mohanty, 170–81. New York: Routledge, 1997.

Hancock, Ange-Marie. *The Politics of Disgust*. New York: New York University Press, 2004.

Hansen, Christian, Catherine Needham, and Bill Nichols. "Pornography, Ethnography, and the Discourses of Power." *Representing Reality: Issues and Concepts in Documentary*, ed. Bill Nichols, 201–28. Bloomington: Indiana University Press, 1991.

Hansen, Miriam. *Babel and Babylon: Spectatorship in American Silent Film*. Cambridge, MA: Harvard University Press, 1994.

———. "Pleasure, Ambivalence, Identification: Valentino and Female Spectatorship." *Cinema Journal* 25.4 (summer 1986): 6–32.

Harper, Phillip Brian. *Are We Not Men?: Masculine Anxiety and the Problem of African-American Identity*. New York: Oxford University Press, 1996.

———. "'Take Me Home': Location, Identity, Transnational Exchange." *Callaloo* 23 (2000): 461–78.

———. "Walk-on Parts and Speaking Subjects: Screen Representations of Black Gay Men." *Callaloo* 18.2 (1995): 390–94.

Harris, Angela. "Race and Essentialism in Feminist Legal Theory." *Stanford Law Review* 42 (1989): 581–616.

Harris, Cheryl. "Whiteness as Property." *Harvard Law Review* 106 (1993): 1707–91.

Harris, Laura Alexandra. "Queer Black Feminism: The Pleasure Principle." *Feminist Review* 54 (1996): 3–30.

Hartman, Saidiya V. *Scenes of Subjection: Terror, Slavery, and Self-Making in Nineteenth-Century America*. New York: Oxford University Press, 1997.

———. "Venus in Two Acts." *Small Axe* 26 (2008): 1–14.

Haskell, Molly. *From Reverence to Rape: The Treatment of Women in the Movies*. 2d edn. Chicago: University of Chicago Press, 1987.

Hemmings, Clare. *Why Stories Matter: The Political Grammar of Feminist Theory*. Durham, NC: Duke University Press, 2011.

Henderson, Carol E. *Scarring the Black Body: Race and Representation in African American Literature*. Columbia: University of Missouri Press, 2002.

Hernandez, Daisy. "Playing with Race." *Color Lines* 7.4 (2004). Accessed 4 June 2013. http://colorlines.com/archives/2004/12/playing_with_race.html.

Higginbotham, Evelyn. "African-American Women's History and the Metalanguage of Race." *Signs* 17.2 (1992): 251–74.

———. "Beyond the Sound of Silence: Afro-American Women in History." *Gender and History* 1 (1989): 50–67.

———. *Righteous Discontent: The Women's Movement in the Black Baptist Church, 1880–1920*. Cambridge, MA: Harvard University Press, 1993.

Hight, Eleanor M., and Gary D. Sampson. *Colonial Photography: Imag(ing) Race and Place*. New York: Routledge, 2002.

Hine, Darlene Clark. *Hine Sight*. Brooklyn, NY: Carlston Press, 1994.

———. "Rape and the Inner Lives of Black Women in the Middle West: Preliminary Thoughts on the Culture of Dissemblance." *Signs* 14.4 (1988): 912–20.

Hoang, Nguyen Tan. "The Resurrection of Brandon Lee: The Making of a Gay Asian American Porn Star." *Porn Studies*, ed. Linda Williams, 223–70. Durham, NC: Duke University Press, 2004.

Hobson, Janell. "The 'Batty' Politic: Toward an Aesthetic of the Black Female Body." *Hypatia* 18.4 (2003): 87–105.

———. *Venus in the Dark: Blackness and Beauty in Popular Culture*. New York: Routledge, 2005.

———. "Viewing in the Dark: Towards a Black Feminist Approach to Film." *Women's Studies Quarterly* 30 (2002): 45–59.

Hodes, Martha, ed. *Sex, Love, Race: Crossing Boundaries in North American History*. New York: New York University Press, 1999.

———. *White Women, Black Men: Illicit Sex in the Nineteenth-Century South*. New Haven, CT: Yale University Press, 1997.

Holland, Sharon Patricia. "Bill T. Jones, Tupac Shakur, and the (Queer) Art of Death." *Callaloo* 23.1 (2000): 384–93.

———. *The Erotic Life of Racism*. Durham, NC: Duke University Press, 2012.

———. *Raising the Dead: Readings of Death and (Black) Subjectivity*. Durham, NC: Duke University Press, 2000.

———. "'Which Me Will Survive': Audre Lorde and the Development of a Black Feminist Ideology." *Critical Matrix* 1 (1988): 1–30.

———. "(White) Lesbian Studies." *The New Lesbian Studies: Into the Twenty-first Century*, ed. Bonnie Zimmerman and Toni A. H. McNaron, 247–55. New York: Feminist Press, 1996.

Hollibaugh, Amber. "Desire for the Future: Radical Hope in Passion and Pleasure." *Pleasure and Danger: Exploring Female Sexuality*, ed. Carol Vance, 401–11. Boston: Routledge, 1984.

Holmes, Rachel. *African Queen: The Real Life of the Hottentot Venus*. New York: Random House, 2007.

Holt, Thomas C. *The Problem of Race in the Twenty-First Century*. Cambridge, MA: Harvard University Press, 2000.

hooks, bell. *Ain't I a Woman: Black Women and Feminism*. Boston: South End Press, 1981.

———. *Art on My Mind: Visual Politics*. New York: New Press, 1995.

———. *Belonging: A Culture of Place*. New York: Routledge, 2008.

———. *Black Looks: Race and Representation*. Boston: South End Press, 1992.

Horton, Andrew S., ed. *Comedy/Cinema/Theory*. Berkeley: University of California Press, 1991.

Howard, Josiah. *Blaxploitation Cinema: The Essential Reference Guide*. New York: FAB Press, 2008.

Hutchinson, Darren Lenard. "Identity Crisis: 'Intersectionality,' 'Multidimensionality,' and the Development of an Adequate Theory of Subordination." *Michigan Journal of Race and Law* 6 (2000): 285–317.

———. "Ignoring the Sexualization of Race: Heteronormativity, Critical Race Theory and Anti-Racist Politics." *Buffalo Law Review* 47 (1999): 1–116.

Ignatiev, Noel. *How the Irish Became White*. New York: Routledge, 1996.

Irigaray, Luce. *Speculum of the Other Woman*. Ithaca, NY: Cornell University, 1985.

———. *This Sex Which Is Not One*. Ithaca, NY: Cornell University Press, 1985.

Jackson, Emily. "Catharine MacKinnon and Feminist Jurisprudence: A Critical Appraisal." *Journal of Law and Society* 19.2 (1992): 195–213.

Jacobson, Matthew Frye. *Whiteness of a Different Color: European Immigrants and the Alchemy of Race*. Cambridge, MA: Harvard University Press, 1999.

Jafa, Arthur. "69." *Black Popular Culture*, ed. Gina Dent, 249–52. Seattle: Bay Press, 1992.

Jakobsen, Janet. "Introduction: Feminism Is Dead (Long Live Feminism)." *Scholar and Feminist* 3.3–4.1. Accessed 30 December 2011. http://barnard.edu/sfonline/sfxxx/intro_01.htm.

James, Darius. *That's Blaxploitation!: Roots of the Baadasssss 'Tude (Rated X by an All-Whyte Jury)*. New York: St. Martin's Griffin, 1995.

James, Joy. *Shadowboxing: Representations of Black Feminist Politics*. New York: St. Martin's, 1999.

JanMohamed, Abdul. "Sexuality On/Of the Racial Border: Foucault, Wright, and the Articulation of 'Racialized Sexuality.'" *Discourses of Sexuality: From Aristotle to AIDS*, ed. Donna Stanton, 94–116. Ann Arbor: University of Michigan Press, 1992.

Jaworzyn, Stefan. *Shock: The Essential Guide to Exploitation Cinema*. London: Titan, 1996.

Jenkins, Candice. *Private Lives, Proper Relations: Regulating Black Intimacy.* Minneapolis: University of Minnesota Press, 2007.

Jennings, Thelma. "'Us Colored Women Had to Go through a Plenty': Sexual Exploitation of African-American Slave Women." *Journal of Women's History* 1 (1990): 45–74.

Jewell, K. Sue. *From Mammy to Miss America and Beyond: Cultural Images and the Shaping of U.S. Social Policy.* New York: Routledge, 1993.

Johnson, E. Patrick. *Appropriating Blackness: Performance and the Politics of Authenticity.* Durham, NC: Duke University Press, 2003.

———. *Sweet Tea.* Chapel Hill: University of North Carolina Press, 2008.

Johnson, E. Patrick, and Mae G. Henderson, eds. *Black Queer Studies: A Critical Anthology.* Durham, NC: Duke University Press, 2005.

Johnson, Eithne. "Excess and Ecstasy: Constructing Female Pleasure in Porn Movies." *Velvet Light Trap* 32 (1993): 30–46.

Johnson, Merri Lisa, ed. *Jane Sexes It Up: True Confessions of Feminist Desire.* New York: Four Walls, Eight Windows, 2002.

Johnston, Claire. "Women's Cinema as Counter-Cinema." *Notes on Women's Cinema,* ed. Claire Johnston, 24–31. London: Society for Education in Film and Television, 1973.

Joshi, Sameer. "Homo Pomo: Experiments in Gay Porn Criticism." PhD diss., University of Kansas, 2004.

Juffer, Jane. "A Pornographic Femininity? Telling and Selling Victoria's (Dirty) Secrets." *Social Text* 48 (1996): 27–48.

———. *At Home with Pornography: Women, Sex, and Everyday Life.* New York: New York University Press, 1998.

Julien, Isaac. "Confessions of a Snow Queen: Notes on the Making of The Attendant." *Critical Quarterly* 36.1 (1994): 120–26.

Julien, Isaac, and Kobena Mercer. "De Margin and De Centre." *Stuart Hall: Critical Dialogues in Cultural Studies,* ed. David Morley and Kuan-Hsing Chen, 450–64. London: Routledge, 1996.

———. 1986. "True Confessions." *Ten 8* (1986): 191–200.

Kakoudaki, Despina. "Spectacles of History: Race Relations, Melodrama, and the Science Fiction / Disaster Film." *Camera Obscura* 17.2 (2002): 109–53.

Kaplan, E. Ann. "Global Feminisms and the State of Feminist Film Theory." *Signs* 30.1 (2004): 1236–47.

———. "Is the Gaze Male?" *Feminism and Film,* ed. E. Ann Kaplan, 119–39. Oxford: Oxford University Press, 2000.

———. *Psychoanalysis and Cinema.* New York: Routledge, 1990.

———. "The Case of the Missing Mother: Maternal Issues in Vidor's *Stella Dallas.*" *Issues in Feminist Film Criticism,* ed. Patricia Erens, 126–36. Bloomington: Indiana University Press, 1990.

Kelley, Robin D. G. *Freedom Dreams: The Black Radical Imagination*. Boston: Beacon, 2002.

———. "Nap Time: Historicizing the Afro." *Fashion Theory* 1.4 (1997): 339–51.

———. *Yo' Mama's Disfunktional!: Fighting the Culture Wars in Urban America*. Boston: Beacon, 1997.

Kempadoo, Kamala, and Jo Doezema, eds. *Global Sex Workers: Rights, Resistance, and Redefinition*. New York: Routledge, 1998.

Kendrick, Walter. *The Secret Museum: Pornography in Modern Culture*. New York: Viking, 1987.

Kennedy, Duncan. *Sexy Dressing Etc.* Cambridge, MA: Harvard University Press, 1993.

Kennedy, Randall. *Interracial Intimacies: Sex, Marriage, Identity and Adoption*. New York: Vintage, 2004.

Khanna, Ranjana. *Dark Continents: Psychoanalysis and Colonialism*. Durham, NC: Duke University Press, 2003.

King, Deborah. "Multiple Jeopardy, Multiple Consciousness: The Context of a Black Feminist Ideology." *Signs* 14.1 (1988): 42–72.

Kipnis, Laura. *Bound and Gagged: Pornography and the Politics of Fantasy in America*. New York: Grove Press, 1996.

———. "(Male) Desire and (Female) Disgust: Reading *Hustler*." *Cultural Studies*, ed. Lawrence Grossberg, Cary Nelson, and Paula Treichler, 373–404. New York: Routledge, 1992.

Koshy, Susan. *Sexual Naturalization: Asian Americans and Miscegenation*. Stanford, CA: Stanford University Press, 2004.

Koven, Mikel J. *Blaxploitation Films*. Harpenden, U.K.: Kamera, 2010.

Kristeva, Julia. *Revolution in Poetic Language*. New York: Columbia University Press, 1984.

Kwan, Peter. "Complicity and Complexity: Cosynthesis and Praxis." *DePaul Law Review* 49.3 (2000): 673–92.

———. "Jeffrey Dahmer and the Cosynthesis of Categories." *Hastings Law Journal* 48.6 (1996): 1257–92.

Lane, Christopher, ed. *The Psychoanalysis of Race*. New York: Columbia University Press, 1998.

Lawrence, Novotny. *Blaxploitation Films of the 1970s: Blackness and Genre*. New York: Routledge, 2008.

Leahy, Michael. *Porn Nation: Conquering America's #1 Addiction*. Chicago: Northfield, 2008.

Lee, Shayne. *Erotic Revolutionaries: Black Women, Sexuality, and Popular Culture*. Lanham, MD: Hamilton Books, 2010.

Lehman, Peter. "A 'Strange Quirk in His Lineage': Walter Mosley, Donald Goines, and the Racial Representation of the Penis." *Men and Masculinities* 9 (2006): 226–35.

———. "Penis-size Jokes and Their Relation to Hollywood's Unconscious." *Comedy/Cinema/Theory*, ed. Andrew S. Horton, 43–59. Berkeley: University of California Press, 1991.

———, ed. *Pornography: Film and Culture*. New Brunswick, NJ: Rutgers University Press, 2006.

———. "Revelations about Pornography." *Film Criticism* 20 (1995): 3–16.

———. "Twin Cheeks, Twin Peaks, and Twin Freaks: Porn's Transgressive Remake Humor." *Authority and Transgression in Literature and Film*, ed. Bonnie and Hans Braendlin, 45–54. Tallahassee: University of Florida Press, 1996.

Leidholdt, Dorchen. "When Women Defend Pornography." *The Sexual Liberals and the Attack on Feminism*, ed. Dorchen Leidholdt and Janice G. Raymond, 125–31. New York: Pergamon, 1990.

Lembcke, Jerry. "Post-Vietnam Masculinity." *Men and Masculinities: A Social, Cultural, and Historical Encyclopedia*, ed. Michael Kimmel and Amy Aronson, 621–23. Santa Barbara: ABC-Clio Press, 2004.

Lemire, Elise. *Miscegenation: Making Race in America*. Philadelphia: University of Pennsylvania Press, 2003.

Levin, David, ed. *Modernity and the Hegemony of Vision*. Berkeley: University of California Press, 1993.

Lévi-Strauss, Claude. *The Elementary Structures of Kinship*. Boston: Beacon, 1969.

Lewis, Jon. *Hollywood v. Hard Core: How the Struggle over Censorship Saved the Modern Film Industry*. New York: New York University Press, 2000.

Lipsitz, George. *The Possessive Investment in Whiteness: Why White People Profit from Identity Politics*. Philadelphia: Temple University Press, 2006.

Locke, Brian. *Racial Stigma on the Hollywood Screen from World War II to the Present*. New York: Palgrave Macmillan, 2009.

Lorde, Audre. *Sister Outsider*. Trumansburg, NY: Crossing Press, 1984.

———. *Zami: A New Spelling of My Name*. Trumansburg, NY: Crossing Press, 1983.

Lott, Tommy L. "A No-Theory Theory of Contemporary Black Cinema." *Representing Blackness: Issues in Film and Video*, ed. Valerie Smith, 83–96. New Brunswick, NJ: Rutgers University Press, 2003.

Lubey, Kathleen. "Spectacular Sex: Thought and Pleasure in the Encounter with Pornography." *differences* 17.2 (2006): 113–31.

Lubiano, Wahneema, ed. *The House That Race Built*. New York: Vintage, 1998.

MacCannell, Dean. "Faking It: Comment on Face-Work in Pornography." *American Semiotics* 6.4 (1989): 153–74.

MacDonald, Scott. "Confessions of a Feminist Porn Watcher." *Film Quarterly* 36.3 (1983): 10–17.

MacKinnon, Catharine. *Feminism Unmodified: Discourses on Life and Law*. Cambridge, MA: Harvard University Press, 1987.

———. "From Practice to Theory, or What Is a White Woman Anyway?" *Yale Journal of Law and Feminism* 4 (1991): 13–22.

———. *Only Words.* Cambridge, MA: Harvard University Press, 1993.

———. *Sex Equality.* New York: Foundation Press, 2001.

———. *Toward a Feminist Theory of the State.* Cambridge, MA: Harvard University Press, 1989.

———. *Women's Lives, Men's Laws.* Cambridge, MA: Harvard University Press, 2005.

MacKinnon, Catharine, and Andrea Dworkin, eds. *In Harm's Way: The Pornography Civil Rights Hearings.* Cambridge, MA: Harvard University Press, 1998.

Maglin, Nan Bauer, and Donna Perry, eds. *"Bad Girls"/"Good Girls": Women, Sex, and Power in the Nineties.* New Brunswick, NJ: Rutgers University Press, 1996.

Magubane, Zine. "Which Bodies Matter?: Feminism, Poststructuralism, Race, and the Curious Theoretical Odyssey of the 'Hottentot Venus.'" *Gender and Society* 15.6 (2001): 816–34.

Maines, Rachel. *The Technology of Orgasm: "Hysteria," the Vibrator, and Women's Sexual Satisfaction.* Baltimore: Johns Hopkins University Press, 1999.

Maltz, Wendy, and Larry Maltz. *The Porn Trap: The Essential Guide to Overcoming Problems Caused by Pornography.* New York: Collins, 2008.

Manlove, Clifford T. "Visual 'Drive' and Cinematic Narrative: Reading Gaze Theory in Lacan, Hitchcock, and Mulvey." *Cinema Journal* 46.3 (spring 2007): 83–108.

Margolis, Harriet. "Stereotypical Strategies: Black Film Aesthetics, Spectator Positioning, and Self-Directed Stereotypes in 'Hollywood Shuffle' and 'I'm Gonna Git You Sucka.'" *Cinema Journal* 38.8 (1999): 50–66.

Martin, Nina K. "Never Laugh at a Man with His Pants Down: The Affective Dynamics of Comedy and Porn." *Pornography: Film and Culture*, ed. Peter Lehman, 189–205. New Brunswick, NJ: Rutgers University Press, 2006.

Martinez, Gerald, Diana Martinez, and Andres Chavez. *What It Is . . . What It Was!: The Black Film Explosion of the '70s in Words and Pictures.* New York: Hyperion, 1998.

Massood, Paula J. *Black City Cinema: African American Urban Experiences in Film.* Philadelphia: Temple University Press, 2003.

McBride, Dwight A. *Why I Hate Abercrombie and Fitch.* New York: New York University Press, 2005.

McCall, Leslie. "The Complexity of Intersectionality." *Signs* 30.3 (2005): 1771–800.

McClintock, Anne. *Imperial Leather: Race, Gender, and Sexuality in the Colonial Contest.* New York: Routledge, 1995.

McClintock, Anne, and Mufti Shohat, eds. *Dangerous Liaisons: Gender, Nation, and Postcolonial Perspectives.* Minneapolis: University of Minnesota Press, 1997.

McConahey, John B. "Pornography: The Symbolic Politics of Fantasy." *Law and Contemporary Problems* 51.1 (1988): 31–69.

McHugh, Kathleen, and Vivian Sobchack. "Introduction." *Signs* 30.1 (2004): 1205–8.

McNair, Brian. *Mediated Sex: Pornography and Postmodern Culture*. New York: St. Martin's, 1996.

McWhorter, Ladelle. *Bodies and Pleasures: Foucault and the Politics of Sexual Normalization*. Bloomington: Indiana University Press, 1999.

Mendelberg, Tali. *The Race Card*. Princeton, NJ: Princeton University Press, 2001.

Mercer, Kobena. "Fear of a Black Penis." *Artforum* 32 (1994): 80–81.

———. "Imagining the Black Man's Sex." *Photography/Politics: Two*, ed. Pat Holland, Jo Spence, and Simon Watney, 61–99. London: Comedia / Methuen, 1987.

———. "Just Looking for Trouble: Robert Mapplethorpe and Fantasies of Race." *Black British Cultural Studies*, ed. Houston A. Baker Jr., Manthia Diawara, and Ruth H. Lindeborg, 278–92. Chicago: University of Chicago Press, 1996.

———. "Skin Head Sex Thing: Racial Difference and the Homoerotic Imaginary." *How Do I Look?: Queer Film and Video*, ed. Bad Object-Choices, 169–222. Seattle: Bay Press, 1991.

———. *Welcome to the Jungle*. New York: Routledge, 1994.

Miller, Matthew. "The (Porn) Player." *Forbes*, 14 July 2005. Accessed 4 June 2013. http://www.forbes.com/forbes/2005/0704/124.html.

Miller-Young, Mireille. "Hip-Hop Honeys and Da Hustlaz: Black Sexualities in the New Hip-Hop Pornography." *Meridians* 8.1 (2007): 261–92.

———. "Let Me Tell Ya 'bout Black Chicks: Black Women in 1980s Video Pornography." *Blackness and Sexualities*, ed. Michelle Wright and Antje Schuhmann, 143–64. Munster: LIT Verlag, 2007.

———. "Putting Hypersexuality to Work: Black Women and Illicit Eroticism in Pornography." *Sexualities* 13.2 (2010): 1–17.

———. "A Taste for Brown Sugar: The History of Black Women in American Pornography." PhD diss., New York University, 2004.

Mills, Linda G. *Insult to Injury: Rethinking Our Responses to Intimate Abuse*. Princeton, NJ: Princeton University Press, 2003.

Mirza, Heidi Safia, ed. *Black British Feminism*. New York: Routledge, 1997.

Mitchell, Michelle. 1999. "Silences Broken, Silences Kept: Gender and Sexuality in African-American History." *Gender and History* 11.2 (1999): 433–44.

Mitchem, Stephanie Y. "What's Love Got to Do? (And Other Stories of Black Women's Sexualities." *Cross Currents* 54.3 (2004): 72–84.

Moore, Patrick. *Beyond Shame: Reclaiming the Abandoned History of Radical Gay Sexuality*. Boston: Beacon, 2004.

Moraga, Cherríe. *Loving in the War Years: Lo Que Nunca Pasó por Sus Labios*. Boston: South End Press, 1983.

Moran, Rachel. *Interracial Intimacy: The Regulation of Race and Romance*. Chicago: University of Chicago Press, 2003.

Morley, David and Kuan-Hsing Chen, eds. *Stuart Hall: Critical Dialogues in Cultural Studies*. London: Routledge, 1996.

Morreall, John. "The Rejection of Humor in Western Thought." *Philosophy East and West* 39.3 (1989): 243–65.

Morrison, Toni, ed. *Race-ing Justice, En-gendering Power: Essays on Anita Hill, Clarence Thomas, and the Construction of Social Reality*. New York: Pantheon, 1992.

Mourão, Manuela. "The Representation of Female Desire in Early Modern Pornographic Texts, 1660–1745." *Signs* 24.3 (1999): 573–602.

Mulvey, Laura. "Looking at the Past from the Present: Rethinking Feminist Film Theory of the 1970s." *Signs* 30.1 (2004): 1286–92.

———. "Visual Pleasure and Narrative Cinema." *The Sexual Subject: A Screen Reader in Sexuality*, 22–34. London: Routledge, 1992.

Muñoz, José Esteban. *Cruising Utopia: The Then and There of Queer Futurity*. New York: New York University Press, 2009.

———. *Disidentifications: Queers of Color and the Performance of Politics*. Minneapolis: University of Minnesota Press, 1999.

Musser, Amber. *Sensational Flesh: Race, Power, and Masochism*. New York: New York University Press, forthcoming.

Nagle, Jill, ed. *Whores and Other Feminists*. London: Routledge, 1997.

Nash, Jennifer C. "Bearing Witness to Ghosts: Notes on Theorizing Pornography, Race, and Law." *Wisconsin Women's Law Journal* 21 (2006): 47–72.

———. "'Hometruths' on Intersectionality." *Yale Journal of Law and Feminism* 23.2 (2011): 445–70.

———. "New Directions in Black Feminist Studies." *Feminist Studies* 38.2 (2012): 463–71.

———. "Strange Bedfellows: Anti-Pornography Feminism and Black Feminism." *Social Text* 97 (2008): 51–76.

Nead, Lynda. "The Female Nude: Pornography, Art, and Sexuality." *Signs* 15.2 (1990): 323–35.

Netto, Priscilla. "Reclaiming the Body of the 'Hottentot.'" *European Journal of Women's Studies* 12.2 (2005): 149–63.

Omi, Michael, and Howard Winant. *Racial Formation in the United States: From the 1960s to the 1990s*. New York: Routledge, 1994.

Ortega, Mariana. "Being Lovingly, Knowingly Ignorant: White Feminism and Women of Color." *Hypatia* 21.3 (2006): 56–74.

Ortiz, Christopher. "Hot and Spicy: Representation of Chicano/Latino Men in Gay Pornography." *Jump Cut* 39 (1994): 83–90.

Paasonen, Susanna, Kaarina Nikunen, and Laura Saarenmaa. *Pornification: Sex and Sexuality in Media Culture*. New York: Berg, 2007.

Paglia, Camille. *Vamps and Tramps*. New York: Vintage, 1994.

Parks, Suzan-Lori. "The Rear End Exists." *Grand Street* 55 (winter 1996): 10–18.

———. *Venus: A Play*. New York: Theatre Communications Group, 1997.

Patterson, Orlando. *Rituals of Blood*. Washington, DC: Counterpoint, 1998.

Patton, Cindy. *Inventing AIDS*. New York: Routledge, 1990.

Paul, Pamela. *Pornified: How Pornography Is Damaging Our Lives, Our Relationships, and Our Families*. New York: Times Books, 2005.

Pellegrini, Ann. *Performance Anxieties: Staging Psychoanalysis, Staging Race*. New York: Routledge, 1997.

———. "Women on Top, Boys on the Side, but Some of Us Are Brave: Blackness, Lesbianism, and the Visible." *Race-ing Representation: Voice, History, and Sexuality*, ed. Kostas Myrsiades and Linda Myrsiades, 247–63. Lanham, MD: Rowman and Littlefield, 1998.

Penley, Constance. "Crackers and Whackers: The White Trashing of Porn." *Porn Studies*, ed. Linda Williams, 309–34. Durham, NC: Duke University Press, 2004.

———, ed. *Feminism and Film Theory*. New York: Routledge, 1988.

Petkovich, Anthony. *The X Factory: Inside the American Hardcore Film Industry*. Manchester, U.K.: Critical Vision, 1997.

Petro, Patrice. *Aftershocks of the New: Feminism and Film History*. New Brunswick, NJ: Rutgers University Press, 2002.

———. "Reflections on Feminist Film Studies, Early and Late." *Signs* 30.1 (2004): 1272–77.

Phelan, Peggy. *Unmarked: The Politics of Performance*. New York: Routledge, 1993.

Pheterson, Gail, ed. *A Vindication of the Rights of Whores*. Seattle: Seal Press, 1989.

Phillips, Layli. "Deconstructing 'Down Low' Discourse: The Politics of Sexuality, Gender, Race, AIDS, and Anxiety." *Journal of African American Studies* 9.2 (2005): 3–15.

Powell, Richard J. *Cutting a Figure: Fashioning Black Portraiture*. Chicago: University of Chicago Press, 2009.

Prestney, Susie. "Inscribing the Hottentot Venus: Generating Data for Difference." *At the Edge of International Relations: Postcolonialism, Gender, and Dependency*, ed. Phillip Darby, 86–105. New York: Pinter, 1997.

Pribram, E. Deidre. *Female Spectators: Looking at Film and Television*. London: Verso, 1988.

Quarles, Mike. *Down and Dirty: Hollywood's Exploitation Filmmakers and Their Movies*. Jefferson, NC: McFarland, 1993.

Qureshi, Sadiah. "Displaying Sara Baartman." *History of Science* 42 (2004): 233–57.

Reed, Ishmael. "Introduction: Black Pleasure—An Oxymoron." *Soul: Black Power, Politics, and Pleasure*, ed. Monique Guillory and Richard C. Green, 169–71. New York: New York University Press, 1998.

Reid, Mark A. *Redefining Black Film*. Berkeley: University of California Press, 1993.

Reid, Rory C., and Dan Gray. *Confronting Your Spouse's Pornography Problem*. Holliston, MA: Silverleaf Press, 2006.

Reid-Pharr, Robert. *Once You Go Black: Choice, Desire, and the Black American Intellectual*. New York: New York University Press, 2007.

Rimmer, Robert. *The X-Rated Videotape Guide I*. Buffalo, NY: Prometheus, 1993.

Rogers, Molly, and David W. Blight. *Delia's Tears: Race, Science, and Photography in Nineteenth-Century America*. New Haven, CT: Yale University Press, 2010.

Rose, Tricia. *Longing to Tell: Black Women's Stories of Sexuality and Intimacy*. New York: Farrar, Straus and Giroux, 2003.

——. "'Two Inches or a Yard': Silencing Black Women's Sexual Expression." *Talking Visions: Multicultural Feminism in a Transnational Age*, ed. Ella Shohat, 315–24. Cambridge: Massachusetts Institute of Technology Press, 1998.

Rubin, Gayle. "Thinking Sex: Notes for a Radical Theory of the Politics of Sexuality." *Pleasure and Danger: Exploring Female Sexuality*, ed. Carol Vance, 267–319. Boston: Routledge, 1984.

Russ, Joanna. "Pornography and the Doubleness of Sex for Women." *Jump Cut* 32 (1987): 38–41.

Russell, Diana E. H., ed. *Making Violence Sexy: Feminist Views on Pornography*. New York: Teachers College Press, 1993.

Ryan, James R. *Picturing Empire: Photography and the Visualization of the British Empire*. London: Reaktion Books, 1997.

Samantrai, Ranu. *AlterNatives: Black Feminism in the Postimperial Nation*. Stanford, CA: Stanford University Press, 2002.

Sansone, Livio. *Blackness without Ethnicity: Constructing Race in Brazil*. New York: Palgrave, 2003.

Sarracino, Carmine, and Kevin M. Scott. *The Porning of America: The Rise of Porn Culture, What It Means, and Where We Go from Here*. Boston: Beacon, 2009.

Scarry, Elaine. *The Body in Pain: The Making and Unmaking of the World*. New York: Oxford University Press, 1985.

Schaefer, Eric. *Bold! Daring! Shocking! True!: A History of Exploitation Films, 1919–1959*. Durham, NC: Duke University Press, 1999.

——. "Dirty Little Secrets: Scholars, Archivists, and Dirty Movies." *Moving Image* 5.2 (2005): 79–105.

——. "Gauging a Revolution: 16mm Film and the Rise of the Pornographic Feature." *Cinema Journal* 41.3 (2002): 3–26.

Scott, Darieck. *Extravagant Abjection: Blackness, Power and Sexuality in the African American Literary Imagination*. New York: New York University Press, 2010.

Scott, Daryl. *Contempt and Pity: Social Policy and the Image of the Damaged Black Psyche*. Chapel Hill: University of North Carolina Press, 1997.

Scott, James. *Domination and the Arts of Resistance*. New Haven: Yale University Press, 1990.

Scott, Joan. "The Evidence of Experience." *Critical Inquiry* 17 (1991): 773–97.

Segal, Lynne, and Mary McIntosh, eds. *Sex Exposed: Sexuality and the Pornography Debate*. London: Virago, 1992.

Sekula, Allan. "The Body and the Archive." *October* 39 (1986): 3–64.

Seshadri-Crooks, Kalpana. *Desiring Whiteness: A Lacanian Analysis of Race*. New York: Routledge, 2000.

Shalev, Daniel. "Silence = Death: (Re)presentations of 'the AIDS Epidemic,' 1981–1990." Undergraduate honor's thesis, Harvard University, 2008.

Sharpe, Christina. *Monstrous Intimacies: Making Post-Slavery Subjects*. Durham, NC: Duke University Press, 2010.

Sharpley-Whiting, T. Denean. *Black Venus: Sexualized Savages, Primal Fears, and Primitive Narratives in French*. Durham, NC: Duke University Press, 1999.

———. *Pimps Up, Ho's Down: Hip Hop's Hold on Young Black Women*. New York: New York University Press, 2007.

Shimizu, Celine Parreñas. "The Bind of Representation: Performing and Consuming Hypersexuality in *Miss Saigon*." *Theatre Journal* 57.2 (2005): 247–65.

———. *The Hypersexuality of Race*. Durham, NC: Duke University Press, 2007.

———. "Making Woman Asian: Racialized Sexuality on Screen and Scene." PhD diss., Stanford University, 2001.

———. "Sex for Sale: Queens of Anal, Double, Triple, and the Gang Bang: Producing Asian/American Feminism in Pornography." *Yale Journal of Law and Feminism* 18 (2006): 235–76.

Sieving, Christopher. *Soul Searching: Black-themed Cinema from the March on Washington to the Rise of Blaxploitation*. Middletown, CT: Wesleyan University Press, 2011.

Sigel, Lisa Z. "Filth in the Wrong People's Hands: Postcards and the Expansion of Pornography in Britain and the Atlantic World: 1880–1914." *Journal of Social History* 33.4 (2000): 859–85.

Simmonds, Felly Nkweto. "'She's Gotta Have It': The Representation of Black Female Sexuality on Film." *Feminist Review* 29 (1988): 10–22.

Sims, Yvonne D. *Women of Blaxploitation*. Jefferson, NC: McFarland, 2006.

Singer, Debra S. "Reclaiming Venus: The Presence of Sarah Bartmann in Contemporary Art." *Black Venus 2010: They Called Her "Hottentot,"* ed. Deborah Willis, 87–95. Philadelphia: Temple University Press, 2010.

Skelly, Julia. *No Strangers to Beauty: Black Women Artists and the Hottentot Venus*. Saarbrücken, Germany: VDM Verlag, 2008.

Skinner, Kevin B. *Treating Pornography Addiction: The Essential Tools for Recovery*. Provo, UT: GrowthClimate, 2005.

Smith, Barbara, ed. *Home Girls: A Black Feminist Anthology*. New York: Kitchen Table Press, 1983.

———. *The Truth that Never Hurts: Writings on Race, Gender, and Freedom*. New Brunswick, NJ: Rutgers University Press, 1998.

Smith, Shawn Michelle. *Photography on the Color Line: W. E. B. Du Bois, Race, and Visual Culture*. Durham, NC: Duke University Press, 2004.

Smith, Valerie. *Not Just Race, Not Just Gender: Black Feminist Readings*. New York: Routledge, 1998.

———, ed. *Representing Blackness: Issues in Film and Video*. New Brunswick, NJ: Rutgers University Press, 2003.

Smith-Shomade, Beretta E. "'Rock-a-Bye, Baby!': Black Women Disrupting Gangs and Constructing Hip-Hop Gangsta Films." *Cinema Journal* 42.2 (2003): 25–40.

Smyth, Cherry. "The Pleasure Threshold: Looking at Lesbian Pornography on Film." *Feminist Review* 34 (1990): 152–59.

Snitow, Ann, Christine Stansell, and Sharon Thompson, eds. *Powers of Desire: The Politics of Sexuality*. New York: Monthly Review Press, 1983.

Snow, Edward. "Theorizing the Male Gaze: Some Problems." *Representations* 25 (1989): 30–41.

Snyder, R. Claire. "What Is Third-Wave Feminism?: A New Directions Essay." *Signs* 34.1 (autumn 2008): 175–96.

Sobchach, Vivian. *Carnal Thoughts: Embodiment and Moving Image Culture*. Berkeley: University of California Press, 2004.

Solinger, Rickie. *Wake Up Little Susie: Single Pregnancy and Race Before Roe v. Wade*. New York: Routledge, 1992.

Sollors, Werner, ed. *Interracialism: Black-White Intermarriage in American History, Literature and Law*. New York: Oxford University Press, 2000.

———. *Neither Black nor White yet Both: Thematic Explorations of Interracial Literature*. Cambridge, MA: Harvard University Press, 1999.

Solomon-Godeau, Abigail. *Photography at the Dock: Essays on Photographic History, Institutions, and Practices*. Minneapolis: University of Minnesota Press, 1991.

Somerville, Siobhan. *Queering the Color Line: Race and the Invention of Homosexuality in American Culture*. Durham, NC: Duke University Press, 2000.

Sontag, Susan. *A Susan Sontag Reader*. New York: Vintage, 1983.

Spector, Jessica, ed. *Prostitution and Pornography: Philosophical Debates about the Sex Industry*. Stanford, CA: Stanford University Press, 2006.

Spelman, Elizabeth. *Inessential Woman: Problems of Exclusion in Feminist Thought*. Boston: Beacon, 1988.

Spigel, Lynn. "Theorizing the Bachelorette: 'Waves' of Feminist Media Studies." *Signs* 30.1 (2004): 1209–21.

Spillers, Hortense. *Black, White, and in Color: Essays.* Chicago: University of Chicago Press, 2003.

———. "Interstices: A Small Drama of Words." *Pleasure and Danger: Exploring Female Sexuality*, ed. Carol Vance, 73–100. Boston: Routledge, 1984.

———. "Mama's Baby, Papa's Maybe: An American Grammar Book." *Black, White, and In Color: Essays*, 203–29. Chicago: University of Chicago Press, 2003.

Spillers, Hortense, et al. "'Whatcha Gonna Do?': Revisiting 'Mama's Baby, Papa's Maybe: An American Grammar Book.'" *Women's Studies Quarterly* 35.1–2 (spring–summer 2007): 299–309.

Stacey, Jackie. "Desperately Seeking Difference." *Feminism and Film*, ed. E. Ann Kaplan, 450–64. New York: Oxford University Press, 2000.

———. *Star-gazing: Hollywood Cinema and Female Spectatorship.* New York: Routledge, 1994.

Stallings, Lamonda Horton. *Mutha' Is Half a Word: Intersections of Folklore, Vernacular, Myth, and Queerness in Black Female Culture.* Columbus: Ohio State University Press, 2007.

Staples, R. "Blacks and Pornography: A Different Response." *Men Confront Pornography*, ed. Michael Kimmel, 111–14. New York: Morrow, 1990.

Stark, Christine, and Rebecca Whisnant, eds. *Not for Sale: Feminists Resisting Prostitution and Pornography.* Melbourne, Australia: Spinifex Press, 2004.

Stecopoulos, Harry, and Michael Uebel, eds. *Race and the Subject of Masculinities.* Durham, NC: Duke University Press, 1997.

Steinem, Gloria. *Outrageous Acts and Everyday Rebellions.* New York: Holt Rinehart and Winston, 1983.

Stockton, Kathryn Bond. *Beautiful Bottom, Beautiful Shame: Where "Black" Meets "Queer."* Durham, NC: Duke University Press, 2006.

Stoler, Ann Laura. *Carnal Knowledge and Imperial Power: Race and the Intimate in Colonial Rule.* Berkeley: University of California Press, 2002.

———. *Race and the Education of Desire: Foucault's History of Sexuality and the Colonial Order of Things.* Durham, NC: Duke University Press, 1995.

Storr, Robert. "Art, Censorship, and the First Amendment: This Is Not a Test." *Art Journal* 50.3 (1991): 12–28.

Strossen, Nadine. *Defending Pornography: Free Speech, Sex, and the Fight for Women's Rights.* New York: Scribner, 1995.

Strother, Z. S. "Display of the Body Hottentot." *Africans on Stage: Studies in Ethnological Show Business*, ed. Bernth Lindfors, 1–61. Bloomington: Indiana University Press, 1999.

Strub, Whitney. *Perversion for Profit: The Politics of Pornography and the Rise of the New Right.* New York: Columbia University Press, 2010.

Struthers, William M. *Wired for Intimacy: How Pornography Hijacks the Male Brain.* New York: IVP Books, 2009.

Tagg, John. *The Burden of Representation: Essays on Photographies and Histories.* Amherst: University of Massachusetts Press, 1988.

Tannenbaum, Judith. "Robert Mapplethorpe: The Philadelphia Story." *Art Journal* 50.4 (1991): 71–76.

Taussig, Michael. *Defacement: Public Secrecy and the Labor of the Negative.* Stanford: Stanford University Press, 1999.

Teish, Luisah. "A Quiet Subversion." *Take Back the Night: Women on Pornography,* ed. Laura Lederer, 115–18. New York: Morrow, 1980.

Telles, Edward. *Race in Another America: The Significance of Skin Color in Brazil.* Princeton: Princeton University Press, 2006.

Terry, Jennifer, and Jacqueline Urla, eds. *Deviant Bodies: Critical Perspectives on Difference in Science and Popular Culture.* Bloomington: Indiana University Press, 1995.

Thompson, Lisa B. *Beyond the Black Lady: Sexuality and the New African American Middle Class.* Urbana: University of Illinois Press, 2009.

Thornham, Sue, ed. *Feminist Film Theory: A Reader.* New York: New York University Press, 1999.

Tsang, Daniel. "Beyond 'Looking for My Penis': Reflections on Asian Gay Male Video Porn." *Porn 101: Eroticism, Pornography, and the First Amendment,* ed. James Elias et al., 473–77. Amherst, NY: Prometheus, 1999.

Vance, Carole S., ed. *Pleasure and Danger: Exploring Female Sexuality.* Boston: Routledge, 1984.

Wacquant, Loïc. "For an Analytic of Racial Domination." *Political Power and Social Theory* 11 (1997): 221–34.

Walcott, Rinaldo. "The New African American Studies: Blackening Queer Studies and Sexing Black Studies." GLQ 12 (2006): 510–13.

———. "Outside in Black Studies: Reading from a Queer Place in the Diaspora." *Black Queer Studies,* ed. E. Patrick Johnson and Mae G. Henderson, 90–105. Durham, NC: Duke University Press, 2006.

Walker, Alice. *In Search of Our Mothers' Gardens.* San Diego: Harcourt Brace Jovanovich, 1983.

———. *You Can't Keep a Good Woman Down.* New York: Harcourt, Brace, Jovanovich, 1981.

Wallace, Maurice O. *Constructing the Black Masculine: Identity and Ideality in African American Men's Literature and Culture, 1775–1995.* Durham, NC: Duke University Press, 2002.

Wallace, Michele. *Black Macho and the Myth of the Superwoman.* New York: Dial, 1979.

———. *Invisibility Blues: From Pop to Theory.* New York: Verso, 1990.

Wallis, Brian. "Black Bodies, White Science: Louis Agassiz's Slave Daguerreotypes." *American Art* 9.2 (1995): 39–61.

Warner, Michael. *The Trouble with Normal: Sex, Politics, and the Ethics of Queer Life.* Cambridge, MA: Harvard University Press, 1999.

Watkins, S. Craig. *Hip Hop Matters: Politics, Popular Culture, and the Struggle for a Movement.* Boston: Beacon, 2005.

Watney, Simon. *Policing Desire: Pornography, AIDS and the Media.* London: Methuen, 1987.

Waugh, Tom. "Homosociality in the Classical American Stag Film: Off-Screen, On-Screen." *Sexualities* 4.3 (2001): 275–92.

———. "Men's Pornography, Gay vs. Straight." *Jump Cut* 30 (1985): 30–36.

Weiss, Margot. *Techniques of Pleasure: BDSM and the Circuits of Sexuality.* Durham, NC: Duke University Press, 2011.

Weiss, Robert, and Jennifer P. Schneider. *Untangling the Web: Sex, Porn, and Fantasy Obsession in the Internet Age.* New York: Alyson Publications, 2006.

White, Patricia. *Uninvited: Classical Hollywood Film and Lesbian Representability.* Bloomington: Indiana University Press, 1999.

Wicke, Jennifer. "Through a Glass Darkly: Pornography's Academic Market." *Dirty Looks: Women, Pornography, and Power,* ed. Pamela Church Gibson and Roma Gibson, 62–80. London: British Film Institute, 1993.

Wiegman, Robyn. *American Anatomies: Theorizing Race and Gender.* Durham, NC: Duke University Press, 1995.

———. *Object Lessons.* Durham, NC: Duke University Press, 2012.

Wilcox, Russell. "Cross-Gender Identification in Commercial Pornographic Films." *Porn 101: Eroticism, Pornography, and the First Amendment,* ed. James Elias et al., 479–91. Amherst, NY: Prometheus, 1999.

Williams, Carla. "Naked, Neutered, or Noble: The Black Female Body in America and the Problem of Photographic History." *Skin Deep, Spirit Strong: The Black Female Body in American Culture,* ed. Kimberly Wallace-Sanders, 182–200. Ann Arbor: University of Michigan Press, 2002.

Williams, Linda. "Corporealized Observers: Visual Pornographies and the 'Carnal Densities of Vision.'" *Fugitive Images: From Photography to Video,* ed. Patrice Petro, 3–40. Bloomington: Indiana University Press, 1995.

———. "Film Bodies: Gender, Genre, and Excess." *Film Quarterly* 44.4 (2001): 2–13.

———. "'Frenzy of the Visible,' Indeed!" *Cinema Journal* 46.4 (2007): 106–8.

———. *Hard Core: Power, Pleasure, and the "Frenzy of the Visible."* Berkeley: University of California Press, 1989.

———. *Playing the Race Card: Melodramas of Black and White from Uncle Tom to O. J. Simpson.* Princeton: Princeton University Press, 2001.

———. "Pornographies On/Scene, or 'Diff'rent Strokes for Diff'rent Folks.'" *Sex Exposed: Sexuality and the Pornography Debate*, ed. Lynne Segal and Mary McIntosh, 233–64. London: Virago, 1992.

———, ed. *Porn Studies*. Durham, NC: Duke University Press, 2004.

———. "Power, Pleasure, and Perversion: Sadomaochistic Film Pornography." *Representations* 27 (1989): 27–65.

———. "Second Thoughts on *Hard Core*: American Obscenity Law and the Scapegoating of Deviance." *Dirty Looks: Women, Pornography, Power*, ed. Pam Church Gibson and Roma Gibson, 46–61. London: BFI Publishing, 1993.

———. *Screening Sex*. Durham, NC: Duke University Press, 2008.

———. "Skin Flicks on the Racial Border: Pornography, Exploitation, and Interracial Lust." *Porn Studies*, ed. Linda Williams, 271–308. Durham, NC: Duke University Press, 2004.

———, ed. *Viewing Positions: Ways of Seeing Film*. New Brunswick, NJ: Rutgers University Press, 1997.

———. "'White Slavery' versus the Ethnography of 'Sexworkers': Women in Stag Films at the Kinsey Archive." *Moving Image* 5.2 (2005): 107–34.

———. "Why I Did Not Want to Write This Essay." *Signs* 30.1 (2004): 1264–71.

Williams, Patricia J. *Alchemy of Race and Rights*. Cambridge, MA: Harvard University Press, 1992.

Willis, Deborah, ed. *Black Venus 2010: They Called Her "Hottentot."* Philadelphia: Temple University Press, 2010.

———. *Posing Beauty: African American Images from the 1890s to the Present*. New York: W. W. Norton, 2009.

Willis, Deborah, and Carla Williams. *The Black Female Body: A Photographic History*. Philadelphia: Temple University Press, 2002.

Wilson, Judith. "Getting Down to Get Over: Romare Bearden's Use of Pornography and the Problem of the Black Female Body in Afro-U.S. Art." *Black Popular Culture*, ed. Gina Dent, 112–22. Seattle: Bay Press, 1992.

———. "One Way or Another: Black Feminist Visual Theory." *The Feminism and Visual Culture Reader*, ed. Amelia Jones, 22–26. New York: Routledge, 2003.

Wing, Adrien Katherine, ed. *Global Critical Race Feminism*. New York: New York University Press, 2000.

Wlodarz, Joe. "Beyond the Black Macho: Queer Blaxploitation." *Velvet Light Trap* 53 (2004): 10–25.

———. "(Un)Making Macho: Race, Gender, and Stardom in 1970s American Cinema and Culture." PhD diss., University of Rochester, 2003.

Wolf, Naomi. *Fire with Fire: The New Female Power and How It Will Change the 21st Century*. Toronto: Random House, 1993.

Wray, Matt, and Annalee Newitz, eds. *White Trash: Race and Class in America*. New York: Routledge, 1997.

Wriggins, Jennifer. "Rape, Racism and the Law." *Harvard Women's Law Journal* 3 (1983): 6–141.

Wright, Michelle, and Antje Schuhmann, eds. *Blackness and Sexualities*. Munster: LIT Verlag, 2007.

Young, Harvey. *Embodying Black Experience: Stillness, Critical Memory, and the Black Body*. Ann Arbor: University of Michigan Press, 2010.

Young, Hershini. *Haunting Capital: Memory, Text, and the Black Diasporic Body*. Hanover, NH: Dartmouth University Press, 2005.

Zack, Naomi. *Inclusive Feminism: A Third Wave Theory of Women's Commonality*. Lanham, MD: Rowman and Littlefield, 2005.

Zimmerman, Bonnie, and Toni A. H. McNaron, eds. *The New Lesbian Studies*. New York: Feminist Press, 1996.

INDEX

New Wave Hookers (Dark Brothers film), 129

Nichols, Bill, 130–31

obscenity, legal definitions, 62

orgasm, female, 18–19

otherness, 130–33, 144–45. *See also* difference

Paglia, Camille, 14–15

Parks, Gordon, 59, 63

Parks, Gordon, Jr., 63

patriarchy, 9, 11, 13–14

Penley, Constance, 19

pleasure: difference and, 131; domination and, 7, 34, 84–85; eroticism and, 54; female orgasm, 18–19; race and, 3–5, 31, 81–82, 84, 87, 93–94, 98–99, 104–6; recovery work and, 55, 58

Pleasure and Danger (Vance), 16

pornography: antipornography feminism, 9–14, 106, 155n37; as benign fantasy, 10; black women as foundation of, 37; as controlling image, 38; elimination of, 12–13; ethnography and, 130–32; feminist porn studies, 18–21; humor in, 108–10; as liberation, 15; male dominance in, 9–10; maximum visibility principle, 68, 72, 73, 78, 100, 167n30; money shot in, 18–19, 77, 95–97, 96, 100–101, 102; oppression of women in, 11–12; pro-pornography feminism, 14–16; queer, 22, 157–58n70; regulation as censorship, 14; sex-radicalism, 16–18; shift in content, 62–63; social functions of, 23–24; videocassette in, 112; violence of, 129–30; violent production of, 12; zoning of, 17. See

also Golden Age pornographic films; racialized pornography; Silver Age pornographic films

"Pornography and Black Women's Bodies" (Collins), 35

pornotroping, use of term, 40–41

Powell, Richard J., 163n80

Powers of Desire (Snitow), 16

Purdie, Bernard Lee "Pretty," 65

puritanism, sexual, 14

queer-of-color studies, 86

Qureshi, Sadiah, 159n3

race: domination, 3–4, 84–85; fictions of, 5, 6, 90, 93–94, 98; hierarchy of, 48–49, 87; humor and, 109–11, 117–18, 126–27; meaning-making, 8, 20; pleasure and, 3–5, 19, 31, 84, 87, 93–94, 98–99, 104–6; stereotypes, 121, 129; taboos on borders of, 19–20

racial iconography, concept of, 2, 3, 5–6, 45–46, 147

racialized pornography: analysis methods, 21–26, 146; as controlling image, 38–39; dangers of fantasy in, 10; degradation of, 38; humor in, 108–10, 117–18, 126–27; injury by, 38–39; overexposure/absence in, 5–6; phallic power in, 65–66, 68, 72, 80–81, 142; spectatorship and, 19; stag films, 132–33; tropes in, 11; use of term, 2

Reagan, Ronald, 111

recovery work, 47–57

Reed, Ishmael, 4

representation: black feminism on, 1–2, 30, 92, 146–47; controlling images, 33–35, 38–39, 46, 105, 147; as epistemology, 35–39; fantasy and,

CPSIA information can be obtained
at www.ICGtesting.com
Printed in the USA
FFHW020459150219
50561250-55882FF

9 780822 356202